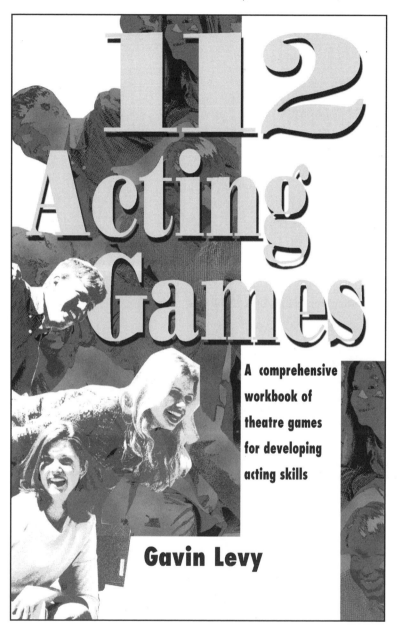

112 Acting Games

A comprehensive workbook of theatre games for developing acting skills

Gavin Levy

MERIWETHER PUBLISHING LTD.
Colorado Springs, Colorado

Meriwether Publishing Ltd., Publisher
PO Box 7710
Colorado Springs, CO 80933-7710

Editor: Theodore O. Zapel
Associate editor: Dianne Bundt
Cover design: Jan Melvin

© Copyright MMV Meriwether Publishing Ltd.
Printed in the United States of America
First Edition

Library of Congress Cataloging-in-Publication Data

Levy, Gavin.
  112 acting games : a comprehensive workbook of theatre games for
developing acting skills / by Gavin Levy. -- 1st ed.
    p. cm.
  ISBN 978-1-56608-106-1
1. Acting. 2. Games. 3. Improvisation (Acting). I. Title: One hundred twelve
acting games. II. Title.
  PN2061.L388 2005
  792.02'8--dc22

                      2005001784

            3   4   5   07   08   09

Dedication

With special thanks to Jennifer Waites

Table of Contents

Introduction

The purpose of this book is to give theatre teachers the tools they will need not just to play a game or teach an exercise, but also to actually understand the reasons they are doing so and the practical benefits of each exercise. This book will also enable teachers to hold a group discussion when necessary, and guide them on how to ask leading questions. So if you are looking for a quick-fix basic game book for drama, this is not the book for you. However, if what you are looking for is something that delves deeper into exercises and their purposes, then read on.

Acting teachers, directors, and instructors at all levels will find many uses for this book. I have discovered many of the activities included here to be just as effective with intermediate students as they are with novices. Also bear in mind that the information and instructions in this book are not hard-and-fast rules; you are free to adapt any exercise to suit your needs. If you disagree with my suggestions, you are under no obligation to borrow them. In fact, if I can get you, the instructor, as well as the students to think, then I have doubly served my purpose.

Many of these games have multiple names; I did not invent any of them. I may have adapted and molded some of them, but they lend themselves to this kind of treatment and you should feel free to do the same. As teachers we must aim to stretch our students in every possible direction and empower them with skills and knowledge — that is the task of this book.

You will find that I use the term "actor" and masculine pronouns consistently throughout the book. This is not because I am sexist, but simply because it is less cumbersome than saying "actor/actress" or "he/she." Please do not take offense, as I am using the terms in their generic sense. (That sounded like a poem!)

Also, you will often see me refer to "the stage" and "the audience." If you are working in a classroom, any area you designate can be the stage. The audience is wherever you decide to put them. The terms are just reference points, but obviously you will not always have the parameters of a formal theatre within which to work. This is just another opportunity for you to improvise.

Again, I did not invent these games. I have discovered them over the past fifteen years, mainly from workshops I have taken. Notice I did not say acting workshops. I have utilized activities from all walks of life and adapted them to the needs of actors. I have also included activities that I was taught as a child. Whether these activities were originally intended for actors or not, it has been my mission to adapt every single one of them to have relevance for the student of acting.

You will notice that I describe the participants using many different terms. This is because I want you to get a taste of how applicable these exercises are to myriad people. Although I wrote these activities with actors in mind, they can be used in many different fields. A theatre director who is using a game before rehearsals might say, "I need two actors to come up onstage," whereas a business employer who uses a selection of these activities to enhance team spirit in his or her company might say, "I need two volunteers to come to the front of the room." An English teacher who uses a character exercise to help the class better understand the characters in a book they are reading might say, "I need three students to come forward and demonstrate this game." We constantly need to ask ourselves, "Who is my audience?" By this I mean, "Who are we trying to affect with these activities?" I find it beneficial to use terminology that will envelop the target audience I am working with.

I have broken the book into chapters to give you some idea of how and where the activities can be used. Again, these categorizations are not set in stone. An activity I have put under "Concentration and Focus" might fit just as well under "Imagination." These labels are just guidelines to help you get on track. Incidentally, you will notice that I have cross-referenced several different chapters, linking an activity in one chapter to an activity in another chapter. This may at first seem redundant; however, the subject matter is so important that I chose to approach some areas again from different angles.

In regards to the information under the "Purpose" subheadings, you may notice there is a great deal of repetition. It is important for actors to train and retrain concepts until they become second nature. Dancers do not learn the basics and then forget about them, they constantly go back to them. You'll also notice that I've separated the "Discussion" and "Purpose" subheads in this book. This is for your benefit, but you should blend the two as you see fit. The point is to encourage you to think outside the box. Look at the suggestions I've given and add your own. Remember, much of what you want to teach will also be picked up through the actual doing of the activity. Break a leg and enjoy!

Chapter 1
Relaxation

1. On the Beach

Have the students spread out to different parts of the room and lie down on the floor. If you can, try to keep the room slightly warmer than usual as the floor may be cold. Dim the lights so that there is just enough light for the students to be seen. If you do not have this capability with your lights, bring in a small lamp. Make sure no two students are touching and that there is some space between them. Have them lie flat on the floor with their legs straight and arms by their sides. Put on some music in the background; it should be mellow, but something the students will appreciate. Repeat the following instructions or something similar.

"Okay, I'd like you all now to close your eyes. Good. With your eyes closed take in a nice deep breath ... good ... and breathe out. And again, take in a nice long breath ... good ... and breathe out. While I'm talking to you, just continue to breathe at your own pace. In a moment you will take in another deep breath, and as you do I want you to flex your feet. Try to isolate your muscles so that you only tense your feet. Try to make this a gradual motion, taking one or two seconds to complete the action. Ready? Now breathe in, tensing your feet. Good. Now hold it ... hold.... Good, and breathe out. Now tense your calf muscles, and only your calf muscles, breathing in ... good.... And relax your calf muscles, breathing out. Now tense your thighs, breathing in ... good. ... And relax them, breathing out. Tense your glutes, breathing in; and now relax, breathing out. Tense your abdomen, breathing in. Remember to isolate this area. Now breathe out. Tense your upper chest (pectorals), breathing in; and relax, breathing out. Tense your hands, making two tight fists as you breathe in. And relax, breathing out. Tense your forearms, breathing in. Good, now relax them, breathing out. Tense your upper arms (biceps), breathing in; and relax them, breathing out. Tense your shoulders, breathing in; and relax them, breathing out. Tense your neck gently as you breathe in; and relax your neck, breathing out. Scrunch up your nose as you breathe in; and relax your nose as you breathe out. Scrunch up your eyes as you breathe in; and relax your eyes as you breathe out. Scrunch up your entire face as you breathe in. Now relax it as you breathe out. And one more time, scrunch up your entire face as you breathe in; relax it as you breathe out.

"Okay, keep taking nice deep breaths as you listen to my voice. In a moment I will ask you to tense up your entire body. As you do this I

3

want you to feel all the tension that is going through your body at that very moment and remember that feeling. Okay, now tense your whole body. Hold it ... hold it. ... Good, and release. And again, tense everything up. Good, and hold it ... hold it. ... Good, and release.

"As you listen to my voice now I would like you to inhale deeply, and as you breathe out allow your body to get heavier and heavier. You might experience this sensation as sinking farther and farther into the floor. As you lie on the floor I want you to be aware of any remaining areas of tension in your body. I want you to imagine that any last areas of tension that you have are now in a liquid form and are floating around your body. I want you to picture them and feel them as they float around your body. Now, I want you to imagine there is a plug at the base of your spine. I want you to mentally pull out the plug now, and as you do I want you to see all of the last bits of tension drain out your body. The tension just drains away and you get heavier and heavier. And by now you couldn't even lift your head if you wanted to because it feels so heavy. Continue to breathe deeply as you lie there feeling totally and utterly relaxed. (Allow about one or two minutes.)

"As you are lying on the floor I want you to continue to breathe deeply; feel your body getting heavier and heavier. I would now like you to picture yourself lying on the beach. As you lie there on the sand you find that the weight of your body starts to pull you gently down into the sand. You can feel the breeze of the warm air as it moves across your body. First you can feel the warm air as it drifts across your feet, causing a slight tingling sensation. Then it slowly moves up your body. It moves up your ankles to your legs, then to your waist, arms, shoulders, and finally to your face. You feel calm and relaxed. As you are lying on the beach you can feel the rays of the sun soaking into your pores and breaking up any last strands of tension. You feel calm, relaxed, and content. You listen to the sounds around you. You can hear the sound of the waves as they crash upon the shore; in fact, you are lying close enough to the oceanfront that you can feel the ocean spray across your feet, and you feel heavier and heavier, and more and more relaxed. In the background you can hear the sound of seagulls flying above as they scout the ocean looking for fish. You listen to the sounds around you and you notice the voices of small children laughing as they build castles in the sand. You lie on the beach and think about the fact that this is the first day of the summer vacation, and that you don't have to go back to school."

(Feel free to adapt some of the language so it fits your audience. I will continue the rest of this exercise with students in mind, but it would

4

be very easy to adapt it for work colleagues or college students.)

"You realize that for the next two and half months you will have no homework, no essays, and no exams, and this realization causes you to smile as you become even more relaxed. You think about what you are going to do over the summer. Perhaps you will go skateboarding with your friend or to that movie you have been waiting to see. As you realize there is nothing you have to do for the entire summer you feel more and more relaxed, and your body gets heavier and heavier, and you sink farther and farther into the sand. After lying on the beach for a while you decide to wade into the ocean. You move toward the water's edge and put one foot into the water. It feels warm and relaxing, so you walk in up to your ankles. After a few moments you go in farther until the water surrounds your thighs and then up to your waist. You decide to move out even farther because the water feels so great. The water is up to your neck now, and as a wave passes by, the ripple effect causes a drop of water to land in your eye. You experience a slight stinging sensation from the salt water as you wipe the drop from your eye. You decide to use the float (raft) that you brought into the water with you. As you lie on your float, you feel heavier and heavier, and more and more relaxed, and the ocean waves gently rock you back and forth like a baby in a swing. You find yourself drifting off as you feel the sunlight across your face and the gentle breeze across your body. You are drifting deeper and deeper into a state of relaxation as your float moves farther and farther out into the sea. You feel fully content and remind yourself of all the free time you have over summer to do exactly as you please. You think of all the friends you are going to see and all the fun you will have. After what seems like a fairly long period of time you open your eyes and sit up slightly on your float. You realize that you must have fallen asleep and drifted out to sea. You decide you need to get closer to the shore, so using your arms as paddles you start to guide yourself back toward land. As your arms propel you, some of the water splashes up, causing you to feel rejuvenated and refreshed. After a short while, you find yourself within view of the shore. You paddle a little farther until you feel you are close enough to stand. You start by testing the water with one foot, and you find that you can stand up even though the water goes up to your neck. You wade back to shore, and as you come out of the ocean you lie back down on the sand feeling cool, refreshed, and relaxed. As you lie there you realize just how calm your mind feels and you sink into the sand feeling heavier and heavier and more and more relaxed. You continue to breathe deeply and the remaining droplets of water on your body evaporate in the sun's rays.

"I want you to continue to breathe deeply for a short while as you think about all of the fun you have had at the beach today. Good. Now I'm going to ask you to get up slowly, in your own time. I would like you to start by just turning onto one side and then slowly rising up from this position. Once standing, I would like you to be still and look out directly in front of you, staying still, grounded, and centered. Notice the feelings that are going through your body at this moment. Good."

Remember that people will be standing up at different rates and in their own time so you may need to allow a little extra time. Do not switch on the lights again until everybody has finished standing. You may choose not to turn the lights all the way up at all, but to keep them at a dim level for the rest of the period.

Variables:

You could vary this exercise in a number of ways. For instance, you can skip the fluid floating around the body section and just close after the tensing and releasing portion.

You can keep this relaxation section as long or short as you like. Remember that the students will probably be lying on a hard, cold floor, so I usually limit this exercise to about twenty-five minutes.

Discussion:

As I stated earlier, I like to keep the lights fairly dim for the rest of the period so the students remain in a tranquil state. When finished, I simply turn to the class and ask them how they were feeling and what was going on for them during the exercise. Was there any part of the relaxation that really stuck out for them? The discussion session often becomes very interesting if you add a scene or a story such as the beach scene. For instance, some students may say they felt very hot and were sweating even though the floor was cold.

Purpose:

To relax through awareness

The relaxation aspects of this exercise can be applied as follows. If you're an actor in a play and you have an evening rehearsal following a busy and stressful day, you have to leave those things behind you. You want to come in and be able to start from a neutral position. A relaxation exercise can allow you to do just that. It can help you put the day's troubles aside and focus solely on acting. Imagine if you were onstage and all you could think about was what an awful day it had been; your performance could suffer terribly.

There are many approaches to relaxation. Lee Strasberg had a particular exercise he liked to do with his students. David Garfield explains, "To promote relaxation, Strasberg has the actor sit in a chair and proceed to find a position in, which if he had to, he could fall asleep."[1] The activity I have used here is just one example of how to find relaxation. Keep searching for other approaches you can use with your students.

Yes, this exercise helps students to relax, but it is valuable for so much more than that. The students will also learn about the body and how specific body parts feel by isolating muscle groups. This ability will be very useful as the students start to delve into character work. This exercise will also help them expand their imaginations as they picture themselves lying on the beach or swimming in the ocean.

2. Breathing

Have everybody stand up and form a circle. Tell your students that they are going to work on breathing for the first part of the day. (You should aim to spend part of your class using exercises such as these, but usually not the whole class. To keep the students stimulated, use these exercises to complement other class material. I find that about twenty minutes on one exercise is sufficient. If you spend too long on one the students may lose interest, which will likely limit their retention of the activity's lesson.)

Now, find a couple volunteers. Instruct one of them to take a deep breath. Then have the second do the same. Have them repeat the breathing as the class watches to see what body parts move. The dialogue may go as follows:

INSTRUCTOR: Sarah, please take in a nice, deep breath. Good. Eric, would you take in a nice deep breath now? Good. Sarah and Eric, take another deep breath and this time I would like the rest of the class to notice what parts of their body move. Anyone?

PAUL: Well, I saw Sarah's shoulders go up.

LIZ: And Eric's arms were moving.

[1] David Garfield, *The Actors Studio: A Player's Place* (New York: Macmillan, 1984), 169.

7

Have all the students take in a deep breath and discover where the movement is in their own body. You are basically finding out where the majority of their breath is going. You should tell them that their bodies are like musical instruments and that when they breathe with just the top half of their bodies they are only expanding a small area of their instruments. In other words, this type of breathing is very inefficient. Now have all the students put one hand on their bellies. Tell them that when they breathe in, this is the area they want the breath to fill. As they inhale, tell them to try to push out their hand with the breath and watch it fall as they exhale. They may find they get a little dizzy because they are taking in a great deal more oxygen than they are used to. It is interesting to note that this is the way we breathe when we are born. We learn incorrect breathing from society and tension.

You may find that not all the students are able to push their hand out at first. This may take some practice and may feel strange. Explain that the area they are filling with air is called the diaphragm. Again, reiterate that the diaphragm is like a musical instrument, which, in this case, contracts as they breathe in and expands as they breathe out. You do not have to go into enormous detail about the diaphragm unless you will be doing a long session on voice work.

Ask the students how they felt doing the activity. Did they get slightly dizzy? You may want to mention that correct breathing is important for actors because it allows them to talk for a longer period of time. In other words, if an actor has a long sentence that would flow much better in one breath, he will need proper breathing to be able to do that.

Because this exercise will probably only take about five minutes, you may want to use the following exercise in conjunction with it. You can do this next exercise sitting or standing, but if you have your students sit, make sure they have good posture. This activity is one I adapted from an audiotape by Gay Hendricks. Gay Hendricks is a phenomenal resource for correct breathing.

3. Breathing for Concentration and Focus

Give your students the following instructions:

"Put your thumb on one side of your nose and press it lightly against the nasal passage so that no air can get in. You are now breathing through only one side of your nose. You should have your forefinger on the other side of your nose, ready to close the other nostril at the appropriate

moment. Now breathe in diaphragmatically, closing your right nostril with your thumb. As you get close to the top of the breath close the left nostril with your forefinger and release your thumb, still breathing in. Now breathe out. Breathe in again and repeat the process. The only time you alternate closing the nostrils is at the top of the breath."
You will want to repeat this exercise for about two to three minutes. If you did this exercise again with the class at a later date you would probably aim for about three to five minutes. Allow them to build up a bit of stamina first. This exercise is excellent for helping a person feel centered and focused.

Variables:

The best way to vary this exercise is to use a different one. There are many breathing exercises you could use with your students. Many bookstores have audiocassettes on breathing. Also, look for workshops on breathing. Do not feel that because you are studying acting you can only take acting workshops. Good breathing techniques can be found in classes such as yoga, meditation, and Tai Chi.

Discussion:

I focused on the discussion in the explanation stage because the feedback needs to be much more immediate. I want the students to understand what they need to do and why they need to develop correct form from the beginning. You may want to discuss with the class where this can be useful. Some examples are if you are sitting in a room waiting to take an exam or just before you are about to go onstage. Ask for their suggestions.

Purpose:

**To help students become kinesthetically aware
of their physical bodies**
The students should be able to feel what is happening in their bodies. The students will learn how to relax their body and ease tensions before a performance or an important event by putting the body in a neutral state. Even though breathing exercises can feel quite calming because they emphasize correct breathing, they also energize the body by increasing the intake of oxygen. Because these exercises enhance focus and concentration they would be excellent to use before a performance. They could also be used right before an exam or any important event. A Tai Chi instructor informed me that this last exercise works the left and

right side of the brain alternately and is an excellent exercise for students who have Attention Deficit Disorder because it helps them to calm down and become focused. All I know is that it works!

4. Sound Sensations

This activity starts off in an identical fashion to "On the Beach." Have the students spread out to different parts of the room and lie down on the floor. If you can, try to keep the room slightly warmer than usual as the floor may be cold. Dim the lights so that there is just enough light for the students to be seen. If you do not have this capability with your lights, bring in a small lamp. Make sure no two students are touching and that there is some space between them. Have them lie flat on the floor with their legs straight and arms by their sides. Put on some music in the background; it should be mellow, but something the students will appreciate. Give the following instructions:

"Okay, I'd like you all to close your eyes. Good. With your eyes closed I'd like you to take in a nice deep breath ... good ... and breathe out. And again, take in a nice long breath ... good ... and breathe out. While I'm talking to you, just continue to breathe at your own pace. In a moment you will take in another deep breath, and as you do I want you to flex your feet. Try to isolate your muscles so you are only tensing your feet. Try to make this a gradual motion, taking one or two seconds to complete the action. Ready? Now breathe in, tensing your feet. Good. Now hold it ... hold. ... Good, and breathe out. Now tense your calf muscles and only your calf muscles, breathing in ... good. ... And relax your calf muscles, breathing out. Now tense your thighs, breathing in ... good. ... And relax them, breathing out. Tense your glutes, breathing in; and now relax, breathing out. Tense your abdomen, breathing in. Remember to isolate this area. Now breathe out. Tense your upper chest (pectorals), breathing in; and relax, breathing out. Tense your hands, making two tight fists as you breathe in. And relax, breathing out. Tense your forearms, breathing in. Good, now relax them, breathing out. Tense your upper arms (biceps), breathing in; and relax them, breathing out. Tense your shoulders, breathing in; and relax them, breathing out. Tense your neck gently as you breathe in; and relax your neck, breathing out. Scrunch up your nose as you breathe in; and relax your nose as you breathe out. Scrunch up your eyes as you breathe in; and relax your eyes as you breathe out. Scrunch up your entire face as you breathe in. Now relax it as you breathe out. And one more time, scrunch up your entire face as you breathe in; relax it as you breathe out.

"Okay, keep taking nice deep breaths as you listen to my voice. In a moment I will ask you to tense up your entire body. As you do this I want you to feel all the tension that is going through your body at that very moment and remember that feeling. Okay, now tense your whole body. Hold it ... hold it. ... Good, and release. And again, tense everything up. Good, and hold it ... hold it. ... Good, and release.

"As you listen to my voice now I would like you to inhale deeply, and as you breathe out allow your body to get heavier and heavier. You might experience this sensation as sinking farther and farther into the floor. As you lie on the floor I want you to be aware of any remaining areas of tension in your body. I want you to imagine that any last areas of tension that you have are now in a liquid form and are floating around your body. I want you to picture them and feel them as they float around your body. Now, I want you to imagine there is a plug at the base of your spine. I want you to mentally pull out the plug now, and as you do I want you to see all of the last bits of tension drain out your body. The tension just drains away and you get heavier and heavier. And by now you couldn't even lift your head if you wanted to because it feels so heavy. Continue to breathe deeply as you lie there feeling totally and utterly relaxed.

(Here is where this exercise differs from "On the Beach.") "Okay, what I would like you to do now is listen to the sounds around you. Try to listen to the most immediate sounds. Can you hear your own breathing? How about the sound of your eyelids opening and closing? Limit your listening to the most immediate sounds around you. Good. Now I would like you to continue to listen for sounds, only this time encompass all the sounds you can hear in this room. Can you hear others breathing? How about coughing? Is someone shuffling in another part of the room? Again, you should attempt to listen to the sounds that are coming from other parts of the room and not from yourself. Good job. (Give them about two or three minutes for each set of instructions so they can really have a good opportunity to listen.) Let's proceed a little further now. This time I want you to listen to all the sounds that you can hear that are coming from outside the room. Try to isolate your listening so that you are only hearing the sounds outside of this room. Can you hear the sounds of cars outside? How about people talking? Good.

"I'm going to ask you to get up slowly, in your own time. I would like you to start just by turning to one side and then slowly rising up from this position. As you stand up I would like you to stand still and look out directly in front of you, staying still, grounded, and centered. Notice the feelings that are going through your body at this moment. Good."

Remember that people will be standing up at different rates so you need to allow a little extra time. Don't switch on the lights again until everybody is finished. You may choose not to turn the lights all the way up, but keep them at a dim level for the rest of the period.

Variables:

See "On the Beach."

You could have a couple of actors recite a scene from a play while the audience watches and listens. Then have the actors recite the scene again, only this time the audience should have their eyes closed. Find out what differences the audience noticed between the two performances. Do not have the actors perform the piece with actions, because we want to make this a pure listening activity. You may find in the first read-through that the audience comments on some of the dialogue, whereas in the second read-through they may start to notice more technical aspects, such as "He stuttered" or "She paused."

Discussion:

"What role does isolation play in acting? Do actors have to isolate themselves from the audience to some degree?"

"Were you able to isolate your listening to a specific area? Talk me through the process that allowed you to do this."

These are all jumping off points for good interaction. If four people come up with four different processes that is okay. If you give a group of students a math problem they may all get the correct answer through entirely different methods. Likewise, the authors of acting books are looking for similar results, but they present various approaches to get there.

Purpose:

To develop and improve isolation skills

In this exercise the actors are isolating their listening skills. They are trying to focus solely on the sense of hearing while blocking out the other senses. In fact, this activity goes one step further as the actors try to isolate their listening to a specific area. Actors use isolation on a regular basis. When about to film a scene, actors may isolate their listening to the immediate area so that they can block out any sounds of moving cameras or technicians that are being made in the background.

The skill of isolation also extends to other senses, including sight. When on set, actors need to focus visually on a limited area blurring a scene. I am not saying they need to do all this consciously through exercising these muscles; eventually these skills will be transferred mostly to the subconscious, freeing the actor to focus on other areas. You may say this all sounds very structured, but I would disagree. The creative paths the mind utilizes to allow the actor to isolate in this manner is an amazing phenomenon. The same can be said for areas such as voice projection and diction. Mastering the technical aspects of acting takes an enormous amount of creativity on the part of the body and mind.

To increase focus

Admittedly, increasing focus and concentration can be a goal of almost every activity used. Remember, I am only giving you a couple of suggestions for the purpose of each activity. It is up to you to emphasize any other benefits you find in each activity. The reason I say "find" is because sometimes after doing an activity with your actors you will discover a purpose you had not thought of before.

In this exercise, students use a tremendous amount of focus to hear the specific sounds required. Do not think of focus as for performance only. Olympic gymnasts do not wake up one morning and become Olympic gymnasts. They exercise and train constantly, never settling but continually pushing themselves. Why should the situation be any different for actors? In the middle of an audition the director may ask an actor to try something different. If the actor is not able to focus because of nerves or trying to remember lines, he might not hear exactly what the director said or be able to transfer the instruction to his performance. The director may interpret this to mean the actor cannot take direction, and thus end the audition.

5. Touch the Sky!

This is a little warm-up exercise you can use to wake everybody up. Have the whole class walk around the room. Have them start off slowly, then speed up to a fast walk, then slow to a snail's pace. After a few minutes, have them stand still and stretch their arms up in the air above their heads. Next have them stand on their tiptoes and stretch as high as they can, reaching for the sky. They should be elongating their bodies as much as possible. Now, have them walk around the room in this position.

After a minute or two, tell them to stop walking and shake their wrists. They should shake them so that they feel as if their wrists are going to fall off. All the time they are doing this they need to use spatial awareness.

Now you can add another step to this activity. Have the students scrunch their hands, making a fist, and then flex them. So they first make a fist, then they stretch their hands out so that their fingers point toward the ceiling. This should happen at a fairly fast pace, and their hands should be in front of them at about face height. Have them repeat this cycle two hundred times. If they are struggling you can cut the repetitions to one hundred times. As soon as they have finished, which hopefully will be at about the same time, have them form a circle. Have them hold their hands up so that their palms are practically touching the actors' palms on either side of them. Ask them to focus on one actor in the circle; that actor does not have to reciprocate because he might be looking at someone else. Have them stand still like this for two to three minutes. Allow everyone to sit down and take a couple minutes to rest after you have finished. Believe it or not, your students will find this activity refreshing and draining all at the same time.

Variables:

This is a wake-up-and-energize exercise. There are many different ways you could do this. You can borrow exercises from aerobics, yoga, Tai Chi, and martial arts. Take some exercises and formulate your own warm-up.

Discussion:

I don't usually have one for this activity. I often like to go from this exercise straight into something else without a discussion.

Purpose:
To bring the body back into homeostasis

This exercise allows the body to feel in balance. Joelle Peeters describes homeostasis as, "bringing about a state of equilibrium or balance within the body."[2] If you are working with teenagers, they may have just had a bad class and be in a bad mood, or maybe Jane broke up with her boyfriend last week and it's constantly on her mind. Perhaps your students are adults and Dirk got into a yelling match with his boss today. If you leave your students

---

[2] Joelle Peeters, *Reflexology* (New York: Barnes & Noble, 2003), 9.

14

as they are, they will bring all of these issues into the class with them. It may mean they cannot really focus on what you are trying to teach. This exercise is physically quite intense, and the actors are usually not able to think of anything else. You are breaking their pattern and enabling them to participate in the present moment. In this way, you are able to shift them into a different gear, even if it is just for a short period of time.

Now, there may be times when it can be interesting not to put your actors in a state of neutrality, but to allow them to play off the events of that day. For example, perhaps Heather performed a monolog last week. The monolog involved the death of her character's cat. When you saw Heather perform it last week she was not very emotional and the piece was acted in a predictable fashion. Today she has come into class and is absolutely ecstatic. Bob, whom she has always liked, has asked her out on a date tonight. She is in a state of euphoria and cannot think of anything else. Then you ask her if you can see her monolog again, the one with the cat. She tells you that she doesn't feel mentally prepared and asks if she can do it tomorrow. You say not to worry about being prepared, to just play it the way she feels. Now you may see some very different results. You may find a lot more light and shade in the performance than you saw last week. This is because even though the theme of the piece may be a sad one, Heather is in a state of euphoria and perhaps some of that will rub off on her interpretation of the piece today. After she finishes the monolog, ask Heather to comment on what, if anything, was different from the last time she performed it.

You will often hear actors say, "I'm going to perform it exactly the same every night because I am a professional." But can we really perform with consistency? Aren't we slightly different people today than we were yesterday? Aren't the events of that day going to at least slightly influence our performance and interpretation that evening? I predict yes, and I also believe that these elements can allow a performance to stay fresh and help the actors believe that this is the first time they have ever uttered these words.

Does this sound like a contradiction to the purpose of "Touch the Sky"? Perhaps, but I feel approaches to acting are often contradictory within themselves. When I read an acting book or meet a director who claims his is the only correct method, I take it with a grain of salt.

To build rapport
In the very last part of this exercise the actors stand together with their palms practically touching. When done with real focus, this will

create a strong group energy. The actors will feel a sense of unity and togetherness. Hopefully, they will experience group rapport. Rapport is really a feeling of sameness. If you have rapport with someone you feel there is something that connects you, perhaps something that you have in common. Anthony Robbins describes rapport as "the phenomenon of people trading and/or sharing particular behaviors."[3] If you were directing a play related to baseball you might discuss the issue of the actors chewing (pretending to chew) tobacco sacks. Baseball players do so because it has been a tradition in baseball for many years, and because this helps build rapport among the players. Other words with similar meaning are *ensemble* and *unity.* These terms do not all mean the same thing, but they are very closely linked. So when you are working with your actors try to use many different words like these.

Similarly, when you use these and other relaxation exercises, instead of using the term *relaxation,* you might say, "In this exercise we are going to work for a feeling of easiness." Do you see how when we change one word we can also change the interpretation? Do not allow your actors to become too robotic or your exercises become predictable. "Oh, we have to relax again!" Always continue to make your students stretch their minds!

[3] Anthony Robbins, *Awaken the Giant Within* (London: Simon & Schuster, 1992), 418.

Chapter 2
Body Awareness

6. Energy Breathing

Get the whole class to stand up and form a circle. By now everyone should understand diaphragmatic breathing, so just give a quick refresher if it is needed. In this exercise, students should breathe in for a count of four, hold their breath for sixteen, and breathe out for a count of eight. They should take all the counts to breathe in and breathe out. This exercise works best when the teacher counts: "Breathing in one, two, three, four, and hold one, two, three, four, five, six, seven, eight, nine, ten, eleven, twelve, thirteen, fourteen, fifteen, sixteen. Breathe out one, two, three, four, five, six, seven, eight. And take a recovery breath. Good. And breathe in one, two ... "

You may wonder how I can breathe in and count at the same time. Good question! The way I like to do this is to snap my fingers to serve as counts so that I can participate in the breathing myself. You should repeat this exercise about five times, and as your students' stamina improves you could work up to five to ten times. Be cautious! There may be some students who become dizzy or cannot hold their breath for long. Tell them to stop if it becomes difficult. I don't want to worry you, but make sure you are observing the students. Safety should always be high on your agenda.

Variables:

You can change the length of this exercise; just make sure you stick to the ratio (1:4:2). So you could have them breathe in for five, hold for twenty, and breathe out for ten. If you are working with very young students you might have them breathe in for two, hold for eight, and breathe out for four.

Discussion:

It is always important to get student feedback, so ask them questions like, "Why do you think we did this exercise? What did you gain from it?" The students will often learn a lot more when they have to think, rather than when you feed them all the answers. Find out if they feel more energized or bored after doing this exercise. These are both valid answers. If they answer negatively, you might respond with, "Okay good, why didn't you like it?" Now that you haven't reprimanded them and you have accepted their answer they will feel like they have contributed, even if that was not their original intention. You may want to reiterate that breathing exercises have many different purposes and that, as they may have discovered, this one can increase energy levels.

Purpose:
To understand the potential of the human body
Through this exercise the students will have a new understanding of their body's possibilities. It is essential for actors to continue to learn as much as they can about the human body, as this is the tool with which they work. This is the actor's instrument. The more aware the students become of their bodies, the more they can manipulate them. As Moni Yakim explained, "Physical expression is as important in its stillness as in its movement."[1]

To energize students
This specific exercise will also help the students come in with energy for a rehearsal or performance. Because this breathing exercise focuses mainly on enhancing energy, it will help oxygenate the blood. The students will feel more alive, and they will be more alert for the task at hand. It can easily be used in a real acting situation. Let us say for a moment that an actor has arrived tired and lethargic for play rehearsal. He finds it hard to concentrate and keeps forgetting the directions he has just been given. The director finds he has to run the same scenes three or four times until he can get what he is looking for. This is not only frustrating for the director, but it is also incredibly time consuming. By utilizing exercises such as these, actors can give their bodies an extra boost. This should leave them alert, revitalized, and ready for rehearsal.

7. Acting Natural
In this exercise you should send about five students out of the classroom. The rest of the students will be sitting at the front of the room as an audience. Tell those who are outside that they will need to number themselves from one to five and that in a moment they will have to come into the room one at a time. When the first student comes in he will need to walk to the center of the room and tell us his name, three

[1] Moni Yakim, *Creating a Character* (New York: Watson-Guptill Publications, 1990), 3.

things about himself, and his date of birth. He will then leave the room and immediately the next person will come in. Once you have given the students these directions, ask them to wait outside the classroom for a moment. Now tell the audience inside the classroom that they should not really pay attention to what is being said, but they should watch the body language. For instance, what are they doing with their hands? Are they standing still or swaying from side to side? Are their arms folded or are they using their hands a lot? Are they smiling or frowning? Ask those in the audience to make a mental note of any specifics they observe with each person. It is important that they do not draw attention to the fact that they are watching the five students very closely. Once the students have made their entrances, invite them all back in. At this point you can tell them the real objective of the activity. You can tell them that they were being observed and that their body language was being watched. I would only use this exercise once because the next group would already know they are going to be observed. This could lead to unrealistic observations.

Variables:

You might ask the students to say their full address and talk about their favorite food for a minute. Be imaginative!

Discussion:

After all five students have completed the exercise, have them come back into the room. Explain to them that the students in the audience were not really interested in what they were saying but what they were doing. Tell them that the class will now make comments based on their observations, not to poke fun but to share with the students what body language was observed. Start with the first person who spoke and have anyone who noticed anything about his body language comment one at a time. Once you have gone through the observations about all five people, ask them for their comments. "Did you know you were swaying from side to side? Do you realize how much you speak with your hands?"

Purpose:

To develop body awareness

For this exercise, explain to the students that actors must be aware of what their bodies are doing. For instance, you might explain, "When you perform in front of an audience you may be very nervous. You may have a great number of lines and movements to remember and it's easy to become very tense if you do not have body awareness. We used the example of just coming into the room and saying a few simple things, and look how much fidgeting we noticed." Explain to the students that at first they will need to be consciously aware of the different forms of fidgeting they are doing, but after a while they will be able to control it without conscious effort.

To encourage students to broaden their horizons
When the students go outside the room, they often spend most of their time thinking about what to say. They want to make sure that they say the right things. When they come into the room and discover that what they said was not an important part of the exercise, they receive a rude awakening. They start to realize that things are not always as obvious as they seem. Actors often need to think outside the box. Let us say the character Emily says to the character Jerome, "I love you." At first glance the actor might play this with love and affection. After reading the play and looking deeper into the text, the actor might find a whole new meaning to this phrase. Perhaps the subtext (the real meaning behind the words) is, "I hate you." This activity encourages actors to look past the obvious and explore the deeper meaning.

8. The Machine

Don't spend much time explaining this activity; just allow the students to discover as they go. Here's an example of how to introduce this exercise:

"I need a volunteer to come up front. Okay, Justine, you are one part of a machine. I would like you to choose an action that your part of the machine will do, and repeat that action over and over. I also want you to add a sound that your part of the machine makes. The only other thing I will tell you is that you have to keep going and you cannot move off the spot. Okay, off you go."

Next give the following instructions to the rest of the class: "Now that Justine has started I need the rest of you to come up one at a time and add your part of the machine. You should add a part that you feel is vital for this machine to continue. It should complement the parts that are already up there; however, it must be different.Your part must also have a sound to go with it."

Variables:

You can play the game, discuss what worked and what didn't, and then play it again. You may think this is the same thing, but it isn't. After the students have commented on their observations they may get totally different results. This is something you can do on most exercises.

You can also have participants come up and perform the action without a sound.

Discussion:

See variables and "The Thing."

Purpose:

To develop body awareness

This is an excellent exercise in body awareness. The students are also learning how to connect the voice and the body. This may sound redundant, but start watching actors onstage and you will realize that many have not developed the resources to connect the two. Although this exercise is not specifically based on teamwork, the performers should be aware of what the others are doing so that they can make their piece of machinery a cog in the machine.

To become part of an ensemble

In this activity there should be an awareness of the group. Even though each student has to come up with his or her own movement, it should complement the rest of the machine. If a student adds an action to the machine that is totally random it may affect the group as a whole. This activity will help the students get away from the "star quality" as they learn to work as part of a unit.

9. The Thing

This game is very similar to "The Machine," so I will not explain it all again. The difference is that this time one person is a traveling thing, and everyone else must join one at a time to the traveling thing. Eventually there is just one big moving blob.

Variables:

See "The Machine."

Discussion:

"How did it feel when you were all trying to move as one organism? What happened as more people started to join in?"

"What worked? What didn't work?"

"Did you have to work as a team?"

"Was one part of the 'thing' more influential than another?"

"Was the leader at the front? Was there a leader?"

Of course the list of questions is endless, so shape your discussion as you see fit. Do not follow my list verbatim; I have just thrown you examples.

Purpose:

To learn to work as a unit, a team, an ensemble

These terms really mean the same thing, and as a teacher you should know and use each one.

To increase body awareness

Moving as a unit means students will learn to develop their sense of rhythm. If some people move in one direction and others move in another, The "thing" will fall apart. The students have to sense where the leader is moving. The students also have to use their bodies to add to any changes in movement or rhythm guided by the leader. The "thing" works much like a pantomime horse, which is usually made up of two actors who fit inside one costume. They have to learn to move as one and to create the impression of a horse with four legs. It is amazing to discover where all of these skills can be incorporated into an actor's performance.

10. Tug of War

For this exercise have the students split up into pairs and find a space in the room. Have the pairs stand with their backs to one another, but keeping a space between them so they are not touching. They then need to bend forward and put their hands through their legs and see who can pull the other one through. Whoever pulls the other one through wins. The pulling should be done in a smooth action so as to avoid injury. Have each team play the best of three and then switch partners. Sensible shoes are also required. (In fact, this should be a given for all acting classes. Often there is lots of movement in an acting class, so have students avoid wearing shoes and clothing that might impede their movement. An example of what to avoid might be high heels. You might make an exception to this rule for a character in a play. If Sarah is playing a lady of good standing, you might ask Sarah to wear her high heels to rehearsals to help her practice walking in them and still keep good posture.)

Variables:

This activity is partly related to strength, but the students also have to use their ingenuity. An activity that exercises similar skills is called "Thumb Wars." Mention this to any of your students and they will know what you are talking about.

Discussion:

"Did you always manage to predict the winner in this activity? In other words, did the strongest person always win?"

"What factors might have played into the end results?"

"Did anyone find a strategy that he thinks is fool proof?"

"Are there any benefits of this activity for acting?" It is very important to see that the students can make this connection.

Purpose:

To utilize body mechanics

In this game the students initially think that strength is the key ingredient. As they explore different strategies, however, they will discover that transference of body weight is the most important factor. By leaning slightly backward they will increase their potential to dislodge their partner. Utilizing their lower body is more important in this activity than using their upper body. The actors have just rehearsed transference of body weight. They have exercised physical and mental muscles. If we say that the body/mind is the actor's instrument, then perhaps we should continue to play it in as many ways as we can.

To break down personal boundaries

You need to decide how suitable this exercise is for your students. I might choose not to use this with junior high students but would be quite comfortable with older teenagers and adults. During the game, the students must work at close range and personal space will almost definitely be invaded. This is to your advantage; the students are now confronted with completion of the task and the invasion of personal space issue. As they proceed with the activity, the personal space barrier usually becomes less of an issue and the object of the activity becomes the main focus. There is no telling how many times in a film or play a character might be put in a position that contradicts the beliefs or normal behaviors of the actor. The beliefs or actions are not the actor's, but the character's; nevertheless an actor must learn to become comfortable with those beliefs and actions. Actors need to learn to portray different situations without having to fight their own internal battles. This activity is a building block for breaking down some of these barriers.

11. Sink to the Floor

In this activity, call one person to the front of the room. Now have this individual stand in a horse's stance. This means her legs should be about a foot apart, parallel to each other, and facing forward. Her knees should also be slightly bent. Now tell her you want her to allow her body to sink toward the floor as if it is being pulled by gravity. She has to imagine that everything is being pulled down toward the earth. Her body should feel very heavy. Now tell her to remember that sensation because you will be coming back to it in a minute.

Call up two more volunteers. Tell them that in a moment they are going to lift the individual off the ground. Explain that they can only use one arm each and that they have to place it under the individual's armpit, one on either side. Tell the first volunteer that she should just stand as she would normally. When the two volunteers are ready they should begin lifting. This should be fairly easy for them. After they have lifted her, tell them to return her to her standing position.

Now tell the student to let her body slump toward the floor as gravity pulls her down. She should still be standing, but her shoulders, legs, arms, everything should be pulled toward the ground. (She should have a sinking feeling.) Give her about a minute to get centered. When she indicates that she is ready, ask the two students to lift her the same way as they did before. This time the results should be quite different. Either they cannot lift her at all, or they lift her, but it is visible that doing so is extremely difficult.

These are the results you should find; however, sometimes there is a lack of focus, and the student is not really allowing her body to sink downward. If this is the case your results probably will not change. This activity is popular with the students as they see something visually, but normally they are not convinced of its authenticity until they themselves have had a go at it. You will probably find most of your students will want to try this activity, so allocate enough time.

Variables:

There are a number of similar games, including "Arm Levitation" and "Arm Zapper."

Discussion:

"Why was it more difficult to lift her the second time?"
"How important was the issue of strength in this activity?"
"How does this activity benefit you as acting students?"
"In what way does the participant have to focus in this exercise?"

Purpose:

To become aware of one's body

One thing I love about this exercise is that the students become more aware of what their bodies can do. It helps to break down limitations they place on their own physical capabilities. The more aware an actor is of his body's capabilities the more he can take advantage of it. Let's say that an actor who is fairly small in stature needs to play a bodyguard. If he is aware of his body's capabilities then he will be able to elongate his spine by standing straighter and push out his chest to appear more built.

By understanding their bodies, the students will also be able to enhance the technical aspects of acting, including vocal skills. Michael McCallion, one of the world's leading voice instructors, explains the voice/body connection: "You cannot separate your voice use from the rest of you. The impulse to communicate vocally comes from and uses your whole person, not merely the vocal organs."[2] So as you use this exercise to help your students develop a sense of awareness about their bodies, be sure to encourage them to explore the different ways they can apply this awareness to other areas of their acting.

To become centered

In order to allow their bodies to feel as if they are being pulled down by gravity, the actors have to center themselves. They have to allow

---

[2] Michael McCallion, *The Voice Book* (London: Faber and Faber, 1988), 3.

their energy to focus toward the pelvic region. One way of doing this is to focus on that area both mentally and physically. Even though character development is not the specific aim of this activity, students will be able to use this experience when they are building a character. (See "Center of Gravity" exercise.)

12. Friendly Hands

Introduce this activity like this:

"Good morning, everyone! Please form a circle in the center of the room. In a moment, I am going to ask you to choose a partner and find a space somewhere in the room. But first of all, let me have two volunteers to go into the middle of the circle. (I will sometimes use volunteers to demonstrate an activity; this can often save a lot of time in explaining an activity. Many students are much better when they are given visual as well as verbal directions.) Simon and Mark, thank you very much. Please turn so that you are facing each other. Good. Make sure you keep your hands nice and relaxed. Now, lift your hands so that your palms are facing each other — they should be almost touching but not quite. Thanks for the help.

"Now everyone, please get with a partner and stand so that your hands are practically touching. I am going to dim the lights slightly and add some music. (I like to use instrumental music here.) Please stand facing your partner in absolute silence. Good. As you stand facing each other, please look into each other's eyes. I know it sounds romantic, but it is actually a great way to increase your concentration. Now keep your hands so that the palms are very close to your partner's and see if anything happens. If everyone concentrates you may find that your hands start moving all on their own. If this happens just observe, but don't do anything. It may appear to you that your hands are actually dancing. This will only work if we all concentrate and work together as a team."

It takes a little bit of time, sometimes five or six minutes, before there is any movement. As the students continue with the exercise, walk around and observe. Then get back together in a circle and discuss the results.

Variables:

You may want to try having three pairs in the center while everyone else forms a circle around them. As the three groups participate in the activity have the rest of the students observe. After a sufficient period of time, stop the activity and ask for comments from those who were observing.

Discussion:

"What were the unexpected results in this activity?"
"What about the importance of the ensemble for this activity?"
"How is keeping the muscles relaxed crucial to this activity?"
"Why is having an open mind important for actors?"

Purpose:

To encourage actors to keep an open mind

When students first come into this activity they are often a little apprehensive or they do not believe it will work. In order to get the desired results, the students have to clear their minds and just go with the activity. By keeping an open mind the students should find the results are more rewarding.

Actors have to keep an open mind in many ways. An actor may interpret a character one way, whereas the director may see the part in a totally different light. The actor has to be open to any ideas or changes the director has. Changes may occur continually and happen in every scene. An actor may be asked to interpret the same scene in twenty different ways; the actor needs to be open to these suggestions. Even though the actors will certainly have opinions of their own, by being open to suggestions they will become more malleable and flexible as actors.

To help actors to get in touch with their bodies

When actors are facing their partners, they need to keep their hands nice and relaxed. If they flex their fingers or tense their hands they will not give their hands the opportunity to react off their partner's. Visually there may not be much difference between tense and relaxed fingers, but kinesthetically, in terms of feeling, the difference is huge.

As the hands start their dance, the actors become more aware of the different capabilities of their bodies. This hand dance is rather interesting in that the hand movements seem to be involuntary. The human body has many mechanisms that work involuntarily, such as breathing and movement. (Although we do have some degree of control over these.) When novice actors get onstage they often become very conscious of these involuntary mechanisms. You will hear things like, "I didn't know what to do with my hands." "I felt like I couldn't breathe!" An exercise such as the hand activity gives the students an opportunity to just let it happen. Students should not try and control the involuntary motions. This will then help them to understand that they do not need to totally control these functions onstage.

27

13. Roller Coaster

For this activity you will only need one actor in your playing area. Have everyone else sit in the center of the room. Now ask the actor onstage to get himself in a physically depressed state. How would his body look when he is feeling depressed? Get some suggestions from the audience to help. You may get suggestions like, "Your head should be looking toward the floor. You should be sitting in a chair. You shoulders can be slumped forward toward the ground. Your knees should be touching, your arms should be folded, and your breathing should be slow and shallow. Close your eyes." If the actor is struggling, you can offer your own suggestions. You want the actor to have an idea of what it feels like to be depressed just by adjusting his body physically. He does not even have to think of a specific experience; simply adjusting his posture will affect his emotional state.

Now tell the actor to keep that feeling of depression, but to begin jumping up in the air as fast as he can. Tell him to continue jumping and raise his arms above his head toward the ceiling. Ask him to keep his arms stretched as high as he can and to paste a big smile on his face while chanting, "Yeah, yeah, yeah." (You can change this to "Woo, woo, woo," or anything you want.) He will most likely feel more energetic and cheerful during this part.

Now, here are some really important elements to this exercise. When the actor is jumping and raising his arms he must jump as high as possible using all his energy. When he raises his arms he must stretch so that he thinks they really will hit the ceiling. When he smiles it must be the biggest smile he can muster, while at the same time trying to stay in that state of depression. Even if he commits 100 percent, it will be virtually impossible for him to remain depressed. We created the depression artificially by putting the actor in a physical state and we broke it just as quickly by contrasting it with another physical state. In neither case did we give the actor a reason to feel depressed or to feel good. You can try this out on different actors. You may want to have a discussion after each actor has taken a turn.

Variables:

You could ask your actors to be really angry in the first instance and then really cheerful in the next. Maybe they are laughing during one part; you decide. The important factor is to make sure that whatever you choose, the two situations are contrasting. Also, make sure you adjust the actor's physical posture quite dramatically and accurately for each emotion.

28

Discussion:

"How did your state change when we changed you physically?"

"Would anybody say they were affected emotionally? Can you explain why?"

"Audience, how did you decide what positions to put the actors in? Let me take that a step further: Why did you think they should be looking down for depression?"

"Is this exercise useful for you as actors? How might it come in handy?"

Purpose:

To show the importance of physicality

This exercise is really effective because the actors discover that without any specific thoughts, their physical body can change their state of mind. You may have noticed that they were given very basic emotions such as depression and happiness. This is because there is very little thought process needed to sustain these general states. The audience just has to decide what kind of posture they assume when sad, happy, etc. It is purely a mechanical process; it is no different from asking them to tell me how to ride a bike. However, if I asked my students to remember a specific time when they were young and got really upset, that would be a different ball game. In that case, the actor has to dig deep and find specifics, and that is not what we are looking for in this activity. We simply want the actor to be aware of the instant affect the body can have on the emotions. Another application for physicality could be playing the role of a drunk. Melissa Bruder and her colleagues at the Atlantic Theatre Company state, "To play a drunk scene, you must first figure out what the physical manifestations of being drunk are — for example, slurred speech, wobbly movements, and difficulty maintaining balance."[3] This exercise could help prepare the students for future work such as this.

To incorporate physical action

Now that we understand what this exercise can do, we want to see where it can be used in acting. One great example could be during an argument. Jo and Grace are talking about whose turn it is to do the dishes. As they are discussing the issue, Jo drops her carefully organized portfolio on the floor and all her papers fall out. As she starts to pick them up, she is becoming frustrated. She starts to snatch them up at a faster pace, but

[3] Melissa Bruder et al., *A Practical Handbook for the Actor* (New York: Vintage Books, 1986) 52.

they just become more entangled and she becomes annoyed. She picks up the pile, slams it to the ground, and screams at Grace that she will not do the dishes! This issue of the dishes has really become secondary to Jo, but the physical action of picking up her papers has gotten her more and more frustrated until she is fuming with rage. So as actors we want to be aware that physical action can be used to drive our emotional states. Great actors such as Laurence Olivier and Benoit Cerstant Coquelin knew the power of physicality. These actors are considered to be among the greatest of all time, and yet they chose a very external approach to acting. Uta Hagen describes Coquelin's reaction when he had a real moment during a performance, "The famous nineteenth century actor Coquelin once apologized to his colleagues in the wings, 'Tonight I shed real tears onstage. I promise you it will not occur again.'"[4] In this book, I do not intend to pass judgment on this or other acting approaches; rather I want to make the students aware of the infinite possibilities in acting.

14. Siamese Twins

After explaining this activity, have the students get into teams of four. Instruct one member from each team to sit in a comfortable position. Whatever positions those members choose, they will need to stay perfectly still, which is why they need to be comfortable. Explain that staying still also includes abstaining from any facial movement. Ask the team members in the middle to keep their eyes closed throughout this experience. Allow them to stay like this for two or three minutes. At this point ask them to explore how they are feeling in general terms. They may feel relaxed, nervous, scared, or whatever comes to mind. They should explore their emotion internally and not share it out loud. They should not signal in any way either. Remind them that they need to hold perfectly still.

Now, ask a second person from each team to sit, very carefully, next to members already in the middle. These team members should arrange themselves in a position identical to the first person. Also tell them that they need to be sitting shoulder to shoulder to the other person. It is very important that there is body contact between the two. When they feel they are in position, ask them to close their eyes. Now the remaining two members of each group are going to physically adjust the

---

[4] Uta Hagen, *A Challenge for the Actor* (New York: Scribner, 1991), 47.

second person so he or she is absolutely identical to the first. The people who are sitting need to allow themselves to be manipulated; however, they cannot make any comments or help in any way. The aim is not just to align the second person's body so its position is generally identical to the first member's, but also to really go into detail. Perhaps one facial cheek needs to be raised slightly, or an arm seems to be too tense. How about breathing patterns? The remaining team members should adjust the second person until they have him or her in a position as close to that of the first as they can. Do not touch the first person! When you are satisfied, wait a few minutes. Now ask the second team members to mentally explore how they are feeling in general terms.

Wait a few more minutes and then ask both of the students in the middle to picture a specific event. They need to decide where they are. They do not need to tell you what they are thinking. Give them a minute or so to do this. Now ask them to make the picture more intense and brighter. Ask them to add sound to the picture, and if possible make it a moving picture. Ask them to intensify these images even more using noises, smells, colors, movement, and even volume. You should ask them to consider these things over about a five or six minute period. Once you have finished, give them another minute or two to just absorb. Then ask them to open their eyes.

This activity is still not quite finished. Ask the first person and then the second to tell you what state they were in at the beginning of the activity. They may say relaxed, calm, tense — whatever was happening for them. Next ask them to talk about their stories. Where were they? What was happening? Sometimes the results of this activity can be incredible. It is quite common to find that the pair has parallels in the first stages, i.e., they both felt relaxed. However, what can also be interesting is that some pairs will have very similar or even identical stories.

After explaining an activity such as this you may want to take a few minutes to answer questions. It is a little complicated and may continue for a good thirty minutes, so you want to give the participants good instructions before they begin. Most likely, you will only use this activity once in a session because of time.

Variables:

You could change the number you have in a group. You might have groups of four with two people doing the adjusting. Or you may choose to have a group of three in which only one person does the adjusting.

31

Discussion:

"In what way does this activity attempt to highlight the connection between body and mind?" "Even though there were individual groups, were there any ways in which the whole room worked together?"

"Why would it matter if the breathing patterns of the two people were totally different?"

"What was the purpose of having the two participants sit shoulder to shoulder?"

"Do you see this activity as beneficial for actors?"

Purpose:

To highlight the mind/body connection

This activity attempts to show that by having people sit in the same positions physically they can create some of the same thoughts and feelings. It does not work on every occasion; however, people seem to come up with a lot of similarities. It gives actors another reference to the interlinking of mind and body. Actors have realized for many years that the physical body is not separate from the mind. By understanding the effects of the body on the mind, actors are able to manipulate the connection to their advantage. You will see this time and time again through character development. It is important for actors to have experiences to back up many of the theories they are taught. This exercise gives actors just such a reference point.

To incorporate the senses

The senses are explored in depth in this exercise. While you talk the actors through the visualization process, you are asking them to engage their senses. They are asked to see a picture, to hear the noises, to smell the sea, to taste the coffee, and to touch the grass. This is a wonderful way of involving all the senses. It is also an excellent way to show the actors the power that the senses have. By incorporating them with visualization in this manner the actors often feel the images become incredibly poignant. I have often seen actors salivate at the mouth tasting whatever food is in their picture. On many occasions the manipulation of the senses is a necessary tool for the actor. To picture an ocean in front of you when you are facing a brick wall takes an extraordinary imagination, and understanding the value of the senses is a benefit of this exercise.

Chapter 3

Observation

15. Group Stare

Split the group so that half of your students are on the stage while the other half are sitting in the audience. Ask the group onstage to simply stand there in silence; do not give them anything to do. They can spread themselves out a little as long as they are standing in the designated area. The audience is going to watch and observe. Those onstage will probably start to become uncomfortable and fidgety. Allow this to happen and do not question it or comment on it. After about two or three minutes give the group onstage an activity to do, for example, counting the tiles on the ceiling. Allow this to continue for another two or three minutes. Once you are ready, switch the groups so that the group that was onstage is now in the audience watching and the second group is onstage. Do not allow any comments until both groups have completed the exercise.

Variables:

You can vary this exercise for the more advanced students by giving them different senses of urgency. For instance, tell them they must count the tiles in less than five minutes or they will be grounded. What will happen if they don't get it done in a minute or thirty seconds? Consider how you can change the intensity. For adults you might say that if the activity is not complete within forty-nine seconds their houses will be repossessed. You only have forty-nine seconds to complete the task and rush to the courthouse. Remember! They must count the exact number; it is not enough to just believe it is correct. It must be 100 percent accurate and the students must have an absolute sense of certainty.

Discussion:

Once the exercise is finished, discuss it with the students. Ask them, "How did it feel when you stood onstage for five minutes with nothing to do? What did you observe as an audience member at the start of this exercise? What were your observations, comments, and opinions? What changed for you when you were given a task? What did you observe as an audience member once the group had been given an activity?" These are some examples of the guiding questions you might want to ask. It is important not to express your opinions to the students until they have shared their views. Always try to avoid telling them they are wrong. Be

i need to correct an answer. You might say, "Good, you are
, the right direction," or "Not quite, but good effort." You may
, is unnecessary, but you want your students to feel relaxed
,n to speak freely.

Purpose:

To know the objective in any given moment

It is common for actors to start fidgeting onstage. Often this is
because they get nervous and don't know what to do with themselves.
This activity allows the actors to experience this, and then to discover
what it is like to be fully engaged in an activity, Because they get so
focused on the activity, they have no time to worry about how they are
standing or what to do with their hands.

To encourage observation and analysis

In this activity it is the audience who is asked to do the observing.
They are also asked to comment on what they see and what meaning
they took from it. So Sarah might say, "Well, they were just standing
there. They looked really bored." Not only did she remember what the
performers were doing, but she also gave us an interpretation of what
their actions meant to her. It is important for actors to know that all of
their actions, or lack thereof, onstage will be interpreted by the
audience. If actors have their arms folded, the audience might interpret
this to mean they are bored, or perhaps they are really mad about
something. Through this activity the students will start to realize that
everything they do onstage has meaning. They will also enhance their
skills of observation.

16. Three Changes

Have two students come up from the audience. (I often ask for
volunteers, but be careful doing this because you may find the same
three of four students volunteering every time. While this shows
excellent confidence and enthusiasm, it can be unbalancing for the
ensemble. So sometimes you may request a volunteer, although often
you should select the people to come up. Sometimes you may instruct
the previous students to choose the next pair to come up. Doing this
takes some of the pressure off you and reduces the possibility of
perceived favoritism.) Now have the two students look at each other for

about a minute. They can ask each other to turn around so they can get a complete view. Then tell them both to turn around so that they are looking in opposite directions. Choose one of them to change three things about his appearance. The actor will want to make these changes fairly subtle, such as slightly rolling up one leg of his jeans or unzipping his jacket. He should not make really obvious changes, such as putting a shirt on backward. The actor can also change personal features, such as his hair, if desired. When you have given the actor about a minute to make these changes, have both actors turn back around and face each other again. Now the other person has three chances to guess all three changes. It is important at the beginning that you do not tell the pair who will be making the changes; this way they both have to observe as they do not know which task they will be assigned.

Variables:

You can alter the number of changes to as many as you like, perhaps five changes with a more advanced group. Look at all these exercises this way: If the students aren't challenged, try to adjust the exercise to stretch them more. I do not mean you want to set them up for failure; it is important that they see themselves succeeding in many instances.

Discussion:

"Why is observation important for actors and actresses?"

"Why did I ask the participants to make subtle changes to their appearances?"

"Why didn't I just tell them at the beginning who was going to be the observer?"

"What did you notice about their body language?"

Purpose:

To be specific through observation

The students have to study each other in detail; they need to get very specific. So if Sarah is wearing a shirt, Fred will want to know that it has green shiny buttons and a bright red butterfly with glitter on its wings. This is an excellent tool to develop actors' observation skills and show the importance of specificity. If you were playing a character you shouldn't say you're about fifteen to twenty. When asked how old we are we don't say, "About nineteen to thirty." We say, "I'm twenty." So observation forces them to pay attention to detail.

To practice memorization

If the students are to notice what has changed, they have to remember what the person looked like to being with. Memorization is important in many aspects of acting, such as learning lines and blocking.

17. Action Whisper

This game is similar to a game called "Chinese Whispers" but is at a more advanced stage. There is a nice little introduction you can do before you actually start this exercise, which goes something like this: "Okay, everyone stand up and form a circle. Today's game is called 'Action Whisper,' but before we start I would like us to do a few small introductory exercises. First, come up with an adjective that has the same first letter as your name. For instance, I might say, 'Great Gavin,' or Tony might say, 'Tough Tony.' Your adjective does not have to be something that necessarily characterizes you, but it can be. I will give you about thirty seconds to come up with something. As you do this, turn to face the outside of the circle and practice your phrase out loud. (This not only gives them an opportunity to hear how it would sound, but also allows them to rehearse without the feeling that their peers are judging them.) Okay, ready? Turn back to face the center of the circle and we will go around the circle and have everyone say his or her phrase one at a time. Good job!

"Now I want to take the activity one step further. You already have your phrase, and what I would like you to do this time is to add an action that goes with your phrase. So for Great Gavin I might flex my biceps like a weight lifter. Angry Andrea might stamp her foot. Take about thirty seconds to come up with something, and as you do this use the same process as before. Face the outside of the circle, and this time practice your action with the phrase. (Give them a few minutes to do this.)

"Okay, good; now as we go around this time I would like for you each to perform your action with the phrase, and then after each person I would like the whole class to repeat the action."

It is up to you as the instructor to make sure this is done in a respectful manner. Of course, people will laugh at each other's actions, and this is fine, as long as it is done in a safe environment. For instance, you may explain, "Because we are all going to look silly at some stage and feel a little embarrassed it's okay. We can all feel silly together. The problem is when someone decides to personalize it and make someone feel bad. I do not allow this behavior and neither should you."

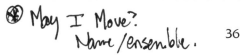

May I Move?
Name / ensemble.

36

After you have completed these introductory exercises, segue into the game as follows:

"Okay, this leads me into our game which, as I have mentioned, is called 'Action Whisper.' To start with, everyone go back and take a seat. Okay, now I'm going to choose half the class to come up onto the stage. Let's have you all stand side by side facing the audience. Here is how this activity works. I will tap the first person on the shoulder and act out a few movements. For example, first I might raise my arms out to the side and then bring them back in. Then I might pat my head and rub my belly. And finally, I might bend forward and touch my toes. (Of course, you could demonstrate this visually in a classroom.)

"Now, at the moment, I have you facing forward so you can see what I am doing, but when we start the activity you will all need to turn and face the side wall so that you cannot see the action. You will be staring at the back of the person in front of you. The first person will tap the second person on the shoulder, who will then turn around so that the two are facing each other. The first person will demonstrate the sequence and then turn around to face the opposite wall. Now the second person will tap the third person on the shoulder and the process continues. Each person should turn around to face the opposite wall after demonstrating the actions. This is done that way so that no one can hint to another player or accidentally show through his or her body language how accurately the other players are performing the sequence.

"If the sequence was too fast, just perform it to the best of your ability. Whoever starts us off will need to come up with his or her own short sequence, as mine was just an example. Also I want you to interpret the sequence to the best of your ability rather than pretending to forget the sequence to entertain us. Believe me, it will be far more compelling for the audience if you address the challenge honestly. There is nothing as interesting as reality. After we have been through the activity we will switch groups and try again. Once we have watched the second group, I will ask the half that is watching to make constructive comments about their observations."

Variables:

See "Chinese Whispers."

Discussion:

"What do you feel were the challenges for this group?"
"Can you pinpoint exactly where the sequence changed?"

"What happened to the sequence after it had been changed?"

"What strategies did the players come up with to improve their results?"

Purpose:

To make discoveries

You may have noticed that I did not give the students as much information as I could have. For instance, at the start of the game the first student will tap the second player on the shoulder and show the sequence once through. The second person may hardly remember it, but will go straight on to the next person. Now if you look back at the game description you will notice I did not tell the performers they couldn't show the sequence more than once. Nor did I tell them that they could not ask to see the sequence again. Everyone just assumed this was the rule, which is the intention. You are making the students think and pay close attention. Sometimes they will gesture that they want to see the sequence again; they will probably look at you to see if this is acceptable. When you do not say anything they will proceed, happy that they have made a new discovery. If, after playing once or twice, no one has discovered this secret, you can pass on the information.

Actors are constantly making discoveries through the rehearsal process. A director might be working on a funeral scene with his actors and find it has become stale. He might decide to have them improvise the whole scene as a comedy. This is not because he really wants it played this way, but because it might help the actors to make some discoveries. Perhaps there are some lighter moments they had not even considered. Antonin Artaud once said, "I'm leaving to search for the impossible; the essence of the real human heart."[1] It is necessary to encourage your students to become independent thinkers and make their own choices. Be careful of creating a submissive actor who mechanically obeys your every whim.

To observe and utilize the senses

The students must pay close attention visually to what the previous person did. We can concentrate and focus in a number of ways, but if I am only listening and not watching I will not be able to complete the task. So as actors we are constantly working on improving all our senses.

---

[1] Gabriela Stoppelman, *Artaud for Beginners* (New York: Writers and Readers Publishing, 1998), 77.

(In this exercise we are working with our sense of sight.) When we utilize our senses to their full potential we are able to get that much closer to the reality of the moment. Edward Dwight Easty comments on how an actor could have taken advantage of his senses: "Suppose he first tried to remember the smell of whisky, as he brought the glass to his lips. Then suppose he had tried to remember how the alcohol feels when it first touches the lips."[2] Utilizing the senses can help create believability in the actor's mind.

18. Murderer

For this exercise have the lights already dimmed when the students come in. Have your students sit in a circle. Now tell them that in a moment they will need to look at the ground and close their eyes. At this point one student will walk around the circle and tap another student on the back once. This person will be the murderer. The student will keep walking around and pat another person on the back twice. This person will be the detective. Now have all the students open their eyes and ask the detective to identify himself to the group. Ask the other students to stand up and mingle. As they mingle they should shake hands with other people around them. The murderer, who has not revealed herself, will also shake hands, however with a slight difference. When the murderer shakes hands she must give a slight tickle to the inside of the victim's palm. This is how the victims know they have been murdered. As victims are murdered they should die dramatic deaths. The role of the detective is to try to guess who the murderer is through observation. Allow the detective to keep guessing until he gets the right answer, or until there is only one person left standing.

Once you have played the activity through, play again. Choose one of the students to lead the activity at this point. Allow your students to be in positions of responsibility as much as possible, positions in which they have to be able to communicate clearly with others. As actors we are always looking to communicate something.

Variables:

To make this activity more of a challenge you can ask people to have a delayed death. They should wait an extra moment or two before

[2] Edward Dwight Easty, *On Method Acting* (New York: Ballantine Books, 1981), 26.

39

actually dying. This will make it more difficult for the detective to figure out the murderer.

There is another version of this game called "Wink Murder." In this version, the students sit in a circle and close their eyes. The leader can still choose the murderer and the detective in the same way as before; however, this time the students stay seated in the circle throughout the game. To murder his or her victim the murderer simply has to wink at another person. As victims receive the wink (make eye contact) they must die a dramatic death. The detective will only get three guesses to try to solve the case.

Discussion:

"How does nonverbal communication play into this activity?"

"Give me some examples of how the actors can die dramatically."

"Discuss this activity in terms of observation."

"Why does the murderer need to be focused at all times?"

"When the leader is choosing the murderer and detective, what must he make sure he does?"

Purpose:

To break down inhibitions

When the students are murdered in this activity they are asked to die a dramatic death. This sounds fake and over the top. To a large extent it is; however, it serves an important purpose. Apart from being entertaining, it encourages actors to break out of their shells. One student will always try to top the previous deaths. This is very useful for directors; it is often considered far easier to bring a performance down, rather than to take it up a notch or two. Learning to lose inhibitions can be very important because it stops actors from mentally checking themselves in the middle of a performance. "Do I look stupid? Am I standing funny? Did I just say that line all wrong?" Oddly enough, when the actors focus on the action of the play, they often find they do not have time to worry about anything; they are too involved in the moment.

To help actors analyze a situation

Encourage your actors to think independently as much as you can. Yes, I know I keep saying this! When the leader walks around the circle he might simply stop somewhere and choose a murderer and a detective. The problem with this method is that it will most likely signal who has been chosen to the people sitting on either side. If the leader analyzes the situation for a moment he might make a number of observations: "If I tap a person while I'm moving it will be harder for others to guess who I chose. Even when I have chosen the murderer and detective I should continue to walk around the circle for a while, as this should further serve to confuse people." By analyzing his strategy before starting the activity, the leader will enhance the activity for everyone. Actors often analyze the script when defining their roles. It can also be useful to analyze scenes in rehearsal. A director might work through the same scene in five or six different ways to see which works best.

There is a slight cautionary note related to analyzing. Once the actor is in performance, the analyzing must stop. If an actor is in the middle of the show and analyzing his work at the same time, there will be a conflict of interest. This seems to be where some directors get confused. There are those who tell their actors they should not analyze at all. This could be dangerous as it cuts out part of the process. Analysis is a necessary tool in the exploration stage, but has no place in the final performance.

19. Stand Up/Sit Down

To play this game you will need three volunteers and one chair onstage. Have your audience in a designated area. Explain the game as follows:

"Okay, I need three volunteers to come up on the stage. In a moment, you are going to be given a scene to act out that will involve all three of you. However, there is a slight twist to this game. At all times one of you must be standing, one of you must be sitting on the chair, and one of you must be kneeling. So two people cannot be standing or sitting at the same time. Now it is also important to keep the exercise moving; in other words, you cannot spend the whole time just sitting in the chair.

"I want to make it even more interesting by adding another rule: You have to justify your actions. Let's say one of you is a doctor, one is a nurse, and the third is a patient. If the patient is sitting because he feels sick, this could be justified. If the nurse was kneeling and stands up to get some medicine this can be justified. If the doctor stands up and says, 'I think I will stand up now,' this seems totally unjustified and without purpose. You must have a purpose if you are going to stand, sit, or kneel; do not just change positions for the sake of it. At the same time, you must also remember who your character is and continue to portray him or her as accurately as you can. Remember, if you can keep it moving at a fairly fast pace it is more interesting and challenging."

You can give the students different locations, such as a hospital or doctor's office, a classroom, a visit with the principal, or an aerobics class. You can choose any scenario, but make sure each person has a defined role. Do not have three people in an aerobics class; instead designate an instructor, a student who is absolutely enthusiastic, and another student who does not want to be there. Be specific!

Variables:
You could add more people and more positions, such as standing, sitting, kneeling, and lying down on the floor.

Discussion:
"When did the movement seem justified?"

"How did projection and diction affect the performance?"

"Bearing in mind that they had to keep the movement going, what were your observations on the way the actors defined their characters?"

Some of these questions may sound complex, but after you have been talking in this manner for a while the students will start to adapt. You want to stretch them even with the terminology you use. If they don't understand, just rephrase the question. When teaching a foreign language, the teacher will often speak in that language. As acting coaches we also have our own language to teach.

Purpose:
To form an ensemble
This is another exercise in which teamwork is essential. While continuing to create a scene, the actors need to know who is sitting, standing, and kneeling. They have to be constantly aware of what other members of the cast are doing. In this respect, they have to support one another.

To improve observation skills
To be able to play this game the students have to continue to observe each other. This is great because, as teachers, you should encourage the students to be observing all the time. A lot of this should take place outside of class in their everyday lives. If they see someone

crying at a bus stop, of course they may be concerned, but they will also learn a lot from watching the process of what happens physically to that person while he or she is crying. This training is invaluable because it is real life.

To act and react

Not only must the actors act and react to what is being said, they must also respond to the standing and sitting aspect of the exercise.

Remember that on these exercises I am not mentioning every benefit; I will leave it to you to add your own ideas. If I included every single thing I could think of, you would see an incredible amount of repetition, with focus and concentration appearing on just about every exercise. More importantly, if everything is handed to you on a plate, you do not have to think for yourself. This is a danger for actors that I would like to avoid.

Chapter 4
Memorization

20. This Is Jane

Ask your students to stand in a circle. Go around the circle and get each person to say his or her name. This exercise is most effective in the first class the students have together because the students do not know each other's names yet. It is useful for the students to pay close attention to each others' names, but don't tell them this yet. Now ask the first person to repeat her name and tell us one thing about herself, such as "I'm Jane and I like shopping." Now the second person must tell us about Jane and then about himself: "This is Jane and she likes shopping. I'm Bob and I have big feet." The idea is to keep going in this manner until somebody gets stuck and cannot remember all of the previous information that has been shared. When this happens, start the activity again with the next person beginning a new round. Challenge the students to see if they can get farther than they did in previous rounds. If they managed to get to four people in the first try, see if they can get to seven people the next time around. Play this activity until everybody has gotten to participate at least once.

Variations:

You could vary this activity in a number of ways; if it is too easy, have each student include two personal facts. For example, "I'm Jane and I like shopping and washing cars." If the students are very young, you might want to start by just having them complete the name section of the exercise. Invent your own variations. Be flexible and use your imagination.

Discussion:

Ask the students why we might play this game. You are always aiming to get the answer from them. You also want to impress on them that something has been learned; it's not just a silly game. If they remembered ten names in a row, ask them, "How do you think you just did that?" If they have trouble answering, ask more pointed questions. For instance, "Okay, so you were talking out loud, did this make a difference in your memorization? You were using your visual abilities because you were looking at each other, how did this enhance your memorization capacity? Why do you think memorization is so important for actors?" You should also mention that everyone said his or her name at the beginning and if they were paying attention they may have a head start on the game. This is not a reprimand; you are just making an observation.

Purpose:

To practice memorization

This is, at the core, a memorization exercise. If an actor can give us a wonderfully meaningful performance but can't remember his lines, he is never going to achieve total mastery of his craft. Russ Weatherford, who invented his own line-learning technique, has the following to say about this particular game: "This exercise gives the class members the opportunity to realize that their own potential for recall is greater than they ever imagined."[1] By participating in this game, students are naturally exercising their memorization muscles. Acting is a fine blend of creativity and technique, as well as other things thrown into the melting pot, and memorization is an important element.

This exercise also reinforces the use of other senses such as sound and sight, from which students will learn that line memorization increases as more of the senses are used. As a bonus this exercise is an icebreaker because people start to feel a little more comfortable with each other when they know each other's names.

I want to stress that even these "fun games" have some real benefits for the actor. I have been in acting workshops and seen this activity used for two minutes and then pushed aside. I felt cheated; I wanted to ask my instructor, "Can you not see the important aspects of this activity?" It is up to us as teachers to completely utilize the games we play. I do not see acting games as a substitution for an actor's training; rather they are a complementary necessity.

21. The Name Game

Have the group stand in a circle. Go around the circle with each person giving his or her name. (Everyone needs to pay attention, but you do not have to mention that at this stage. Part of the discovery process in these activities is facilitated by not explaining everything beforehand. The issue of paying attention might be raised later on in the discussion.) Now one person (Player One) must go into the center of the

---

[1] Russ Weatherford, John R. Weatherford, and Ruth Warrick, *Confidence and Clarity* (Hollywood, Calif.: The Weatherford Group, 1992), 2.

circle and approach someone in the circle (Player Two). The person Player One walks toward must make eye contact with a third person (Player Three) and that individual must call out the name of Player Two before the Player Two gets tagged. Confusing enough for you? The only person who can call out the name is Player Three. Sometimes a different person will call out the name, but unfortunately this does not count. The students will sometimes find they cannot get anybody's attention. Of course, this is all part of the activity. If Player Two (the starer), is tagged, he has to be in the middle. If he isn't tagged and Player Three calls out the right name, Player One must now walk toward Player Three. Make sure the students are walking at a reasonable pace. If they go too fast or too slow it will change the dynamics of the entire activity.

Variables:

I have not used any variables for this game; however, if you are feeling really courageous you could put two people in the middle at once. I am sure it would prove very exciting, if not chaotic. You might also want to vary the speed at which the actor may move. If the game is too easy, have the individuals in the middle walk toward people at a faster pace or tighten the circle.

Discussion:

"Who learned some new names today? How did you do that?"

"What part did the pressure play in helping you to learn names?"

"You had to call a name before somebody else got tagged so you really had to pay attention. Did your senses become heightened during this game? Which senses?"

Purpose:

To break the ice

As much as anything, this game is a great icebreaker. I have sometimes used this as the first exercise I do and found that students who didn't know each other were able to break down barriers very quickly. This is of vital importance because, as we move on, the students will participate in activities where they are taking risks (in terms of acting) and they need to have a level of comfort and trust with the other students. When a new cast is put together for a show, they might only have two weeks to rehearse. Any activity that can help them break down barriers early on will be very useful.

47

To use a sense of urgency to enhance memorization capability
This can really be translated as absolute focus and concentration. These games are so important because while having fun the students are equipping themselves with a variety of tools that they can draw upon as necessary. The first time you give them lines to learn, they will already know that reading them out loud will be of more use than trying to learn the lines in their head; they will know that if they use absolute focus they will have to spend less time learning the lines than if they do it in a lethargic manner. They just learned about twenty names in ten minutes; you have expanded their confidence in their own abilities.

22. Name Spring

Here is another variation of a name-memorization exercise. This activity is one that I recommend you use in the first day or two, before the students get to know each other's names. You might explain it like this:

"Please come and form a circle. I need everyone to stay standing for this exercise, and let's all take a step back so there is about six inches of space in between each person. Good, now this activity is fairly simple. In a moment I will give one of you this beanbag, which you will throw to someone else in the circle. As you throw the beanbag you have to say the name of the actor you are throwing it to. You cannot throw it to the actor on your immediate left or right. The idea is to try to remember the names of as many people as you can. Each time the beanbag comes back to you, try to throw it to someone you have not thrown it to before. Let's keep this moving at a fast pace, so as soon as you get the beanbag you have to throw it to someone else. As well as remembering names you must also concentrate so that you do not drop the beanbag. There are no 'outs' in this activity, so do not see it as a competition. Okay, let's begin."

Variables:

Here is a variable that will make the game more difficult. Instead of the thrower calling out the name of the catcher, have the catcher call out the name of the actor who threw the beanbag to him. So if Fred throws the beanbag to Bob, Bob will say, "Fred," and Fred does not have to say anything. This is a challenge because the receiving actor has no time to prepare and may not remember the name of the thrower.

Discussion:

"What were the challenges that arose with throwing the beanbag and saying the name?"

"Which senses were used in this activity?"

"How might this activity help us to break down barriers?"

"Did you like this activity? Why or why not? What would you have done differently?"

Always give the actors the opportunity to challenge what you are saying. Allow them to express their opinions and feelings; perhaps they do have an idea that would work better. Try to steer yourself away portraying a godlike quality. My favorite teachers and directors have always been the most humble.

Purpose:

To use memorization with distractions

Remember, actors are always juggling different priorities. These objectives may include blocking, memorizing lines, voice projection, and acting and reacting. In this activity they have to throw and catch the beanbag, but they also have to remember all of their classmates' names. I love to give the students what I call "confusing tasks" in which there is not a singular objective. The students are then forced to cope with multitasking.

To break down barriers

Of course, as soon as the actors have learned each other's names they have broken down an initial barrier. This may sound obvious, but read on. When I was at drama school in London, teachers and directors alike would call all of us "Darling." At first it felt like a term of endearment until we realized it was because they could not be bothered to learn our names.

Anything that can bring the actors closer together will only enhance their acting. I remember a story an acting teacher once told me. She said that there was a huge storm one day and that students could not go home or leave the property. Everyone was somewhat scared and it was flooding outside, so all of the students and the teacher went into the costume room and huddled together for the next three hours. While they were there they shared stories and bonded. From that day forth there was a change in their work. That experience united them and it was evident in each performance. I am not telling you to go lock yourselves in a room; however, I am saying that the group is more important than the individual.

23. Baffling Ball

You will need a soft ball about the size of a tennis ball for this activity. I like to use a juggling ball, which is made of a synthetic leather material. Have your students stand in a circle and throw the ball across the circle. As they do this they need to say the name of the person to whom they are throwing the ball. Now here is the tricky part. Once the ball has gone to every member of the circle, the students need to start again. The challenge is to throw the ball to everyone in the circle in exactly the same order as they did previously. They need to do this without prompting each other, and if they drop the ball they have to start over. Make sure the participants continue to repeat the names at the same time. If they complete the activity successfully, start again with a different pattern.

Variables:

You can do this activity without saying the names. This is actually more difficult as the actors will have no auditory cue to help them remember. Also, if you want a really big challenge, you might try introducing two balls at the same time.

Discussion:

"How are teamwork and memorization linked in this activity?"

"Identify possible challenges with this activity."

"Give some examples of why memorization is important to the actor."

You can ask this last question after different activities where it applies. You want to make sure your students have a thorough understanding of the benefits of this skill; really drive it home.

Purpose:

To enhance multitasking skills

In this activity the students have to coordinate different skills at the same time. They have to throw the ball, remember names, remember the order, and work together all at the same time. So if they remember the order, but are not paying attention, they might not catch the ball. The students need to be focused on all the tasks at once. This is something actors must do constantly. For instance, actors on a film set have to make sure they hit their marks on the stage, know their lines, know their blocking — and these are just some of the technical aspects. As actors we are constantly juggling many different tasks all at once. Through games and activities students can learn to feel comfortable doing this.

To exercise motor skills

As the students throw and catch the ball, they are utilizing their hand-eye coordination. They also have to remember to whom they threw the ball. Mind and body are intertwined in this activity. As actors we are constantly tapping into this connection. Just as the ball bounces off different stimuli along its path, as actors we bounce our interpretations off different stimuli to form our decisions. After reading *Richard III* an actor might decide to interpret the main character in a physically grotesque manner. The actor in this situation is choosing to utilize the mind/body connection.

24. Camera Game

To start with have the students sit in various parts of the room. Ask them to take a good look around the room and, using their hands as a lens, take some "photos" of the people in the room. Now choose one person to leave the room and tell him that when he goes outside, five people will move to somewhere else in the room. His job is to come back in and figure out which five have moved. Once your volunteer has left the room, explain to the students that they do not want to give away who the five people are, so they want to make sure they are not staring or giving any sort of indication. It is up to them to work together. As you choose the five people, ask them to move in silence. When everyone is situated, ask the person outside to come back in. Before he attempts to name the students, ask him to look through his camera's "lens" one more time. This is to remind him of where he thinks people were sitting originally. When he feels he is ready, ask him to guess which students moved. Tell the students that no one should comment until the student who left has made all five guesses. At this point, ask the students who moved to raise their hands. If you have time, try this activity again with someone else going outside.

Variables:

Instead of asking the students to move to a different place you can actually have them leave the room. This is easier if your room has more than one exit. Then the person who was outside has to identify who is missing.

You could also change the number of students who move. I gave five as an example, but you might choose to use three or six.

Another way of doing this activity is to have two people take the pictures at the beginning. These two will then leave the room and they can work together when they come back in.

Discussion:

"What do you think the benefit is of taking the imaginary photographs at the beginning?"

"In what ways is teamwork important in this activity?"

"What is the purpose of having the actors move in silence?"

"Explain the benefits of this activity as you see them for the actor."

Purpose:

To enhance memorization skills

This exercise is obviously heavily linked to memorization, but what really caught my attention with this activity was taking the mental photos at the beginning. The students are now given what seems like an extra tool for remembering. By taking mental pictures of the people in the room, they have just doubled their capacity for memorization.

Memorization seems to be an area that is often given little attention in acting. Actors are often told, "Learn your lines." This seems strange; you very rarely hear a director say, "Direct the play by yourself." If we want our actors to become efficient at memorization then we have to give them the tools to do this.

To drive home the importance of the ensemble

It is often in the simplest of activities that the importance of the ensemble can be seen most clearly. When the observer comes back into the room he will search his own memory to try to work out who is missing or who has changed places. Sometimes he does not even have to use his own memorization to do this. If someone in the room is laughing at a certain person or staring at someone, this might be enough to give the answer away. All the students need to sit in a manner that gives no clues or indications to the observer. This can be quite challenging at times. Only if all the students do their part can this exercise be utilized fully. The great thing about this activity is that even if some students thought they had nothing to do, they now realize they have a very important role to play. Every person involved in a production has a vital part to play.

25. Describe Me if You Can

For this game, choose two volunteers to come up onstage. A little note about choosing volunteers: You want to make this as equal as possible. I sometimes ask the student who has just performed to choose the next volunteer. Another technique I like to use is to ask for volunteers who have not participated in an activity that day. One of the aims of the instructor should be to get as many students involved as possible.

Tell your volunteers to take a good look at each other and really try to remember everything the other person is wearing. Give them one minute to do this. Now choose one of them to close his eyes. The one you choose must now attempt to name everything the other person is wearing. This description should include as much detail as possible, such as color and texture. When the student has mentioned everything he can ask him to open his eyes. Turn to the audience to find out what items were missed. Now you can ask two more volunteers to come onto the stage and repeat the task.

Variables:

You could have both actors onstage close their eyes and then have them take turns to see what they can remember.

You could have all the students close their eyes, including the audience. Then ask the people onstage to say what they remember. Once they have finished, see if students in the audience, who also have their eyes closed, can remember anything else.

Another way you could do this activity is to talk to the actors onstage while they close their eyes. You can ask them general questions about their day or anything you like. Continue this for a couple of minutes, then ask them what they remember. Asking the questions will count as a buffer and a distraction to the actors, which will make recall more difficult.

Discussion:

"What strategies can you use in this activity to help you remember more effectively?"

"Who was surprised about how much they could or couldn't remember?"

"Why do I ask you to be as specific as you can?"

"What role does the audience play in this activity?"

Purpose:

To practice preparation

After the actor onstage has remembered as much he can, the audience is asked to comment on what he missed. I do not tell the students in the audience that I am going to ask them to do this. In this way I find out if they were really prepared. Audience members may not always be paying full attention during an activity because they feel that they are not the main focus. I like this activity because it can jolt the audience into participation. This parallels actors onstage who are not paying attention to the lines spoken by other actors. They may think that because it is not their line no one is really watching them. Or perhaps while the other actor is talking they are going through their own lines in their heads. This is a danger for actors and can lead to a very artificial performance.

Preparation is important in many aspects of an actor's career. While explaining the methods for getting work Andrew Reilly says, "a professional actor does not wait for a phone call or strike poses in sidewalk cafes. She gets on the phone, or gets to a desk to write letters or cards."[2] This activity will help the students think about preparation, which they can then use in many acting contexts.

To encourage the actor to be specific

The actors onstage are asked to name everything they can remember. This in itself may not be too difficult. It is when the actors have to remember specific details that the activity becomes a greater challenge. For example, Simon might say, "John is wearing a green shirt." If he were going to be more specific he might say, "John is wearing a dark green and light green striped shirt. The stripes form a crisscross pattern with tiny diagonal white stripes through the darker lines. The shirt looks like flannel and the buttons are plastic and white."

Actors are always looking for specifics. Let's say a director asks you to come up with the age of your character. You look through the script and find no mention of an age, so you have to come up with one yourself. You go back to your director and tell her you think your character is in her twenties, but she tells you to be more specific. So you decide she is twenty-one. She tells you she still needs more specifics and suggests you even make up a birthday for your character. The more

---

[2] Andrew Reilly, *An Actor's Business* (Fort Lauderdale, Fla.: Vintage Press), 15.

specific you can be with your characters, the more real they will appear to you. Try to stay away from generalities.

26. Twenty Objects

Before you start this game you should have prepared twenty separate items on a tray and covered them up. Do not allow any of the students to see the tray. Ask one of the students to come forward, and as you take the cover off the tray, tell the student she has one minute to remember as many items as she can. After one minute cover up the tray again and see how many items she can remember. If you want to play with many students, have lots of little items you can quickly change over each time you start again. You do not have to put twenty new items, just mix them up a little.

Variables:

You can change the number of items you put on the tray.

Something else I like to do to make this activity harder is to have a time lapse between when I cover the tray back up and when I ask the student to recall the items. I will talk to the class for a minute or two or may ask the individual some questions, such as how well she thinks she did. I am trying to throw her off and make her forget some of the items by making her think about something else.

Also, you can change the detail required of the answers. Instead of saying, "A matchbox," the answer might be, "A yellow matchbox with red stripes made out of cardboard and a silver sulphate stripe."

Discussion:

"Why do you think you could not recall many items?"

"Why was it more difficult when there was a time lapse?"

"Did having other people here help you or make it more difficult?"

"Why might we play this game? Could you use visualization to help you in this activity?"

Purpose:

To practice memorization techniques

We are touching on memorization, which is vital for every actor. If actors cannot remember their lines then they will be very limited as an actor. In this activity, the students may have discovered a number of different methods to help them remember. Perhaps they said the name of the item or maybe they associated one item with another. This activity will help the students realize that there are many techniques to help them with memorization. They do not have to just cover their lines with a piece of paper to learn them; they should look to use more of their senses. Russ Weatherford points out some of the advantages of actually saying your lines out loud: "We say lines out loud to take advantage of the sense of hearing, as well as the sense of sight."[3] The more of your senses you involve in the process, the better retention rate you'll get; and the more creative the memorization technique, the more powerful it can be.

To be prepared

As you take the cover off the tray, the students will need to be fully focused. They only have a minute to memorize as many items as they can, and the more focused and prepared they are the better they will do. If you gave an unprepared student five minutes, she would still probably remember less than a prepared student who was given one minute. Actors can use preparation in many ways. Before going to an audition an actor might visualize him- or herself actually getting the job. This activity is at its core a memorization activity, but it is the preparation that will enhance the memorization.

27. Same Time Story

In this exercise have two people come onstage and face each other while each one shares a short story. While telling his own story each needs to remember the other person's story as well. When they have finished, have one repeat the other person's story as best he can. When he has said as much as he remembers, ask the original storyteller to tell him what he missed. When the storyteller has finished, go to the audience and see if they can find anything that the original storyteller missed in his own story. Finally, have the other person repeat the story. Once you have finished, let two more volunteers have a turn.

[3] Weatherford, *Confidence and Clarity*, 9.

Variables:

Try this activity with three people telling their stories at the same time and see who can remember the most.

Discussion:

"Why do you think you couldn't remember much of the other person's story?"

"What might you have done to make it easier for you?"

"Was there anything that the storyteller did that made it harder for you?"

"Audience, what tricks helped you to repeat a story?"

Remember, I am just giving you examples of questions, but these discussions will go off on many different tangents. Often a discussion will start to lead itself; however, make sure you are the one who is guiding it.

Purpose:

To help students understand where to direct their focus

Concentration is a vital part of this exercise as the volunteers try to relay their own stories while absorbing another person's. Focus is also a key aspect, because although you may be concentrating, if you are focused exclusively on the story you are telling then you may not remember anything the other person says. This activity helps the students to understand the importance of directing their focus where it needs to be. An actor may be concentrating so hard on his next lines that he loses focus of what the other characters are saying to him. This can lead to one-sided dialogue, which the audience will not buy as realistic unless the scene is purposely set up this way.

To practice preparation

When neither member can completely recall the story it is the audience that attempts to remember. Even though at the start these students appear to be merely observers, by the end they could be vital to completing the exercise. This means that the audience needs to be paying attention right from the start. It might be worth experimenting with this a little. When you play this game for the first time, do not tell the audience they will be asked anything. This way you can see who is paying attention and who is not. This is not intended to be a trick but to remind them that as actors they must constantly be prepared.

Preparation for the actor comes in many forms: listening,

responding, learning lines, rehearsing, character development, seeking out a dramaturge if needed, and much more. Robert Cohen explains the value of preparation in a classroom setting: "A good classroom performance requires preparation. First, take the time to set your scene properly: put the furniture in the proper place, decide where the imaginary door is, where the stove is, and what real properties are represented by substitute items."[4] You have not covered all of these bases during this activity, but you have hopefully triggered the benefits of preparation in the students' minds.

Sometimes I like to explain the games first, and other times I like to get the cast (volunteers) together before I begin. It is sometimes interesting to get them ready when they have no idea what they are about to do, and the students seem to enjoy that element of surprise.

Remember that most of these exercises are suitable for students from the ages of about ten to a hundred, and many of them can also be played with six- and seven-year-olds when adapted to that age group. What changes with each age group is how deep you go in your discussion and your purpose.

28. Mix and Match

This is a very simple activity and yet it is very useful. To start, choose a participant to come forward. Then have about ten students form a single-file line in the middle of the room. Tell the participant she needs to study the order the other players are in. Give her about a minute and then send her out of the room. Now tell the players that they need to remember their original order, and ask them to change places. They should do this so that they are now totally mixed up from their original positions, but it is important that they are still standing in a line formation. Now invite the volunteer back into the room and ask her to put the players back into their original order. I would give her up to five minutes to do this. She can do this by telling the players where to move, or if she prefers she can physically move them herself. When she has finished, ask the students to raise their hands if they are in the correct place. If some were incorrect, ask them to move back to their original

[4] Robert Cohen, *Acting One* (Mountain View, Calif.: Mayfield Publishing Company, 1998), 98.

positions. Once you are finished, switch the contestant and the players and have another go.

Variables:

This activity works well with about ten players, so if you have a large class you might have half the class observe while the other half participates. If you have a small class you may have everyone involved at one time. Of course, you can change the numbers as you see fit. If you are using this activity with very young students, you might want to use five participants. If you have a large group of more experienced students who are finding the activity easy, increase the number of students. There are no restrictions; use your imagination to adapt this activity to fit the needs of your students.

To add another layer, have the players say their names in the order in which they are standing. This will give the contestant a little extra help in memorization.

You might try involving the audience by asking them to have a noisy conversation. This should disrupt the concentration of the contestant and increase the difficulty of the task.

Discussion:

"Who needs to be concentrating for this activity?"

"What methods could the contestant use to help her succeed in the task at hand?"

"If the players say their names once they are all lined up, how will this help the contestant?"

"How did the audience talking loudly affect the memorization of the contestant?"

Purpose:

To promote variables in memorization

As soon as this activity begins, the contestant is using her sense of sight. She will look at all the players to remember their order. If the players do not say their names out loud perhaps the contestant will choose to say them out loud herself. While looking at the players, the contestant might choose a distinct thing about each that sticks out. Perhaps it is an item of clothing, a hairstyle, or a facial characteristic. This might also increase her ability to memorize the correct order.

Often when actors are learning their lines they learn them one line at a time. They do this by sliding a piece of paper down the page so only one line can be seen at a time. They then say the line inside their head. Not only is this very inefficient, but it is also boring. This exercise will encourage actors to think about different techniques of memorization, such as visualization and reciting out loud.

Employing a variety of memorization techniques is important for a number of reasons. First of all, people have different learning styles, including visual, auditory, and kinesthetic; one method of memorization will not work well for all actors and all situations. Also, relying on only one method for memorization may lead to a great deal of confusion. If actors learn their lines in visual form only (reading from a script), they may become internally confused and forget them once they have to add movement (kinesthetic) and react to the lines of others (auditory) during rehearsals. When this happens, actors may become frustrated and panicky, thinking they will never be able to learn their lines.

We have talked about memorization in terms of line learning, but it has many other values for actors. When actors rehearse a play, they need to learn their blocking for each scene. This will come partly in the rehearsal process, where the actors can physically remember their blocking through repetition. However, the actors should also use other techniques, such as visualizing their positioning on the stage. The blocking may constantly be changing, so actors may not be able to learn and relearn their movements through physicality alone.

To remind the students that there are no small roles

At the start of the activity the contestant is told she needs to remember the order the players are in. However, it is also necessary for the players to remember their positions in the line. Even though this is a simple task, it is still a requirement. Imagine if three players did not bother to remember their positions. They might dispute the contestant's answers even if she was correct. The activity would be disrupted and the results would be hard to validate. The actors are reminded that their commitment to the activity is a vital one.

Chapter 5
Sensory Awareness

29. What's the Object?

I used to play this game with five- and six-year-olds, but it can be just as rewarding for any age. Have the students sit in a circle close together so that there is no space between them; they should be elbow to elbow. Then give the following instructions.

"Okay, in a moment you will pass an object around the circle. Only you are not going to pass it in front of you; you will pass it behind your backs on the outside of the circle, so you will all have to sit with your hands behind your backs. When the object comes to you, take a moment to really try and figure out what the item is. Do not call out an answer; just keep it to yourself. Once we have gone around the circle I will choose someone to make a guess. The first person to get the right answer will win a piece of candy." Of course you do not have to give them anything, or you can come up with a different incentive. I am constantly amazed at how excited a student will get over a tiny piece of candy.

Now suggest that the students close their eyes. You may want to discuss the reasons why this might help. The discussion might go as follows:

INSTRUCTOR: Now I am going to recommend that you close your eyes. Why might that be? Jenny?

JENNY: Because it will be more fun in the dark.

INSTRUCTOR: Good, what other reasons? Liz?

JENNY: So we can concentrate better.

INSTRUCTOR: Good, you're on the right track. Can anyone be a little more specific as to why we can concentrate better? Eric?

JENNY: Is it something to do with our senses?

INSTRUCTOR: Good! Yes, if you close your eyes you will have lost your sense of sight. What this means is that your other senses will become more heightened; so, for instance, your sense of touch will become stronger. Okay, let's begin.

Variables:

You could have more than one object going around at a time.

Instead of sitting in a circle, you could have one person come up and sit in a chair. Put an object in his hands (behind his back). Give him twenty guesses to get it right. You could also allow him twenty questions, to which the audience would respond with yes/no answers.

Discussion:

"How did you decide what you thought the object might be?"
"In what way did you involve your senses in this activity?"
"Did other people's body language give you any clues?"
"Is there a different way you could have done this activity?"
"What was the purpose of having you sit so close together?"
"Would this activity work just as well standing?"

Purpose:

To utilize the senses

As mentioned in the description, this game certainly exercises our senses. Why is this important to an actor? Let's say you are doing an exercise that strengthens your sense of smell. Six months later you are in a play that is set in a rundown orphanage. You might want to create the smell of staleness and dust and dankness, and thus a more believable situation. This exercise may give you the resources to recreate this situation. Remember, if you do not buy into the world you have created for your character, neither will the audience.

You may feel this information is good for the teacher, but way over the heads of some of the younger students, but don't be so sure. I have had such discussions with ten-year-olds in which they fully comprehended what was being said. If you treat them as if they are naive then that is just the type of actor you will create.

Endowment of an object

When the object is being passed around from one person to the next, the students are formulating opinions as to what the item is. They are using their imaginations and the sense of touch to create a reality in their minds of what the object could be. Actors often have to create a reality in their minds for the meaning behind an object. The way they pick up a pen might be totally different if it was something the character bought for fifty cents versus a pen that belonged to their recently deceased grandma. While this activity is not endowment of the object as such, it does encourage the students to link meaning to the object. They cannot see it, and yet they still have to formulate an opinion as to what it is or what it could be.

30. Where's the Object?

This game is very similar to the last game in that an object is being passed around the circle behind people's backs, only this time the students have to guess where the object is. Choose one student to sit in the middle of the circle while the object is being passed around. At some point ask the students to stop passing the object and have the person in the middle take a guess as to where he thinks the item is (he can swivel around). If he does not guess correctly on the first try, have the students continue passing the object and choose a time to shout, "Stop." The person in the middle should be allowed a total of up to three guesses. After three guesses, switch the person in the middle and give someone else a shot. You can pass around any handheld item, such as a ball, an orange, a hairbrush, or anything else you can think of.

Variables:
You can have everyone stand up.

Discussion:
"How easy was it to disguise where the item was?"
"Did it make a difference if the item was passed around fast or slow?"
"How were you able to guess where the item was hidden?"
"What clues did people give you? Did body language help you in any way?"

Purpose:
To be able to read and understand body language
We are again trying to stretch our senses in this exercise. This time it is our sense of sight that is of utmost importance.

This game also helps students learn about body language. They realize that everything we do physically means something to the observer. If you smile in this game, it may mean that you are trying to hide the fact that you have something. If you are acting out a scene, and you suddenly break into a smile because you felt nervous, you have just given your audience a signal as to how you are feeling or what is going on for you. This may be a totally contradictory message that had nothing to do with your character. That is why it is so important for the actors to get used to their bodies and learn to control them so that they can become free from them. The less students need to concentrate on what their body is doing, the more they will be able to focus on and respond to each moment in any given scene.

To break down physical barriers
In this activity the students have to sit pretty close together. Their hips and arms should be touching so that there are no visible gaps. At

63

first some students might feel a little uncomfortable at this prospect. Once they get involved in the game, the fact that their arm is touching someone else's tends to pale in significance. This is a useful exercise because physical contact is a common occurrence in acting. You may see a play in which a young couple is holding hands or a husband and wife are hugging. Students need to become comfortable with basic physical contact. If a husband and wife look uncomfortable holding hands because the actors are uncomfortable, the whole message of the scene may be misinterpreted or lost.

31. Alphabet Soup

This exercise works best with about twenty or more students. You also need quite a lot of room for this exercise. To start with, have the students split up into teams of four to six. Designate an open space for each group and ask them to sit down as a team while you explain the rules. This game is quite simple, and loads of fun. You will need a piece of paper and pencil to keep score. After explaining the exercise, call out a letter, let's say c, and have the teams form that letter using their bodies. They must be lying on the floor and everyone on the team must be used for each letter. The first team to complete the letter gets a point. This game is fast-paced, so do not give them too much time in between letters.

A word of warning: It is very hard for you, the judge, to find out who won each point, so you must be assertive and make your decision final. Sometimes you may find there is a tie between three teams. In this case you can give a point to all three teams. Make sure you stress that this is for fun because students may get a little upset if they don't win. Remember, it is the first team to complete the letter that gets the point, not the first team to say they are finished!

Variables:

You could use numbers instead of letters. You could also ask them to form items, such as a house, a tree, and a dog. Of course, this would be more difficult and subjective to judge.

Discussion:

"What did you like about this exercise? What didn't you like?" (Probably the unfair judging.)

"What did you need to focus on to be successful in this activity?"

"Which sense became vitally important during this game?"

"Talk to me about physicality in relation to this exercise."
"How important are listening skills for this exercise?"

Purpose:

To stretch the senses

The students are required to stretch their senses. The students need to feel where the other students are to form the letter correctly, so the sense of touch is engaged. They need to see where their teammates are placed and that they are all where they should be. They have to listen to know which letter to create and to communicate well within the team.

Actors are constantly involved in listening moments. This can happen on- and offstage. A director might be giving notes after a rehearsal; if some of the actors are not listening properly they might miss the notes or misinterpret them. Directors hate having to give the same note twice, so listening skills are imperative. This activity encourages the students to utilize their senses to their full capacity. Doing so requires practice and effort, but as Ned Manderino noted in *All About Method Acting,* "Pianists, dancers and singers devote many hours of the day to their creative gifts, even when the gift is working well. The amount of time you spend depends on the extent to which you wish to perfect a gift and keep it in shape."[1] Using an activity such as "Alphabet Soup" is a step in the right direction.

To become physically comfortable with oneself

As the actors form the different letters they are literally rolling around on the floor, moving their bodies in many different directions and angles. Through this, they become more comfortable with physical expression using the body. Later on, they can translate this idea into character work. The more they experiment with their bodies, the freer they will become. Joan Snyder and Michael Drumsta talk about physicality in terms of its value for character work: "Once the actor has completed an analysis and fully understands the character, the physical and psychological parts of the character must become comfortable on the actor."[2] This exercise will hopefully enable the students to feel a level of comfort in using their bodies as a physical tool.

[1] Ned Manderino, *All About Method Acting* (Los Angeles: Manderino Books, 1976), 8.
[2] Joan Snyder and Michael P. Drumsta, *The Dynamics of Acting* (Skokie, Ill.: National Textbook Company, 1981), 79.

32. My Vacation

For this activity, place a chair onstage facing out toward the audience. Tell the audience that you would like all of them to think of a place that they love to go, a place that relates to nature. Some examples are the beach, an open field, a forest, and a mountain. Now ask one of the actors to take a seat in the chair. Tell him to look down for a few minutes and really picture his place. Tell him that when he looks up you want him to have a visual of this place. Allow him to continue in this manner for at least two minutes. While this is happening, ask the audience to pay close attention. Next, ask the actor to stay with his place, and at the same time ask the audience to comment on where they think they are. You want them to get as specific as they can. For instance, if one actor says, "He looks like he's on the beach," push him for more information. You may then get an answer such as, "He looks like he is on the beach looking out toward the ocean. He has a calm look in his eyes, so I think the ocean is calm and there is a cool breeze blowing." This means you will want your actors to make their pictures quite specific. Switch out and have different members of the class take a turn in the chair.

Variables:

I chose places as the focus for my students because I really enjoy their reactions. You could use an array of topics that would work just as well. Perhaps you could have them visualize their favorite meal.

Discussion:

"What clues did the actor give about his choice of place through his body language?"

"How do you need to prepare for this activity?"

"Are there any benefits in this activity for the actor?" (The benefits are not just for the actor onstage; they could be for the audience as well.)

"What senses did the actors onstage use during this activity?"

Now, in a way, this last suggestion is a trick question. The audience may reply with "sight," because of course they have to visualize the place; however, they may involve other senses as well. Let us say they were picturing the ocean. To make this image more powerful they might hear the sound of the ocean waves, they might feel as if their feet are burning as they touch the hot sand, and they might smell the sea salt as the gentle breeze blows over them. Expand your questioning to see if you can pull these types of answers from your students.

Purpose:

To stretch the different senses

This activity is very useful in having the actors utilize their different senses. As mentioned in the discussion, for the actors to really picture their chosen environments, they will want to involve multiple senses: to hear the sea, to touch the sand, to smell the salt air, and so on. This is not a substitute for visualization; rather it is a complementary tool.

When describing a sense activity for taste, Yoko Nomura says the purpose is "to sharpen the sense of taste."[3] I think this definition contains a good metaphor. If we do not keep our senses sharpened they will become dull and blunt. The idea behind this activity is to make sure we continue to stretch our senses on a continual basis.

To create audience awareness

The audience really has to pay attention to every detail in this activity, though the object is not necessarily for them to get the correct answer. They may come up with something that the actor onstage had not even thought about, and yet this was what the audience member felt was being conveyed. This can be a very powerful tool to help students learn that what we think we are portraying and what is actually being understood from our behavior can be very different. The audience has to be aware of everything if they are to be able to make these judgments with any authority. I love activities that ask actors to observe others, because observing others encourages them to do this in their everyday lives. In my opinion, observation of our surroundings on a constant basis is a fundamentally important part of an actor's training.

33. Now You See Me ...

In this game your students are going to be walking around the room with their eyes closed (or blindfolded, if you prefer), so you will need to clear a large part of your playing space so that there is nothing on the floor for them to trip on. You can also dim the lights at the start of the game. If you want to do this activity on a stage, make sure that you have someone watching to be sure nobody gets too near the edge. Explain the game as follows:

---

[3] Yoko Nomura, *Pinch and Ouch* (Tokyo: Lingual House Publishing, 1982), 22.

"To start this activity I am going to need everyone to come and form a circle. Turn to your right so that you are facing the back of the person in front of you in a clockwise direction. Now put your hands on the shoulders of the person in front of you. For some of you this is going to be a little more difficult than others depending on how tall the person is in front of you. Take a good look at the person and make sure you remember who he or she is. Okay, now I would like you to close your eyes and feel from the shoulder to the head and neck area with your hands. Become familiar with the shape and contour of this person's body. I will give you about two minutes to do this.

"Now move without talking to a corner of the room until you come up against a wall. Your task is to find the actor who was standing in front of you and get back into the circle so at the end we should be back in the same circle that we started with. The only challenge is that you are going to do this without the sense of sight. You are going to have to move slowly and carefully around the room so as not to crash into anyone else. As you move around the room, do so in absolute silence. As you find the person you presume is your original partner, put you arms on his shoulders, and stay with him until he finds his partner, and so on until you are all back in the circle. Do not ask each other any questions; stick with the person you think is your partner. You will only find out if you are correct at the end when you are all in the circle and I ask you to open your eyes. Is everyone ready? All right, off we go."

One challenge to this activity is that at its conclusion the actors will not always be 100 percent sure they have found the right person. This is okay because the process and exploration is more important than the end result.

Variables:

If you are doing this activity with younger students you may want them to start with their eyes open so they will know at the end of the activity whether they found their actual partner.

Discussion:

"What convinced you that you had found your partner?"

"Did any of you choose a partner and then change your mind? What was the turning point in your decision?"

"Which sense is heightened during this game?"

This last one is a trick question because by asking the question in this manner, your students may come back with only one answer. The sense of touch is the obvious one, but the senses of smell and hearing will also be enhanced. Do not hand them everything on a silver platter; it is okay to make them work for the answer. The aim of a question such as this should be to get the students to question you. In other words, it challenges them to develop their own ideas and not take everything you say as gospel. Help them to build independent thought processes, which, in turn, will enhance their creativity.

Purpose:
To heighten the senses
The more we can isolate our different senses, the more we can manipulate them. So by closing their eyes in this activity, the students automatically start to shift more toward listening initially to try to locate the other people. Then the sense of touch becomes heightened as they search for their partner while also trying not to crash into anyone or anything. As they find a person they will rely mainly on their sense of touch; however they may also involve their sense of smell (perhaps their partner is wearing a perfume).

Let me go off onto a sidetrack here and show how using the different senses can play a part in line learning. By reading the lines out loud an actor sees the lines, says the lines, and hears the lines all at the same time. Many people find that the more senses that are involved in the line learning process, the better their ability to learn and retain their lines.

To break down barriers
I have mentioned this before, and I don't mind mentioning it again. The actors have to get used to touching each other. Obviously, not in a lascivious manner, but being comfortable putting their hands on another human being is vital for actors. Acting is often linked to human interaction and communication, and physical contact is a common thread. For a massage therapist the goal of touching another might be to break down muscle tissue; for the actor the goal of the handshake might be to convey a feeling of gratitude or perhaps of disdain.

As with most of the activities in this book, the exercise itself has many indirect benefits for the actor. After all, there was no mention of character breakdown or objective and motivation in this activity. However, you could take an activity such as this and build it into a larger picture. Perhaps after this game you could do scene work involving characters and relationships.

69

34. Mafia

For this exercise have your students form a circle sitting on the floor. Tell them that in a moment you will say, "It's nighttime." When this happens they should all look toward the floor and close their eyes. At this point, you will walk around the circle and pat one of them on the head once, indicating that this person is the murderer. The murderer must stand up and point to someone; this person is the victim. The murderer will then sit down and look at the floor again. At this point, you should choose a detective by patting someone on the head twice. Now tell everyone it is morning and that they should all sit up and open their eyes while you tell them what has happened. For instance, you might say:

"During the night Ben Harper decided to go fishing. He caught a couple of catfish and was having a really good time when suddenly he was pushed into the water and drowned. Someone in this room murdered him. We are very lucky today to have Detective Lana Edwards with us. She has told me that she knows who the murderer of Ben Harper is. Lana, could you please tell us who you think the murderer is and why?" (You must make sure that the names you use for the detective and the person who was murdered are the students who were just chosen.)

Once you have asked the detective, you can open up the questions to everyone else. Whenever a student says who he thinks the murderer is he must give a reason why. After you have asked a number of people, you should tell them who the murderer was. You can then choose a student to lead the game and play again. Select a new leader for each round.

Variables:

You should change the story each time you play. Ask the new leader to come up with a different story. An example might be, "Sarah was driving her brand new car, but little did she know someone had fixed the brakes."

Discussion:

"How does this activity stretch the imagination?"

"How does the sense of hearing play a part in this activity?"

"Can you explain to me some of the differences between being creative and being imaginative?"

"In this activity a student has to take on the role of leader. In what way do actors need to be leaders?"

Purpose:

To increase sensory awareness

When the murderer has been tapped on the shoulder he must stand up. At this point it is possible that the people on either side of him may sense his movement. Other people may also become aware by hearing some shuffling. Therefore, the murderer must stand up while causing as little commotion as possible, and it is also beneficial for the other participants to keep their ears open for any telltale sounds.

As actors we should constantly be looking for opportunities to develop our senses. An actor might be given a cup with nothing in it and be told to make it look as if she is drinking a hot cup of tea. In order to do this she may recollect past experiences, but to recreate the moment she will want to involve her senses. How does the tea taste? How does the tea smell? How does the cup feel? Is it hot? Is it too hot?

To develop agility

When the narrator points to the murderer that student must stand up with as little commotion as possible. In this sense he will need to be quite agile. If the other students can hear him, then it may be obvious who the murderer is. Actors needs to have a sense of agility for a host of different reasons. Actors performing in a musical will want to have developed fluid movements. When actors walk across a stage they will want to be able to do so in a way that is fitting for their character. A character may need to appear clumsy at times, which is fine. However, if the character needs to appear more refined with a touch of finesse, the actor should be able to do this. This is one reason the directors always want to see actors who have an understanding and control of their bodies.

35. Everybody Touch Someone Who ...

This is an activity I have used with elementary students; however, I think it can be used with students of any age. Have the students spread out to different parts of the room. Tell them that in a moment you will start to call out instructions for them to follow so they need to listen closely. Begin each instruction with "Everyone touch someone who ..." The game might progress as follows:

INSTRUCTOR: Everyone touch someone who is wearing green. (At this point the students simply look around the room for someone wearing green and go over and touch him with one finger.)

INSTRUCTOR: Everybody touch someone who has blonde hair. (Students find and touch someone with blonde hair.)

And so on.

Now you can also change your instructions to inanimate objects: "Everybody touch something made of wood. Everybody touch a wall." You might want to start off by being the leader yourself and then letting some other people have a try. This is not a game that ends with a winner. It is simply a warm-up activity I like to use.

Variables:

If you want to create a competitive mood, you could say that the last person to complete the action each time is out.

Discussion:

"What makes this a great warm-up?"

"Detailed observation is a key ingredient in this activity. Can someone explain what this statement means?" (If no one can come up with a response, you might illustrate with a scenario: "Let's say Sarah had to find someone wearing blue. She looked at Katie and thought she was wearing blue items. She was about to look somewhere else when she noticed Katie's blue nail polish. Through detailed observation Sarah was able to complete the task more efficiently.")

"How is this activity useful for the actor?"

Every time you ask this last question, your students will find reasons. At times, they will discover benefits you hadn't even thought about.

Purpose:

To develop listening skills

You need to be listening in a focused manner to participate in this activity fully. If you are only half listening your mind might wander elsewhere. Let me give you an example of how this can be a very real challenge in acting. If you go for a film audition you may be given some sides (a scene from the movie) to read. Let's say you go into the audition and the director asks you to state your name and agent and then profile left and right. You are really trying to concentrate on the sides you are about to read so you turn the wrong way when you are giving your profile. You don't realize the mistake because you weren't really listening in the first place, but this error may have just cost you the job. The director may decide that even if you give a great read, you would be too much of a risk because you have a problem listening to direction. So honing in on listening skills is key for actors. Of course, I am only giving you one of the benefits of listening, which are many.

To warm up for rehearsals and performance
This activity is great for getting your actors ready for the larger task at hand. If you want to start rehearsal in five minutes you can use this activity to help your actors get focused. In the three or four minutes the game lasts your actors will utilize their listening skills, develop their ability to react, and enhance their observation capabilities. You want to have them at a resourceful and receptive place before you begin rehearsals or a performance.

36. Detective

This is one of my favorite games! You will need a set of keys and two blindfolds to play this game. Have all the students sit in a large circle so they are an arm's length apart. (This game is not really good with less than about fifteen people because you need a large circle.) Explain the game as follows:

"Today we are going to play a game called 'Detective.' In a moment, I will choose one of you to be the thief and one of you to be the detective. The detective's job will be to try to catch the thief, and thief's job will be to try to find the keys. Now it sounds simple enough, but there are a few catches. Both the detective and the thief will be blindfolded and they will not be walking around the circle, but moving on their hands and knees inside the circle so they are not heard by the other person. This exercise is not about running around as fast as you can, but moving like a snail so that it is virtually impossible for the other person to hear you. I recommend you take off your shoes for this activity. The slower you move the more interesting this game is to play and watch. Detective, if you find the keys, try not to make any sound with them. It is not your objective to find the keys, so if you come across them you must leave them and move on.

"In a moment I will ask someone to silently place the keys somewhere in the circle. The detective and thief will also be placed somewhere in the circle by two other students. They will be spun around in both directions so that they lose their bearings. Those of you who are forming the circle are playing a vital role. You must not make any noise whatsoever. Also, you cannot laugh if the players get close to each other. You do not want to give them any clues as to what is happening. I have you sitting at an arm's length apart so that they can cover the entire circle between you. If they appear to be about to move outside the circle, put out an arm and gently guide them back in. Do not push them back, just guide. Everyone must be concentrating at all times. Remember, safety is of utmost importance. Detective and thief, do not worry if someone guides you back in; I will tell you if you have been caught. Remember that you must move slowly and as quietly as possible. Okay, let's begin."

Variables:

I do not recommend two thieves and two detectives because this would become very confusing. However, you could try two detectives and one thief.

Discussion:

"When you were the detective, what helped you find the thief?"

"When you were the thief, how were you able to find the keys without getting caught?"

"If you were in the audience, how were you able to stay so quiet?"

"How important do you feel the audience's role was in this exercise? What happened when there was laughter from the circle?"

"If you were a thief or a detective, did circle noise help you in any way or make it more difficult?"

"What senses are we using for this exercise?"

"How might this exercise be useful for you as actors?"

Purpose:

To develop teamwork

Your students are certainly developing their sense of hearing as they lose their sense of sight. I also find many students comment on the importance of their sense of touch, which is enhanced during this exercise. Teamwork plays a big part, too; if the people in the circle do not work together and stay focused, this game will fall flat on its face. The more opportunities you can give the students to take responsibility for each other and work together the better. You want the students to feel that even when they are just a small part of the game (sitting in the circle) they are still a vital part of its success. At a future date when they have a tiny part in a play, hopefully they will be able to transpose this information and apply it. (There are no small parts!)

Chapter 6
Concentration and Focus

37. Leave Me Alone

Have your students sit so they are facing the performance area and call up two actors. Tell Actor One that he is going to do some math and that Actor Two is going to come up with some math problems. Actor One will be given the questions out loud and he will have to work out the answers in his head. The questions should consist of addition, subtraction, and multiplication, or a combination of the three so that they are fairly easy to solve.

After Actor One has answered a few problems, make the game a little more challenging. Give Actor One a plastic chair and tell him that while solving the problems he has to keep the chair balanced in the air. He can only hold it with one hand by one leg of the chair. You might prefer to give him a wooden broom and tell him to balance it with one or two fingers. Make sure you consider safety when doing this exercise.

Now try the exercise for a third time, and this time, instead of the chair, Actor One has to juggle three or four tennis balls. His aim is to answer all the math problems and juggle the tennis balls successfully at the same time. Switch out the actors and try the exercise with different people.

You should find that as the activities become more difficult, so does the task of solving the math questions. Sometimes the actors will forget or they may just become much slower in responding. You might want to have a list of math questions already prepared so the students can quickly verify their answers before moving on to the next problem. Try this activity a number of times with different actors. If they are completing both of their assigned tasks with ease, try giving them a more challenging activity to do while solving the math problems. Keep the activities really physical.

Variables:

You can give the participants all kinds of activities. They could stack a pile of chairs, rearrange the desks in a certain order, or hula-hoop.

You can also do this exercise with an extra actor. The third actor can come in and ask questions to Actor One, such as "How was your day?" "Are you having a lot of fun at the moment?" This actor can also make general conversation about anything he wants. Actor One does not have to respond, but he cannot cover his ears. Actor Three cannot shout, because we still have to be able to hear the math questions.

Discussion:

"Why did we do that exercise?"

"Who got frustrated when trying to solve the math problems? Why do you think that happened?" "How do you think you could achieve better results in this activity? Was one type of problem more challenging than another?"

Purpose:

To highlight concentration

The reason I say we are highlighting concentration is because we are approaching it from different angles. The students have to concentrate mentally at the beginning to solve the math problems. Then when we add the chair or broom they have to concentrate physically as well so that they can balance the item without letting it fall. They are still using concentration, although now there is a mesh between physical and mental. Which do they prioritize more? Do they start forgetting the math problems, but keep the broom balanced? Or maybe they seem torn between the two and cannot complete either task successfully. This is all linked to the multitasking an actor has to do in a performance. Lines, blocking (movement or positioning), characterization, and objectives, to name a few, must all be balanced. So as actors we are constantly multitasking and linking the mental and physical. In discussing the subject of concentration, Richard Boleslavsky explains that, "Concentration is the quality which permits us to direct all our spiritual and intellectual forces toward one definite object and to continue as long as it pleases us to do so."[1] This exercise is great for highlighting this valuable skill.

38. Count Off

Explain this game as follows:

"Please come and form a circle, but stay standing. You are about to see how high you can count. Sounds easy enough, doesn't it? The challenge is that you are not doing this on your own, but as a group. So as a group you have to see how high you can count with no number being said by more than one person at any time. For instance, if you get to five and three people say, "five," you have to start again. There is no

---

[1] Richard Boleslavsky, *Acting* (New York: Theatre Arts Books, 1990), 22.

leader; when someone is ready he or she should begin. I think I've told you enough for the moment, so let's begin." (Allow the actors to start the activity, but they probably won't get much higher than seven or eight at first. Now stop the activity and give a little advice.)

"Okay, good, let me stop you for a moment. I have been watching the activity, and everyone is making a really good effort. I did notice one thing, though: at the start of the activity you seem to prepare yourselves individually, but not as a group. Try to get focused as a group for about thirty seconds or a minute before anyone says the first number. Although you are saying individual numbers, you want to work as if you are one person." (Now have them repeat the activity a few times and see if it makes any difference. After they have tried a couple more times you might want to offer another suggestion.)

"Okay, you are getting higher numbers now. Let me give you a couple other things to think about. You might want to try standing closer together so that you are shoulder to shoulder; this might help you to feel more like one unit. Also, you may want to try the activity with your eyes closed so that your sense of hearing will become more heightened."

Make these suggestions sporadically. The students may pick up on some of these ideas on their own. You don't want to make all these suggestions at the start of the activity; remember, a lot of the learning comes through the discovery process. Continue with this exercise until you feel your students have explored enough paths. You don't want to continue activities to the point that the students become lethargic or fed up. I often stop my activities when the students' interest is at a peak. One reason for this is so I can come back to the activity in future sessions and know that my students will already be motivated and charged.

Variables:

See "One Word Story."

Discussion:

"What difference, if any, did it make when you took a moment of silence before starting to count?"

"Can you give me some reasons why you could sometimes count much higher than other times?" "Was it possible to have a leader in this activity, and if so, in what capacity?"

"In a play the director might say, 'You are only as strong as your weakest link.' Explain this comment in relation to this activity."

Purpose:

To enhance the students' intuition

Although listening is of vital importance, in this activity the students need to go one step further. They have to sense when they should call out the next number. They have to feel the right moment. This feeling is not something they can get through an equation or a formula; it is only something they can get by sensing the moment. In acting we see this all the time. Actors always say that comedy is a great challenge because of the need to have "comic timing." The actors don't just count to three and say their lines. They have to sense and feel the moment. The further the actors get with the counting activity, the more they will feel their intuition develop.

To further cooperation and teamwork

If you have twenty students participating in this activity and they work as twenty individuals, the game will be immensely difficult. The actors have to learn to work together. If they decide they are going to try to focus for thirty seconds at the start of the activity and one person is talking or making jokes, this one individual will change the whole energy of the group and affect the results. The students will be able to see the importance of a supportive atmosphere where there are no stars, but a mesh of separate minds. Only if all the members of the team do their part will the team progress in this activity. This activity may help the actors realize that whether they are an extra on a movie set or the lead in *Othello* they must have the same commitment. If one person does not pull his weight, the whole project will be affected.

39. Bing, Bang, Bong

The whole group should stand in a close circle so that they are practically elbow to elbow. Tell the students that the selected person must put her hands together and point toward any person in the circle, except the person on her immediate left or right. As she points she must say the word "bing." Now that person must point at someone else and say "bang." Finally, that third person should point at someone else and say "bong," and the students should continue on in this manner, repeating the phrase "bing, bang, bong" over and over again.

Now if someone points at Mark and says "bing," and Mark says "bing" to the next person, Mark is out. Or if Amanda freezes and doesn't say anything, she is out. In order to stay in the game you must say the next part of the phrase without pausing. When participants get out, they must sit down in their spot in the circle. For the best results, this game should be played at a rapid pace. Make sure that when the students are pointing at each other it is very clear whom they are pointing at. This is one reason they have to keep their hands together as they point; it is more clear and direct.

Variables:

You can vary this game by changing the speed at which it is played.

You could also try starting two people at the same time; this will lead to lots of confusion and interesting results.

You do not have to stick to the words given. Perhaps you could use "zipity, zapity, zop."

Discussion:

Come up with your own discussion. I am not going to suggest you must have a discussion after every exercise; that is entirely up to you. If you have a discussion after every exercise, the students may start to dread it or mentally switch off. However, if you feel a discussion can enhance an exercise or learning, use it!

Purpose:

To enhance motor skills

This game is excellent at improving motor skills. Students must have excellent hand-eye coordination. In this game, somebody acts (points his hands at another student and says "bing") and somebody reacts (points his hands at someone else and says "bong"). So we could reduce this to acting and reacting. This is something actors should constantly be doing during a performance. They should react to the actions and comments of those around them. They should be in a position to respond to what has just been said. They can only do this if they are listening to what is being said instead of thinking of their next line.

To develop listening skills

The students have to involve their listening skills so they know what word comes next. It is not enough to know that it is their turn, but they must also be aware of what they have to say. Active listening is a skill actors start to develop as they grow in confidence and experience. Novice actors will often not be listening to what is being said because they are desperately trying to remember their next line rather than trust in the moment. This activity reminds actors to listen.

40. Can You Hear Me Now?

To start this activity, have half of the class find a partner and form two straight lines facing their partners. Have them stand in the center of the room so all the paired students have plenty of space behind them. The other half of the students should be sitting at the sides of the room observing. The aim of this exercise is for the paired students to have a conversation with their partners. They can talk about whatever they want, but the challenge is that all the other groups will be having conversations at the same time.

There is another challenge to this activity. Every thirty seconds you should blow a whistle signaling the students in both lines to take a step back. They should get farther and farther away from their partners. When a team reaches a point where they can no longer converse with each other, they should not go back any farther. They should move forward until they find the farthest point at which they can still talk with each other. Ask those watching to come up with some observations for the discussion. Once all groups have gone as far as they can, switch the audience and the participants.

Variables:

Instead of having the students talk about anything, have the audience give each pair a topic to discuss.

You may choose to have all the students start the activity at the same time rather than asking half to observe.

Discussion:

"Which of you found that you were shouting to communicate with your partner and which of you think you were projecting? Explain the difference."

"If you found you could not communicate with your partner, what tactics did you use to correct this?"

"Could someone who was watching the activity comment on some of the observations you made?"

"Do you think it would make a difference if we changed the number of players for this exercise?"

"What part does focus and concentration play in this activity?"

Purpose:

To encourage correct use of voice

In this exercise the students have to find a way to hear and be heard by their partners. Some may choose to scream at the top of their lungs, which may work; however, they will probably end up with a sore throat. Those who use their voices correctly will project to their partners. This will include using their diaphragm as part of their breathing apparatus. These students will most likely be making clearer sounds than those who are shouting, but they will also be pain free.

This activity could be useful as part of an introduction to a voice section. Correct use of voice is a fundamental part of an actor's training. A professional play will most likely run eight times a week. The actors have to put their voices through an enormous amount of work. Not only are they using them constantly, but they also have to project so they can be heard at the back of the auditorium. An exercise like this one can help to highlight the importance of correct use of voice. (It is interesting to note that babies can scream at the top of their lungs and not get a sore throat. This is because they are breathing correctly. It is only as we age that we start to breathe incorrectly. This comes partly as a result of mimicking those around us, but also because we start to place our tensions around the neck, shoulders, and upper body.)

To enhance concentration and focus
In this activity it is not enough for actors to project and be heard, they must also find a way to hear what their partner is saying. This would be easy enough except for all of the noise from those around them. The students will have to be incredibly focused to blot out all of the noises around them. They will also need to concentrate so they can hear what's being said and be in a position to respond. Through focus the students should attempt to blur out the other voices as distant noise and concentrate solely on the voice of their partner. This can be an immensely difficult task to complete and for that reason this exercise can be an excellent resource for the actors.

We have talked about the importance of focus and concentration throughout this book. One reason for this is that there are so many places where they are important. Let us say a multimillion dollar movie is being filmed and the director is shooting an important scene. The scene goes wonderfully and everyone is very happy, but unfortunately the cameraman was not concentrating and forgot to press record on his camera. Now the whole scene must be shot again. Not only did this lapse in concentration cost time, it also cost a great deal of money. Now you may say this sounds like a far-fetched example; however, it is actually based on a true story. You might also say, "What does the cameraman have to do with acting?" Remember that the whole cast is part of the same team. This includes technicians, producers, costumes, makeup, dramaturge, etc. Who knows why the cameraman lapsed in concentration? Perhaps he was talking to an actor who also was not concentrating. So concentration and focus should be like a virus that spreads among those involved in a project.

41. Eye to Eye

To start with, have everyone form a circle — just kidding! In this game your students can actually sit at their desks or on the floor, provided they are facing the stage or an area you have designated as the stage. Set up two chairs onstage so that they are facing each other and are positioned parallel to the audience. Explain the game as follows:

"I need two volunteers to help me demonstrate this game. Okay, Andrew and Craig. Andrew, sit in the chair on the left and Craig, sit in this chair on the right. Now, in a moment I am going to ask you to look down at the floor, and when you look up I want you to look into each other's eyes. Isn't that romantic! As you are staring, if either one of you smiles or laughs, you are both out. There is no second chance! Audience, you can try to make them laugh; however, you must stay in your seats and you cannot say anything rude or derogatory. The pair who stares for the longest time will win some very inexpensive candy."

Adapt this however you want depending on the age group. Remember, even with adults you want to keep a safe environment, so you should steer clear of personal comments from the audience. Also, I would set a time limit. You might decide that if the participants make it to five minutes, they have succeeded. This may mean that you end up with more than one pair of winners.

Variations:

You can manipulate how you want to use the audience. You can make them silent observers, or you could allow them to come all the way up to the front to try to make the competitors laugh (without touching).

If the students are very young you may want to suggest that the players can smile but that they cannot laugh.

Discussion:

I usually stop the game somewhere in the middle and start a discussion.

"Okay audience, you are shouting lots of comments but there seem to be some groups you couldn't crack. Why do you think that is?" (You may want to offer some suggestions, such as, "Do you realize that when you all shout at once it just sounds like noise? In fact, in a way you are probably helping the competitors. So perhaps you should try working as an ensemble. Maybe only one person should talk at a time; you decide. Also, try to be a little more creative; what else could you do rather than just shout out statements? What about a song? If something isn't working, you have to try something else.")

"John and Frank, you lasted the longest. Why do you think that was?"

Purpose:

To break up the intensity

This game is great fun and the students love it. I know I have said this a lot, but remember, some of these activities will be more demanding than others. With this knowledge you should decide how long to use each game and how often. An exercise may not be the most popular, but you must also look at what skills it can teach. If a director is in the middle of rehearsal she may choose to take a ten-minute break to play a fun activity. This might help the actors to break some of the intensity of the rehearsal process. The director might find on returning to rehearsal that her actors are more refreshed and focused.

To increase the actor's ability to focus

This game is very specific in its benefits for focus. Actors in a play or a film are aware of the audience or of the technical crew; however, they must know how to block them out and act as if they were not there. If their attention is drawn toward the audience or anywhere except where it is supposed to be, the magic is broken. The audience will now stop believing in the reality of the performance; they are taken out of the land of make believe. In this exercise the partners are able to control their laughter by not succumbing to the distractions around them. By staying focused on one another they are able to blot out the sounds and distractions around them.

42. Clap Focus

Make sure there is plenty of open, available space in the room and have everyone spread out to different areas. One person will start by clapping toward another person. In other words, the first person should point at another person, keeping his arms close together, and clap. It is better for the pointer to point with his arms because it is much more obvious whom he is pointing at. As he points and claps he also has to take a step toward the middle. Now the person he clapped at will clap toward someone else and take one step in. The idea is that everyone will start quite far apart and will end up bunched together in the middle as one unit. This exercise is called "Clap Focus" because participants really have to focus on the person they are clapping at. Otherwise, the game will become very disorganized and several people may think the clapping was aimed at them. The students must be specific. Demonstrate, have a quick practice, and then begin.

Variables:

Discover your own!

Discussion:

"What happened if you did not direct your clap at a specific individual?"

"What did you notice happened when someone was not paying attention?"

"What started to happen as the group got closer to the center?"

"Talk to me about this activity concerning clarity."

Purpose:

To develop clarity

You have to be clear in this exercise. Whenever it is your turn to clap toward someone, you have to make sure that person knows the clap is directed at him. This forces the actor to know his objective. If he says to himself, "Well, I'll just clap in that general direction," then three or four people will probably assume the gesture was for them. So the player has to commit to the action. In the same way, an actor must commit to his objective. Instead of saying, "I hate Jane," which is very vague, the more experienced actor might say, "Jane took my only child away from me, the one true love I had in my life, the one thing I had left to hold onto." This activity helps the student to move away from generality and develop a sense of clarity.

To break down physical barriers

The actors will end up closer to each other as the activity progresses. They will often get in each other's physical space. You can limit how close they get depending on whether they are young children or adults. The point is that they will get a feeling of discomfort. This is very useful because as they grow accustomed to it, it becomes easier for them. If your junior high boy has to sit on a bench next to a girl in a play, he may protest. Exercises like this will hopefully ease the process of becoming comfortable sharing physical space.

43. Don't Think of the Color Black!

In this example I have integrated all the different steps for you so that you can see how everything pieces together. I will cover the discussion, the purpose, and possible variables in a simulated conversation with students. Remember to be flexible with your actors and the formatting on the activities! Have your outline, but then go with the moment at hand.

This is another of my favorite exercises. Inform your class that you will tell them the name of this game in a moment, but don't offer it yet. Instead begin with instructions similar to the following:

"Okay, ladies and gentlemen, I would like you all to close your eyes for a moment. Good, now while you have your eyes closed don't think of the color black. Whatever you do, don't think of the color black. I am serious — really, really, really don't think of the color black. That's right, black. I said the color black, black, black, black, black. Just in case you did not hear me, the color black. Okay, good, put your hand up if you pictured the color black."

You should find a large number of your students saw the color black. We will get into why it worked in a moment. You can now tell them the name of the game before continuing.

"All right, let's try that one more time. This time, do not think of a cow. Whatever you do, don't think of a cow, cow, cow, cow, cow. No cows, not one cow, see no cows, no cows whatsoever. You got it, not one cow, cow, cow. All right, how many of you pictured a cow that time?" You may find fewer people put their hands up this time around.

"Why do you think so many of you saw the color black or pictured the cow?"

"Because you told us not to see it," John offers.

"Because you kept saying black and I couldn't think of anything else," says Sue.

"I didn't see the cow. When you mentioned cow I blotted it out by thinking about my dog," inserts Allen.

"All right, let me add a few more possibilities as to why this exercise works. Could we say it is like a form of hypnosis? Think about a time when you said, 'I hate school. I really hate school. I absolutely hate school.' How did you feel about school that day? You probably hated it. I feel that there is a similarity in this exercise in that I mention the cow and the color black so much that the mind becomes hypnotized until it can picture nothing else."

Claire interrupts, "But you told us *not* to think of the color black."

"Excellent point. But what happens when you tell yourself not to do something? 'I won't be late today, I won't be late.' The mind tends to fight you and want to do the opposite. Remember, the mind does not like being told what to do. And consequently you end up being late.

"Now let's take this one step further. What possible benefits could this have for acting?"

Sherieka offers, "It could help our imaginations."

"Excellent suggestion, can you tell me in what way?"

"Well, it helps us to picture something in our head," she explains.

"Good, can anyone else add to that?"

"It can help you when you are onstage, say in a production," Nigel notes.

"Nice, can you give me an example?"

"Sure. Let's say I was supposed to be in a forest. It might help me think about the forest."

"Excellent, so what I am hearing Nigel say is that sometimes we can use repetition to our advantage. If I walked onto the stage and said in my head, 'Wow this forest is big and dark! Look at all these trees,' do you think I might be able to imagine I was in a forest? You bet. What if I said, 'This stinks! This is just a stupid stage and I feel dumb walking around a stupid stage!' Now, what do you think I would be picturing?"

"There is no way you would see the forest, and you would seem fake to the audience," Sherieka chimes in again.

"All right, you say I would seem fake to the audience. In what way?"

"Well, if you don't believe there is a forest, then why should we?" she asks.

"Nicely put, Sherieka. Excellent input, everyone. So what I heard you all say was that if we, as actors, do not utilize our imaginations, if we do not picture our environment, then how can we expect the audience to?"

As always I am not telling you this is what you must do onstage; on the contrary I am just showing you different possibilities and giving you things to think about. Take everything you learn and use what works for you, and if it doesn't or you disagree, toss it out.

44. Crazy Talk

You will need three actors for this exercise. Have everyone come and sit in the middle of the room and have your three actors come up onto the stage. You will want three chairs next to each other, one for each actor. The two actors sitting on the outsides are going to hold a conversation with the actor in the middle. The challenge is that they must carry on two separate conversations at the same time. You can ask for topics from the audience. One actor may want to talk about what an awful day he has had and the other might start a conversation about a boy she likes. While these conversations are going on simultaneously the actor in the middle must try to maintain them both.

The actors sitting on the outsides must also ask questions. "I'm having a terrible day. How is your day?" You should also stress that what they say should, in their eyes, be of the utmost importance. There should be a sense of urgency in trying to get their story across. The actor in the middle cannot ignore them, but must be attentive to both conversations. The two actors on the outsides should not acknowledge each other. They should continue as if the other actor is not there. In fact, the only person they should acknowledge is the person in the middle. Also, they should not get into a shouting match with the actor on the other side; there is no need if they do not know the other actor is there.

This exercise is a great challenge. Remind the actor in the middle that he cannot just keep one conversation going, but must constantly be involved in both. This means that the actors on the outsides should constantly be talking to and asking questions of the person in the middle.

After you have played with three people, switch the actors out and let another three try. Remember, you can continue your discussion through the exercise. I often stop after we have looked at an exercise once, have a short discussion, and then continue.

Variables:

How about having four people having two conversations across each other at the same time?

Vary this activity in any way you like. Once you have the basic idea you can run with these activities in any direction you choose.

Discussion:

"How hard was it to keep two conversations going at once? Is there any way the actor in the middle could make this easier on himself?"

"Did you feel at any stage someone was dominating a conversation? Explain."

Any time your actors criticize one another; it is up to you to make sure it is constructive. You may think negative criticism is not going to happen with your class because they are adults; however, an adult might say, "I didn't believe her." Although this is not malicious, it is not explained. It can help to question further:

"Okay Sam, what didn't you believe about Jenny's performance?"

"Well, she seemed fake and she kept exaggerating her actions."

Obviously you could keep going with this line of questioning; you want to make sure that your actors get specific with their remarks. If the comments are not helpful in some way, then they are best left unsaid. I am not saying you should yell at someone who says, "I thought it was good," but you should press for more. "Great, what was good about it?"

Purpose:

To be able to multitask

In this exercise the actor in the middle must be constantly involved in two conversations at once. He must be engrossed in each conversation as if it is the only one he is having.

We have already discussed how actors are constantly multitasking during a performance, but let's also look at how it can be beneficial for you as a teacher or director. If you are leading this exercise, you will be watching the actors onstage. You should also be paying attention to the audience, looking at their facial expressions and observing their reactions while noticing if one of the actors onstage momentarily loses concentration. Perhaps you can make a note on a piece of paper while you are observing. You are also busy planning your class time: When you decide to stop the activity, are you going to pause for discussion or simply switch out the actors? Are you going to move on to another activity? How are you doing for time? So you as a teacher are constantly multitasking.

To keep the attention where it is supposed to be
In this activity there are two conversations going on at once. Remember, I told the students they could not shout over one another; they were not allowed to simply drown the other one out so that theirs was the only voice that could be heard. This would upstage the other player and force the conversation to become totally one-sided. Instead, each actor had to use the importance and urgency of what he had to say to try to keep his friend engrossed in the conversation.

45. Rapid Numbers

This game can be explained as follows:
"Okay, I need everyone to come and stand in a circle. Do you all have your energy up? (I sometimes like to drop hints like this so the actors will already have an impression that they are going to have to be extremely alert for the following activity.) I need you to number off, going around the circle and remembering your numbers. Let's start with Paul. (Wait for them to complete this task.)

"This game is quite straightforward; however, you do need to be alert. Paul, in a moment you are going to randomly call out a number between one and twenty-six. Now, let's say Paul calls out number six, which in this case is Claire. Claire, your goal is to call out another number before Paul can say your name. If she succeeds Paul will have to name the person with the number Claire has just called out and so on. Let's say Paul said Claire's name before she called out another number. Claire would now be 'it.'

"This game, although simple in process, can become a real muddle unless everyone is alert and focused. Make sure you are paying attention to the numbers called. It is important to remember that if you hear your name called before you can say another number you are now 'it' and you must call out a number. Don't think too much; this game has to move at a fast pace if it is to be effective, so keep it moving at all times. All right, is everyone ready? Then let's begin!"

If need be, clarify some points again and allow one or two questions, but do not get bogged down with too many questions. I sometimes tell the students I will take a maximum of three questions. Play the activity and you will find that most of their questions will be answered through doing it. If there is still some confusion, stop the activity and review it again.

Variables:

See "The Name Game," "Bing, Bang, Bong," "Clap Out," and "Clap Focus."

Discussion:

"In this activity there is action and reaction. Explain."

"When I was explaining the game I told you that it needed to be played at a fast pace for it to be really effective. In other words, you had to be aware of your pacing. Can anyone tell me how pacing can be an important tool for the actor in performance?"

"Is there any point to this activity?"

I know this last suggestion sounds like an incredibly negative question, but sometimes it's okay to be blunt. See what responses you get. A question like this can be a reality check for you. Am I getting across the information that I would like my actors to gather from this activity? Is there something missing in my presentation? Am I communicating in a congruent manner? For instance, if I look confident, do I also sound confident? I might speak with confidence while playing with my hands and swaying from side to side in a nervous manner; this would be incongruent. This is a prime example of where miscommunication can become a factor.

Purpose:

To help actors understand the need for pacing

This activity will only work effectively if it moves at a rapid pace. When this happens there is a sense of urgency that makes the activity more of a challenge. Pacing can also be an important part of an actor's performance. You will often hear a director instruct her actors to "pick up the pace." This can be dangerous because the director might not be giving any justification for the change. From the actor's perspective, it may seem like a purely technical, unmotivated request. However, by following through with the request, the actor may discover a whole new outlook on the scene and thus create a whole new dynamic. I would suggest that actors experiment with the pacing in different scenes and see if anything comes out of it. Of course, there are many different variables that affect a scene. Pacing is not just linked to movement. In this activity it is the verbal pacing that is of utmost importance.

To enhance active listening

The only way this game will work is if everyone is listening at a heightened level. If students are half listening, then they will probably only hear half of what is being said. I think actors can incorporate active listening into their everyday lives. Another word for this might be eavesdropping. There is so much we can learn about human behavior by watching and listening to people we see and hear in our day-to-day lives. Most of actors' resources are right in front of their eyes if they decide to take advantage of them. This does not mean that after your students have played this game they will run out and start listening to everybody's conversations, but it might provide a segue into the importance of active listening at a later date. A lot of these games are excellent in that they can be used as a reference. If I were talking about active listening, I might remind my students of the time they played "Rapid Numbers." The lesson becomes more powerful because you have given them their own reference point.

Chapter 7
Ensemble

46. Activity Starter

This game is similar to "The Machine" and "The Thing." To start with, ask everyone to come sit in the center of the room. Why do I keep repeating where people should sit or stand? Believe me, if you just let them stand anywhere, you will have absolute chaos. You must have total control and be working in a safe environment to do these exercises. Explain the game like this:

"In a moment I will choose a volunteer to come forward and mime an action, for example, painting a fence. Then, one by one I will need the rest of you to come forward and help out, so you will also be painting the fence; or perhaps you can help by opening the paint cans. Do not go up and help until you know what is being done. If you are not sure what action those in the front are miming, sit a moment longer until the action becomes clearer. You must complete this exercise through mime, and by the end of the scene you should all be involved in completing the task together. You do not have to do the exact same task as the person who starts, but it must at least be something that complements the initial action. If I see the first person painting a fence, I might go and make them a glass of ice tea because it looks like thirsty work. The first person to go up has an important decision. You will set the tone for the whole group, so make sure you have a clear picture of what it is you are trying to accomplish."

Variables:

You could have the first person choose a topic out of a hat to start the scene.

Discussion:

"What were the challenges in starting the activity?"
"How did it feel to come into the activity in the middle?"
"Did you enjoy this exercise?"

Some of my questions will be very specific and some very general, but you will get interesting feedback both ways. It is okay for the students to make what seems like a negative comment; you can then turn it into something positive. The only comments I do not allow are malicious or rude ones. As a drama teacher you should be looking to instill model behavior in your students. An actor who is amazingly talented but has poor manners or is not a team player will lose many roles for that reason.

Purpose:

To enhance the imagination

Not only do the students have to perform a task, but, because it is imaginary, they also have to visualize it in front of them. If they are painting a fence, then the fence has to be within their mind's eye. They have to visualize its height and the width and the color they are painting it. If they need to pick up more paint, is it heavy or light? If the actors believe what they are doing, then so will we.

To become spatially aware

This starts off as an individual exercise and finishes as an ensemble piece, so the actors' movements will have to fit in with of the group as a whole. As more and more people are working in the same area it is necessary to know the space you have to work with. Often a scene will be performed in a small area (a stage), which has to reflect a much larger space (a battlefield). To convince an audience, the actors must know their space in the same way dancers would know theirs. If the stage simulates a battlefield, then three steps might simulate half a mile. The actors will have to be aware that taking large strides across the stage could compromise the audience's acceptance of the battlefield image.

47. Chinese Whispers

To begin, you could have the students sit in a circle, or you might find it more interesting to have them stay at their desks. Have one of the students come up with a short phrase, which he has to whisper to the person next to him. That person will then whisper what she heard to the next person until it has gone all the way around the circle. It is important for each student to whisper clearly what he or she heard. In other words, one student cannot turn to the person next to him and ask her to repeat the phrase, or say he didn't hear anything; once the sentence has been passed on it cannot be repeated. It is each student's responsibility to be paying attention and then to repeat the phrase loudly enough so that the person next to him can hear, but nobody else.

Once the sentence has made it all the way around the circle, have the person who started and the person who finished both come up onstage. Ask the original person to say his phrase, for instance, "I like peanut butter." Then ask the last person to say what she heard; it may be something like, "I have a really bad stutter."

Before you start this activity, you may want to talk to the class about appropriate language. You will probably get one student who decides it would be funny to say something rude, so address this before you begin. Also, other students like to change the phrase on purpose. Talk to the class about the fact that they could do that, but that it is too easy and very childish. I find if I raise these issues before we start they are a lot less likely to occur.

Variables:

Students could pull a phrase out of a hat, or you could have two whispers start at the same time at opposite points of the circle.

Discussion:

"Why do you think the phrase changed so much?"

"What happened when someone said a different phrase on purpose? How did this affect the activity?"

"How was teamwork a factor in this activity?"

Purpose:

To encourage ensemble discoveries

One of the reasons I like to play this game in class is because of the teamwork aspect it raises. You see, if one person messes the sentence up on purpose by saying something rude or incorrect to amuse friends, the whole exercise loses its meaning. This is quite a valuable lesson because the students realize that unless everyone cooperates, no one can complete the task. When you first play this game and someone says something silly on purpose, the class seems to enjoy it, but afterward they get frustrated because they want to see what would really happen if they played correctly. They are starting to take responsibility for the group.

To improve concentration

If you are not actively listening you may miss what the person next to you says. The fact that students cannot have the sentence repeated will often frustrate them, but it also reminds them of their responsibility to be listening and involved in the moment.

48. Time Bomb

I like to include this exercise alongside the previous one because it reinforces the same principle of one person passing something along to the next. In "Chinese Whispers" it was auditory and in "Time Bomb" it is kinesthetic.

95

Have the students form a circle holding hands. Now have one couple let go of each other's hands so that you have a beginning and an end. Mime taking out a big match and lighting a fuse, which is the beginning of the circle. The person who has just been "lit" will now squeeze the hand of the second person, who will then squeeze the hand of the third person, and so on. The impression we are giving is that the fuse is being burned farther and farther down. When the students are squeezing the hand of the person next to them they should do so as subtly as possible. The idea is not to let anyone else know where the squeeze is in the circle. Of course, they have to squeeze hard enough so that the person next to them feels it, but that is all. By the time it gets to the last person, there should be an element of surprise so that no one expects the explosion. Once the last person's hand has been squeezed they should make a loud booming noise and jump up and fall to the ground to represent the bomb. The other students should follow suit and fall down in the same manner. After you have played this, try it a few more times and switch the first and last person. And don't be surprised if your students love this exercise.

Variables:
You could break the class up into two groups and have them light two fuses at the same time and see what happens.

Discussion:
I'm not going to give you any examples here. Remember I do not always discuss every single activity; however, sometimes I will revisit an activity we did two months earlier as a reference.

Purpose:
To create an ensemble
Yes, you have seen me mention this term over and over again. Get used to it! If one person does not squeeze another person's hand, the activity cannot be completed. If one student lets go of another person's hand for whatever reason, the link is broken and the activity cannot be completed. If one person is not paying attention and has to be nudged, the element of surprise is gone and the effect of the activity is dulled. The students have to pull together as one unit.

To have fun
Although this could apply to many of the exercises we have looked

at, I want to remind you of it every now and then. We want to foster students' curiosity and pleasure in acting. Perhaps they have been acting for many years — the last thing you want to do is steal their dreams. So make sure you emphasize at times that they are allowed to laugh and just have fun. Am I saying this should be the basis for the class? No way! But I am saying that fun should be an element of the class. Why would I train in something I do not enjoy?

49. Rug Flip

You will need a small rug for this activity. A good size would be about two feet by four feet. If you do not have a rug then you can use a beach towel of about the same size. Have a group of about eight to twelve students stand on the rug so that there is a fairly tight squeeze. Their task is to flip the rug over because it is on fire and they have to extinguish the flames. The challenge is that they cannot get off the rug and their feet and hands cannot touch the floor. They will need to communicate and work together.

You may want to set a time limit of about ten minutes. If this activity becomes too easy or difficult, you can adjust the time. Have the rest of your students sit and observe, and once the first group is finished, switch groups. Make sure you discuss safety before you begin.

Variables:

To vary this activity you could allow verbal communication the first time the students complete the task, but make a rule that they cannot talk in the second round. They will have to find other ways to communicate.

Another way to make this activity more challenging is to use a smaller rug or increase the number of participants. You can also decrease or increase the time limit.

Discussion:

"In what way is teamwork an essential part of this activity?"

"Explain the benefits for the actor in participating in this activity without talking."

"Is there a need for someone to take on a leadership role in this activity? Explain your answer."

"Tell me about the importance of balance and coordination and how they apply to the actor."

Purpose:

To introduce elements of mime as communication skills

The second time the students do this activity they should communicate without talking. They will need to mime instructions to one other. This is an excellent way of developing their nonverbal communication skills. This activity will also help the students to become more expressive through using their bodies. If their movements are not clear, other members of the group may misinterpret them. All of these elements fall under a larger heading of communication. Actors are always communicating; the audience needs to know what is being said, but the actors must also convey the message of the story. What is the play trying to tell us? If their communication skills are not clear then the message will also become blurred.

To show examples of raising the stakes

This game has potential to raise the stakes in a number of different ways. This activity is about taking an event and making it more important, intensifying the moment. The students are told they have to flip the rug, but while being a challenge, it does not necessarily create a sense of urgency. The stakes are raised when the students are told the side of the rug on which they are standing is on fire. Now it becomes very important that they flip the rug. The instructor can raise the stakes even further by telling them that they have to complete this task within five minutes. You can even tell them that they will lose everything they own if they do not complete the task on time. I would adjust time depending on the age and maturity of the students.

Raising the stakes is something that can be a useful tool for the actor. Let us say you are a maid in a play. The director tells you that you are being too lethargic and that you need to create a sense of urgency when cleaning. In this instance the actor might decide that if she does not get the room cleaned within five minutes she will lose her job. She has just raised the stakes and given herself an incredible incentive to get the room cleaned.

50. Shipwrecked

You can explain this game in the following manner:

"Today's game is called 'Shipwrecked.' In a moment I will split you into two teams; one team is going to sit on the outside edges of the room and the other team is going to go to one end of the room. I will give the second team two towels, which will serve as rafts. The members on this team are actually stranded on a desert island and will need to get their whole team across to the other side of the room, which is actually the mainland. Everything in between is ocean and you are not allowed to touch the water in any way, so you must use the rafts.

"It is up to you how you do this; you might decide to put more than one person on a raft at once. Remember that once you get across, you still have to get the rest of your team across, but you cannot walk around and bring the raft back. You may want to throw it, or perhaps you have another method. You cannot hit the ceiling if you throw it or the whole team starts again. If your hands or feet come off the edge of the raft, the whole team starts again. Also, if you have made it to safety and then step off the edge back into the ocean, the whole team must start again.

"You will have a time limit of ten minutes; if in that time you do not get your whole team across, then I will count how many people you did get across and the other team will need to get more people across to win. The other team cannot stop just because they got more people across; they have to keep going until the time is up or they get their entire team across. It is very important that you think about safety first. You may not pull the raft out from under anyone's feet. Use your common sense."

After you have explained the rules, split the class in two. If you have an uneven number, one person may have to play twice. You should try to play this game at least twice through to minimize any advantage the second team had of watching the first team.

Variables:

Tell them they need to not only get across, but also get back again.

Discussion:

"How important was teamwork in this exercise?"
"How hard was it for you if you had to go first?"
"What did you do when something didn't work? Can you give me an example?"
"What skills are involved in succeeding in this exercise?"
"How did you improve when you played it the second time?"

Purpose:
To teach the students how to work as a team

You cannot be successful in this exercise unless you work together. Remember, if one person makes a mistake, everyone starts again! Brie Jones is an actor who has taught many improvisation workshops. She says that, "The three most important words in ensemble acting are trust, support, and cooperation."[1] In this activity some actors might cross easily, but if they do not encourage and support their teammates, the group as a whole will suffer. This is an excellent learning experience that the actors will be able to utilize during stage and film work.

To expand imaginations
When the students first start this exercise they may have a preconceived idea of what is going to work, but the longer they continue, the more varied their ideas become. This is an excellent way to stretch the imagination.

To learn to move in an agile fashion
Agility may seem unrelated to acting, but without an understanding and certain level of control of the body, an actor may give off certain physical signals without realizing it.

To have fun!
I mention this time and time again, but student's young and old, elementary to advanced want to have fun. In fact, when they are enjoying themselves the learning will be that much more intense.

51. Heartbeat

Have all of your students form a circle so that they are arms' length apart. Bring out a large beach ball and tell the students that this is the heart and the most important part of this activity is to keep the heart alive. To do this they simply throw the ball around from one person to the next. Choose a direction and stick with it, and make sure the ball goes to every student. If they drop the ball, the heartbeat stops, which is not very good news.

While they are passing the ball around the students may start off laughing and giggling and trying to throw it so others will miss it, but remind them that the most important thing is to keep the heartbeat going. This is their goal. They should also try to keep it going at the same rhythm.

Once the ball has been around the circle one time, stop for a moment and add another step. This time, as they keep the ball moving they must bend (bounce) with their knees. Everyone should be doing

---

[1] Brie Jones, *Improve with Improv!* (Colorado Springs: Meriwether Publishing, 1993), 21.

this as a synchronized movement.

Stop them once the ball has been around and add another step. Take a beanbag and tell them that this time, while the heart is continuing to beat, they will have to throw the beanbag across the circle. If they drop the beanbag then the heart will stop beating. Choose one person to start with the beanbag; the ball can continue from where it was. Allow them to play for a few minutes and just observe. They may have no problems; however, more than likely someone will drop the beanbag or the ball.

Tell them they also have to problem solve in this activity and that it is their responsibility to work out what went wrong and keep the heartbeat going. Some of the comments my students have come up with in the past are that some people throw the beanbag too high, that it is difficult to maintain two objects, and that the people with an object need to signal before throwing it so that the recipient is expecting it. Don't get involved in their discussion; however, you might want to give a time limit of two minutes. It is good to keep that sense of urgency going.

Following the discussion, have them try again with the two items. Remind them again that the heartbeat is the most important thing. By now, they have probably come up with some strategies that have allowed them to sustain the game, so now you can add a third item. This time bring in a small ball (say, a tennis ball) and tell them that they have to add this item, which has to be rolled across the circle. The ball should be rolled across different parts of the circle, and the receiver cannot miss it. Allow them to play for three minutes and then ask them to problem solve again. As I said, you should just observe; do not give any input in these discussions.

Have them play again with the three objects and see if they have improved significantly. If not, you may want to raise one or two questions, such as: "If we said that the heartbeat was the most important thing, should I throw the beanbag toward a person who is about to receive the heartbeat?" or "At the start, I had you throw the beanbag in one direction only; do you think you could change this rule?"

Have them resume play one more time, but before you do, add in one more item, let's say a hacky sack, which they also have to throw across the circle. Have them play for a little while and see how they do. This game can go on for a good twenty or thirty minutes, and you may go up to a much higher number of objects than four.

The students have two objectives: one is to play the game and the other is to solve any challenges they have along the way. This game is very interesting for the teacher because you have to sit back and just let your students work it out. Make sure that no one is shouting at someone else, etc., but don't give advice or even facilitate the discussion until the latter stages, and only then if you really think they need it.

Variables:

You can keep increasing the number of items you add. I knew one teacher who got his students up to twenty-four items. They were so advanced that they had added a chair you had to sit in, get up, and pass on to the next person. They used to play this game as a warm-up for each rehearsal. Do you think they learned to work as an ensemble?

Discussion:

In this exercise I like to keep my discussion going all the way through. The reason is that the problem solving is a large part of the activity. Most of the discussion, therefore, will come from the students. At the end you can hone in on certain issues.

"What was interesting about that activity?"

"What was a key element to being successful in this activity?"

"Did this activity need leaders? How so?"

"How did it affect you when a new task was added?"

Purpose:

To develop problem solving skills and experimentation

To be successful in this activity, the students have to be willing to problem solve. They need to stop every once in a while and try to figure out what is not working. They can discuss these issues and experiment with different ideas to see what works best. I love this activity because it forces the group to take total responsibility for the outcome of the activity. When a group of actors rehearse a scene the director may tell them it's not working and that they should try something else. They might be asked to do a scene again fifty different ways, so it is great for actors to utilize these skills.

To connect physical with cerebral

How? Stretch yourself, and continue to come up with your own reasons. It is very important that you are not just handed everything on a plate. Think for yourself!

Chapter 8
Characterization

52. Animal Farm

This exercise works best with ten to twenty students. Have the students sit on the floor (they do not have to be in a circle) and number off one through five. Choose a farm animal to assign to each number, i.e., one = cows, two = pigs, three = chickens, four = donkeys, and five = goats. Now ask the students to go sit in groups according to their numbers, and explain the rest of the game as follows:

"In a moment I will call out two animals. The members of those two groups must make their way to the middle of the room with their eyes closed. Move slowly so that you do not get hurt. Those who are left should create a large circle around them so that we now have a controlled and safe environment. Once you are in the middle and I say go, you must try to find all the other animals in your group. You must keep your eyes closed and you must move in the same manner as your animal, either upright, on your knees, or crawling. You must also make the same noise as your animal. The first group to finish wins, but safety is of primary importance, so please be careful and considerate of others. You may not talk to anyone except by making the sounds of your animal."

Get two groups to try this out first. You will find that this game moves very quickly and that you will want to use a lot of variety. Make sure you think of safety first. There is a lot of opportunity for head banging if you are not careful.

Variables:

You can vary the number of groups you put in the circle. You may get to the stage where you put all five groups in at once. You should build up to this point gradually.

Discussion:

"Explain the benefits of this activity in terms of characterization."
"Give me an example of the importance of safety as it relates to acting."
"Why might we play this game?"
This is a simple question, but sometimes the answers you get are invaluable. My students often come up with reasons that I had not thought of.

Purpose:

To develop characterization skills

I love the fact that everyone gets to feel goofy when playing this game. Barriers break down as students get to be silly together. They start to develop characterization as they attempt to emulate the physical and vocal characteristics of the animals. In order to imitate their animal they have to know something about it. For example, the students usually know that a cow makes a "moo" sound. They have some prior knowledge of this character. If a student has to play a naval officer in a production perhaps he won't have any prior knowledge of that character. He will realize that it might be necessary to do some research on his character. In this game, if the students don't define their characters in a clear manner, their teammates will not be able to find them.

To create sensitivity in touch

As the students have their eyes closed other senses become heightened. Their sense of hearing will become more defined; their sense of touch will also become more sensitive. This can be a very useful skill for actors to have. Let us say that some actors are in a scene in which they have to put their hand over the side of a boat and dip it in the ocean. We have to see their responses not only on their faces, but also through their entire bodies so we have an idea what the temperature of the water is supposed to be. These responses come in large part from the actors using their imaginations, but also through understanding the sensitivity of touch. This exercise will guide students in the right direction.

To take risks

Gradually you should guide the actors toward taking risks. I don't mean risks as in jumping off a cliff; I mean, for example, freeing up their characters. In this activity all of the students become animals, which can be quite embarrassing for some. If a twelve-year-old girl is playing an eighty-year-old lady, a risk might be hunching over her back and using a croaky voice. You may want to explain to her that with old age some people will develop scoliosis, which is a curvature of the spine. This may be embarrassing for her initially, especially if it is the first character she has ever performed. You will want to make sure the classroom is a safe environment. Do not allow the other students to mock or tease each other in a way that is cruel. Of course people will laugh, but you need to clarify the difference between fun and ridicule.

53. Center of Gravity

You can explain this game as follows:

"Today I want to explore the 'Center of Gravity' exercise with you. This exercise should be a lot of fun. During this activity everyone will get to look a little silly at times. Remember that this is unimportant because we are working in a safe environment. We can laugh with each other as long as it is in a supportive manner. I also want you to have the courage to take risks. Do not hold back because you feel you might look silly. Explore each activity to its fullest.

"Now, let me have this half of the room come up into the performance area while the rest of you sit at your desks and observe. In a moment I am going to ask the group in the performance area to move around the room. As you do this I would like you to lead with your head so it is protruding forward. As we move most of us have a point or origin in our bodies that leads our movement. Most people will have a combination of more than one area; however, one part is usually dominant. Gravity seems to allow the chosen area to lead the body. So, first of all, I would like you to lead with your head. The aim is to isolate the movement to just the one area. Please exaggerate the action as much as you can. Having said this, do not make any sudden movements that could cause injury. Those of you who are observing, please pay close attention. Okay, off you go."

As the students perform the activity, you may wish to incorporate suggestions and discussion. The dialogue might go as follows:

INSTRUCTOR: Good, really exaggerate the action. Sarah, can you exaggerate it even more? Allow the head to really protrude forward. Excellent, that is much clearer. (Allow this to go on for about a minute.)

Very good! Now let me ask those of you who were observing, what type of person might move in this manner?

CLAIRE: A geek?

INSTRUCTOR: All right, any other ideas?

ZACH: An older person.

INSTRUCTOR: Could be.

JANE: Someone who is feeling nervous.

INSTRUCTOR: Good, who else?

MARK: Someone who is very intelligent and always thinking.

INSTRUCTOR: That's an interesting answer. If this is the part of the body that leads the most, then more than likely this person is constantly thinking and utilizing his brains.

Let's try another one. This time as you move around the room, please lead with your shoulders. So the center of gravity this time is pulling on your shoulders.... Excellent, really exaggerate the action. Okay, let me ask those of you who were observing, what type of person might move in this manner?

MONICA: A depressed person.
INSTRUCTOR: Nice, who else?
FRED: An old person.
INSTRUCTOR: Okay, why do you think that, Fred?
FRED: Well, when people get older their bodies start to hunch over.
INSTRUCTOR: Very good, as people get older their bodies do start to curve and hunch over. What other observations did you come up with?
ANGELA: A drunk person?
INSTRUCTOR: Okay, I can see that.
SIDNEY: A monkey!
INSTRUCTOR: Yes, they did look a little bit like monkeys there.

Go through two or three more changes in center of gravity with this group and then switch students. I like to take plenty of comments from those who are observing, and everyone has an opportunity to comment once you switch parts. Some other areas for the center of gravity are the hips, the knees, and the chest. Although each center will lead to many different interpretations, see if you can get your students to come up with a major theme for each one. For the head we came up with studious and intelligent and for the shoulders we came up with depressed or old. You want your students to be as specific as they can in their observations. Make sure you allow about fifteen to twenty minutes for this activity.

Variables:
Work with different centers of gravity.

Discussion:
Obviously, we cover a lot of the discussion for this activity during the exercise, but here are some more possible questions to pose.
"How is physicality important for actors?"
"This exercise explores our body language. What signals do we give off through this medium?"
"Most people lead with more than one area of gravity. Why do you think this is so?"

Purpose:

To increase the students' powers of observation

While half of the students act out the different centers of gravity, the other half observe. Although the movement in this activity is exaggerated, it is still relevant to their everyday lives. I ask my students to start observing people subtly in shopping malls and the park, or any other public places. They will be quite surprised when they see the different centers of gravity people lead with. So much of acting comes from our observations of others that it is imperative that we encourage this skill in our students as soon as possible.

To develop characterization through physicality

After watching the students moving around the room leading with different parts of their bodies, the other actors comment on what type of person they believe would move in this manner and what state of mind that person might be in. They may say that a person who leads with his shoulders is depressed and when they do they are making judgments about people based on physical demeanor. This helps the actors to understand that an audience will scrutinize all of their movement and body language. Everything they do onstage means something, whether they realize it or not. When working on a character an actor might want to use the center of gravity exercise as a starting point. Although the exaggerated posture is supposed to be just that, it can be modified after the actor has experimented with it and got a few ideas.

54. Story Time

For this exercise you will need four to six volunteers to come up onto the stage and tell a story together. The student who starts has to keep going with the story until you tap him on the shoulder, at which point he stops. Immediately tap another student on the shoulder to continue the story. You should be standing behind the storytellers so that they do not know when they are going to be tapped, and do not go in order. Allow the story to continue for as long as it is interesting. You can get topic headings from the audience.

Variables:

Another great way of playing this game is to give each of the storytellers a different genre to use. In other words, the first person should tell the story in the genre of a detective story, the second a romance, the third a horror story, and the fourth a comedy. Obviously whatever each storyteller says has to be a logical continuation of the story. This is really exciting to watch, but it's a game I like work up to through other storytelling games.

Another interesting way to play this is to have the students tell the story as famous characters. One person might be James Bond or Britney Spears. Let the audience choose the people so that they can relate to the characters. Remember, all the basic rules we have already discussed still apply. Be careful that the storytellers do not just do great impersonations but pay no attention to the story. This is not what we are looking for; rather there should be a balance between the continuity of the story and the interpretation of the character.

Discussion:

"What did the storytellers do to help define their genres?"
"When a story went really well, what made it work?"
"How would you have done this game differently?"
"Is there a way the audience could have been more involved?"

Purpose:

To develop characters

When the students perform the story as a personality they will probably take on that person's mannerisms and body language; they will start to develop a character, even if it is mainly though external means. This would include using the body, voice, and face and not involving an internal thought process. Russell Grandstaff comments, "Regardless of the approach, all good actors, professional and nonprofessional, seek a common goal — a characterization that audiences will find believable."[1] I like this activity because the characterization aspect is indirect. The students are usually more concerned about coming up with a good story. We can get the students used to doing things without them even knowing it.

To utilize your life experiences

In order to tell a horror story you have to have some knowledge of horror. Perhaps you have seen a horror movie or read a frightening book

[1] Russell Grandstaff, *Acting and Directing* (Lincolnwood, Ill.: National Textbook Company Publishing Group, 1975), 25.

or had some kind of scary experience. In other words, the students can begin to use their life experiences in their acting. They will start to become observers of their own lives. To create an experience it may be beneficial to have references from which to pull. Uta Hagen uses the example of sleeping to discuss the importance of drawing from personal experiences: "If a playwright or director specifies that I should be sound asleep and then wake up at the play's opening, and I haven't learned what is physically entailed in sleeping or waking up, I will probably lie down and fight for relaxation while, actually, my muscles tense and my nerves tingle with anxiety."[2]

55. Gibberish

This game is similar to "Expert" from the Imagination chapter in that it is an interview format. You will need three people for this activity. The difference in this game is that the person who is being interviewed speaks a language that only he and one other person can understand. I like to call the language gobbledygook. The language is anything they come up with that has audible sounds. It must not be based on any real language, but can be any unusual sounds that come out of their mouths. You should also ask them to physicalize as they talk (to move and/or express themselves using their hands and bodies).

The interviewer will ask the questions in the style of a news reporter, in a confident and clear manner. The interviewee will answer in his made-up language. As I said, only one other person — the interpreter — can understand the gibberish. Interpreters should always interpret the answers with total understanding and clarity. They should also try to make the answers creative and, to some degree, humorous. Here is an example:

INTERVIEWER: Are you happy to be in the United States?
INTERVIEWEE: Oggoo boogoo ba mungi mungi wiggady wig mon sabba sabba dan ofti calpi son day la basda don nosco un telo bosh.
INTERPRETER: He says yes.

It is important that interpreters keep a straight face as if they are giving a literal translation. The person being interviewed can be from a made-up country or a different planet or anything you decide. Get a

---

[2] Uta Hagen, *A Challenge for the Actor* (New York: Scribner, 1991), 53.

topic for the interview from the audience. This game is much more effective when the interviewee is not afraid to "take risks." This means that in this game students should not hold back physically or vocally, but be as varied and as interesting as possible. This game works really well when all three participants commit to their character.

Variables:
You could interview a group of people instead of just one.

Discussion:
"What methods did the interviewees use to physicalize their characters?"

"At what point did the interviewer become more believable?"

"When was the translator not as interesting to listen to?"

"What happened when one part of the trio seemed to lose focus?"

"Explain the idea of 'forcing the humor.' Why do I not want you to force the humor?"

Purpose:
To create a character
The interviewees really need to emphasize their physicality and expression. We certainly do not understand their words so they want to make us understand through the commitment to their actions. Although this activity is not strictly classed as mime it does share some common ground. In order for the actors to be understood they are going to have to express themselves through the use and manipulation of their bodies. So if they say "Hello" in their language, they might choose to wave at the same time. People move in totally different ways from one another. This is why actors will often look for clues as to what type of physical expression is best suited for their character.

To enhance comedy without playing the comedy
This exercise can be very funny to watch. It literally can have the audience in tears. The problem is when the students try to play the humor. Playing the humor to get laughs will often make the actions seem forced. It is far more interesting to watch when the students just play the honesty of the moment. If the interpreter were to say, "She said that her favorite shoes are made out of shoes," it would be far more interesting if this were told in a very matter-of-fact manner. As Michael Shurtleff

puts it, "Humor is not being funny. It is the coin of exchange between human beings that makes it possible for us to get through the day."[3] Actors who try to be funny are at best entertaining, but never moving.

56. As You Will

This exercise is one I like to use in conjunction with a play that we are working on at the time. Have your students come to class as their characters. For about thirty minutes ask the students to mingle and interact with each other as their characters. Do not give them anything specific to do. If you are doing the play *The Crucible,* perhaps John Proctor goes over to talk to Liz Proctor about his concerns about the charges of witchcraft in Salem. Allow the actors to explore the possibilities.

This exploration period should be fluid, so at no time should the students break character to ask you a question. Some actors might sit down and have a discussion over a relevant issue; others might play a game of some sort. Whatever they do, it has to be relevant to the play in some form. So if we were doing the play *The Roses of Eyam,* which is related to the plague of London, it would make no sense if some of the actors started to play a Nintendo Game Boy. However, it would be absolutely fine if a group of the actors got up and started to dance in a circle and sing "Ring Around the Rosie" because this children's song is actually all about the plague. None of the students should have any speeches prepared before class. Also, you don't want the actors to perform a scene from the play they are doing. This time should be pure improvisation and exploration.

Having said that, there is some preparation that goes into this activity. I would recommend that you tell your actors about this activity a day or so in advance. When they arrive to class for this session you want them to walk into the room as their character, so some advance notice is helpful. Also, although you do not want your students to prepare any dialogue, telling them about this activity in advance will give them another opportunity to think about their character. I like to give my students about twenty minutes for this exercise, but if you have a two-hour session you might want to spend an hour on this activity.

[3] Michael Shurtleff, *Audition* (New York: Bantam Books, 1978), 74.

Variables:

If you are using this with younger students you might want to make it more fun by having them come in as a famous person. If you do, let them choose their own characters. Remember that our definition of who is famous might be totally different from that of a nine-year-old. With younger students, you may want to put a lot of emphasis on making sure they have a costume as they usually really enjoy the dressing up aspect of acting.

Discussion:

"How did it feel to come into the room already in character?"

"I told you not to prepare a speech or any dialogue; were there any ways in which you did have to prepare for this activity?"

"Did you make any new discoveries about your character? Were there any moments that you would consider 'eureka' moments when something suddenly clicked for you or you saw something in a different light? This could be related to a character or perhaps it is related to a technical aspect of acting."

I witnessed an example of a "eureka" moment in an improvisation exercise similar to this one. I watched a young student instantaneously become freer and looser in her acting. I asked her what she attributed this to and she said, "It was great, I spent the whole time communicating and listening without worrying about remembering my lines." This was a "eureka" moment for her because she realized that in order to be free in performance she had to be free of her lines. She started to look for different approaches to line learning, of which there are many.

Purpose:

To free the actors from constraints

During this activity the actors can forget all the technical aspects of acting. They do not have to think about diction, projection, line learning, or blocking, among other things. They also feel no pressure to perform for the audience because there is no audience. Consequently, the actors start to relax in ways they may not have felt able to in the past, and through this there may come an array of new discoveries. Of course, the eventual aim is to incorporate all of the technical aspects of acting with the artistic side and still feel this freedom in the work. This activity may give your students a taste of where they want to head. It is so powerful for the actors to experience the learning for themselves.

To help the actors be prepared

I know this sounds strange when I have just said that the students should not come with any rehearsed lines or blocking, but there are some ways they can prepare. As they walk into the room they should already be in character, so they need to be prepared at least for the moment they walk into the room. Maybe they will have some questions they ask themselves to get ready: "How does my character move? Where is his center of gravity? How does she feel right at this moment? Where have I just come here from?" Perhaps they decide just to take a few minutes to be on their own and get their body back to neutral before entering the room.

This preparation could apply to film and theatre in the following way. Let's say an actor is shooting a film set in the 1500s. While on her lunch break, she might go eat some pizza and watch MTV. She knows that MTV and pizza were not around in the 1500s and does not want these things to impact her performance. So upon returning to the set, she decides to take a few minutes to get her body and thoughts back to a neutral setting and away from the environment she has just been in. I like to use the term *homeostasis,* which means putting the body back into balance. Of course, this is also a medical term meaning recovery from illness.

Now let's look at an example of preparation for the theatre actor. Let us say John is playing the messenger in *Medea.* He is waiting in the wings for his entrance in a very important scene in which he must inform the king, Jason, that his children are dead. So part of his preparation might be to ask, "Where am I coming from?" Typically a novice actor might say, "I'm coming from Stage Left." However, a better choice might be, "I've just come from the prince's room where I found the children dead." This is just one example of preparation an actor might make.

All of the suggestions I make for these activities are just that, suggestions. If you think you have a better way of presenting an activity or feel you could use a different angle to relate to a specific group of students, use it. Everything I am writing is to give you ideas, and hopefully complement whatever goals you have for your class. Take what works for you and disregard the rest. This is what I have done. If I go to an acting workshop and like only one idea, then that is all I keep.

57. Bear, Fish, Mosquito

Explain this exercise as follows:

"Ladies and gentlemen, this next activity we are going to work on is very similar to the game 'Rock, Paper, Scissors,' with a few twists. In a moment, you will form two rows and the rows will start off back to back and shoulder to shoulder so that everyone has a partner. When I blow my whistle you will turn to face your partner. At that point, you must make a sign of a bear, a fish, or a mosquito. (The explanation for each of these creatures works much better in a visual demonstration, so I will let you decide with your students on a sign for each one. For the bear you might put two hands up in front of your face and make claw-like gestures. For the fish the students might pucker up their lips, and for the mosquito they might flap their hands like wings. Whatever actions you agree on, you must be consistent and stick with them.)

"Now here is where the fun begins. The bear eats the fish, the fish eats the mosquito, and the mosquito stings the bear. So if you turn around and do the bear and your partner does the mosquito, you are out. The person who is out should sit down to the side, and the surviving partner needs to go find a new partner for round two. If you and your partner pick the same animal, you need to go again quickly. Otherwise we will have an odd number in the next round. Eventually there should be only one winner.

"Let me make a couple of suggestions before we begin. Be brave! What I mean by this is that if you choose a mosquito, flap your little wings for all they are worth. I want you to become your chosen animal. Also, fully commit to your decision; if you turn around and see that the other person is a bear and you were going to be a fish but now you quickly change it to a mosquito, that is not good sportsmanship. You should have already committed to your creature before you turned. Remember, a lot of acting is about working together and developing trust, and I would not see this tactic as a good way to develop trust. All right, is everyone ready? Let's begin!"

Variables:

You could vary this activity by changing the animals. For example, you might have an ant, an aardvark, and a tiger. The tiger eats the aardvark, the aardvark eats the ant, and the ant bites the tiger.

As an extension to this activity you might split the students into teams of four or five and have them invent their own sequence and teach it to the rest of the class. Give them about ten minutes to prepare.

You might use "Rock, Paper, Scissors" as a preparation for this activity.

Discussion:

"In this activity the actors have to make quick decisions and change with relative ease. What do I mean by this?"

"Once students are out, they become observers; explain how this role can be of particular use to actors."

"How does this activity challenge students to have fast reaction skills?"

"Discuss this activity as it relates to fair play. Why is reliability and honesty so important in acting?"

Purpose:

To develop the actor as an observer

Once students are out they should sit to the side and observe. This can be a very beneficial time for the actors. As they sit, they can watch the surviving competitors prepare. They should try to predict what animal people will choose based on their body language. For instance, perhaps one of the competitors has decided he will be a bear in the next round. He might not practice the action, but he might stand a little bit taller and command more space. The students can look for these subtleties.

This activity serves a number of purposes. The actors are able to hone in on body language and nonverbal communication. It also shows them that even though they are out of the game, they still have a vital role to play. They are still able to grow from the performance of others. Too often actors onstage feel they can relax when they don't have lines; they feel as if no one is watching them. This activity may remind them in subtle ways that they always have a role to play. If their character's role is to be listening to the conversation then that is what they need to do.

To encourage actors to take the easy way out

Actors should strive to take the easy way out. If an actor is in a scene but has no lines he might choose to become disinterested while he waits for his next line. He is not listening to what is happening around him even though he knows that this is what he is supposed to be doing. So now he pretends to be listening even though he is not. This is really difficult to do convincingly and would take a really accomplished actor. This is why I say the actor should take the easy way out. If you are supposed to be listening to another character, then listen!

58. Box Full of Hats

To start this activity, have your students sit so that they are facing the stage. You should have a big box of hats at the side of the stage. Choose a volunteer to come onto the stage. He should quickly take the first hat he sees out of the box, put it on, and assume a character related to his hat. So if he pulls out a chef's hat he might choose to show us a short scene related to cooking. If he pulled out a nurse's hat, perhaps we would see him giving someone medicine. It is important that the hats you put in the box are distinctly different from one another. Once the first person has gone, find another volunteer to take out the next hat, and so on. It is important that you do not allow the performers to search through the hats. This activity should move at a fast pace. As soon as one person has finished the next should be ready to go. In fact, you may want to give each student a number to keep the pace moving.

Variables:

You might want to have two actors go onstage at the same time. This means they can be in a short scene together. This might make for an interesting scene if, for instance, one of them pulls out a top hat and the other pulls out a pirate hat.

Discussion:

"Why do I ask you to pull out the first hat you see?"

"Could you explain to me how this activity is related to improvisation?"

"Why is it important that I have a large variety of hats available?"

"In your opinion, what is the relationship between the costume and the character?"

"Can you explain the terms *internal* and *external acting* and tell me how they could be applied to this activity?"

Purpose:

To establish character-building methods

In this game the actors come onto the stage as themselves. As soon as they put the hat on their heads they take on the role of a new character. They must define their character based on the hat they have picked. To some extent, this can be described as acting externally. All the actors have to go on is a costume piece and they must pull as much as they can from their limited resources. What will often surprise them is that they can come up with a whole array of ideas just from wearing a hat.

In this respect, your actors have learned that one method they might use to help define their characters is a costume. An actor who is playing the role of a clown will want to have his costume just right. If he does not have a red nose he might feel something is missing; he might know his character is not quite complete. There are those who believe that any form of costume is contradictory to the needs of the actor. Jerzy Grotowski believes that, "By gradually eliminating whatever proved superfluous, we found the theatre can exist without make-up, without autonomic costume and scenography, without a separate performance area (stage), without lighting and sound effects, etc."[4] While this view may differ from your own, it is important to explore all avenues.

To learn to accept the moment

In this activity the students are told to pull out the first hat they see. They are not given the opportunity to rummage through the box and find the perfect hat they had in mind. As soon as they take their hat they must start their scene. In other words, they must accept the moment. A young actor who wanted a crown but pulled out a sailor's hat must accept the situation and go with it, taking on the role of a sailor. This can be quite a challenge for the students. It does, however, have some great advantages. It teaches the students to become more flexible in the moment.

I know of an actor who was faced with the following dilemma onstage. In the scene taking place he was supposed to wait for the phone to ring and then answer it. The whole phone sequence was to go on for the next three or four minutes. The problem was that the phone ringer forgot to ring the phone. So what should he do? He could have just stood onstage and apologized to the audience that the phone didn't ring. He could have picked the phone up as if it had rung, although this may have confused the audience. In the end, he went over to the phone and made the phone call himself. He went with the moment. Actors have to be flexible and learn to accept the situation at hand. While this activity is just a low-risk example of accepting the moment, it is opening up a valuable pathway for handling future dilemmas.

---

[4] Jerzy Grotowski, *Towards a Poor Theatre* (London: Methuen, 1991), 19.

Chapter 9
Imagination

59. One-Minute Wanders

For this game, you need to have a prepared list of topics written on separate slips of paper that are placed in a container of some sort. Each slip should be folded up so the students cannot simply look in and read them. Some examples of topics are, "Why I love the color green," "I think peanut butter is great because … " and, "I hate clouds because … "

Call up a student and have him pull out one of the slips. Once he has looked at the topic he has to attempt to talk about that subject for one minute. His opening sentence will start with the prompt: "I think peanut butter is great because you can put it on your toast … "

It sounds simple enough, but there are some other requirements. Students cannot say the words, *and, but, uh, erm,* or pause at any time, and they cannot speak extra slowly. This sounds easy enough, but believe me, it is not. Make sure you have enough slips for each student to take a turn without repeating a topic. Make sure every student has a chance.

Variables:

You can change the length of time that the students have to talk, or change the banned words, i.e., "You may use the word *and,* but not *the, they, he,* or *us.*" Be creative!

Purpose:

To encourage participation

It is very important that every student take a turn in this game. Participation means that every student will be onstage alone and have to perform. This is a huge leap for some of your more introverted students. They may not realize it, but this is a big step toward being comfortable performing in front of others. Some actors are naturally outgoing, but others are quieter and more introverted. Through their training, these quieter students must find a way to leave the introvert at home when performing, and this activity will help them do just that.

To work with improvisation skills

Students must also be quick thinkers. In fact, they really do not have time to analyze at all; they simply have time to respond. This is also the case in a performance; all of your thinking and problem solving should take place in rehearsal; in performance it becomes spontaneous. The students must learn to trust in themselves and just allow it to happen. As Constantin Stanislavski put it, "This kind of creativeness gives a freshness and an immediacy to a performance."[1] "One-Minute Wanders" demands creativity from the students if they wish to sustain their performance for any given period of time.

60. Expert

Have your students sit in the center of the room facing the performance area. It is often beneficial to arrange the students in this way as it helps create a sense of performance for the players in each activity. Choose two people from the audience to come up onstage. (I like to use two chairs for this exercise.) Assign one of the players the role of interviewer and the other one the expert and ask them to sit down in the chairs. Tell the interviewer that during the game he has to sit how he feels an interviewer might sit, be confident when asking questions, and make sure he addresses the audience. The expert is going to be an expert on a topic that either you assign or the audience suggests. An example could be, "Sarah is the world's expert on cheese making." Whatever subject the actors are given they must answer the questions with complete authority. Even if their answers are totally incorrect, for this game everything the experts say is fact.

You can give some topics, but you should also ask the audience for ideas, as theirs may be more relevant to the students. When answering the questions, those playing the expert should never say, "I don't know," for as the expert they have to know! Also, you want to express to them that their answers should be filled out. You do not want simple yes or no answers, but rather long and complex ones; often when people are experts on a topic it is hard to for them to stop talking because they have so much knowledge they want to pass on. This makes it more interesting to watch and more challenging for the expert. Make sure the interviewer accepts the answers as totally correct and does not betray looks of surprise at the answers.

---

[1] Constantin Stanislavski, *An Actor's Handbook* (New York: Theatre Art Books, 1994), 78.

Variables:

You could use themes for this activity. For a music theme, one person might be an expert on singing, another on playing the guitar, another on tuning a piano, and so on. Perhaps the interviewer could ask the expert on singing to stand up and sing a song.

Discussion:

"What made an expert more believable?"
"What were some of the reasons you did not believe the expert?"
"What were some funny moments?"
"How did the interviewers control the conversation?"
"What skills were utilized in this exercise?"

Purpose:

To enhance the imagination

By asking the experts to expand their answers so they are more complex they are forced to stretch their imaginations. This becomes an even greater challenge when they are experts on a subject they know nothing about.

To focus

If the experts laugh and giggle we will not buy any of their explanations. They have to stay focused on their topic, and not on how funny their answers sound. This will be difficult if the audience reactions distract them, but it is a crucial lesson for an actor to learn.

To improve improvisation

The actors are learning to think on their feet, to react to each other and respond without any concrete direction or rehearsed lines. So a mini-scene is performed in front of a live audience.

61. Twenty Questions

This is a pretty famous game that almost everybody knows. Ask your students to sit down in a circle and choose one person to pick a visible item or object in the room. The student must not let the rest of the group know what object he has chosen. Next, go around the circle and allow each student to ask a yes or no question to try and figure out what the item is. This means those asking the questions have to be really specific. If someone asks, "Is it big?" the student cannot answer, "Compared to what?" but must simply say yes or no. This may result in some misleading answers. A better question would be something similar to "Is it over a foot tall?"

I like to set another rule, stating that we must have gone around the circle asking questions at least once before anyone can start guessing. I then tell the students that they will get three guesses total, which must be utilized before we have been around the circle twice. If at that stage they still have not guessed correctly, the person who chose the object wins. Once you have finished you can play again and switch the person who chooses the object. If you have played for a while and your students really love it, stop the activity. You want to stop them while they are still enjoying it, not when they are fed up with it. This will enable you to utilize it again at a future date.

Variables:

You could play the game as it was originally intended with only twenty questions. You must then decide at what point you want the students to start guessing. Are they allowed to guess right away or do they have to wait until a certain number of questions have been asked?

Discussion:

"Why did I not let you just guess right away?"

"What were some good items that were chosen? What made those items more difficult to discover?"

"How was body language important?"

"What visual cues did you discover? For example, was the player looking toward the item to remember what it looked like?"

Purpose:

To expand the imagination

When we teach these exercises one of our aims is to enhance the actors' skills. The reason I have all the students ask a question before they start guessing is because they really have to stretch their imaginations to form questions. It's easy if you're the first person to ask a question, but if you are number twenty you really have to dig deep, and the students are not allowed to repeat the same question. Again, this forces them to think. Remember, we are not just playing these games to have fun; we must develop the covert lesson. Similarly, actors in a comedy might say they are in a funny play. They might then discover that the hidden meaning in the play is related to love and honor. As actors we should always be looking to delve beneath the surface.

To interpret body language

As we discussed earlier, body language is very important for actors. Julius Fast says body language is "any non-reflexive or reflexive movement of a part, or all of the body, used by a person to communicate an emotional message to the outside world."[2] In this exercise the students who are guessing look at the player to see if he will give anything away. Sometimes the player looks toward the item without thinking; the students really have to concentrate to pick up on this. Because the students who choose the object can only answer yes or no, their faces will sometimes go into a frown or wince as they struggle with which is the best answer. The students will only notice these clues if they are paying close attention to body language. As actors, we always have something to communicate to our audience. Let us not ignore the huge influence that body language can play in the communication process.

To improve focus

The students need to pay attention to the questions that have been asked previously not just so they do not repeat them, but because they are then able to put this information together so they can work out what the object is.

62. Brain Drain

The explanation and discussion for this game might go as follows:

INSTRUCTOR: I am going to need one actor for this exercise. All right, Mark, come up here onto the stage. Mark, under this sheet I have an object. In a moment, I am going to remove the cover for thirty seconds. In that time I want you to remember as much as you possibly can about this object. Then I will cover the object back up with the sheet and ask you to tell us everything you remember. Ready? ... Go!" *(The object in this example is a banana.)*

---

[2] Julius Fast, *Body Language* (New York: Pocket Books, 1971), 2.

MARK: *(After the banana is covered again.)* It's yellow with a little black tip and it has little brown marks all over it. It is about medium sized. It is a little bit soft in the middle. It smells like a vanilla yogurt, and that's it.

INSTRUCTOR: Good job, Mark. What did Mark talk about that stood out a little? Katie?

KATIE: Well, he mentioned what it smelled like, which was kind of different from the other things.

INSTRUCTOR: Yes, he mentioned smell, so he was not just using his sense of sight. Good job, Mark. Now I need another actor for the same exercise. Okay, Emma, come up onto the stage. Remember, I want you to tell me everything you possibly can about this object. *(The object is a toothbrush.)* All right, your time is up. Oh, before you talk to us, Emma, I would like to ask you a couple of questions. Is that okay?"

EMMA: Sure.

INSTRUCTOR: How was your weekend?

EMMA: It was okay.

INSTRUCTOR: Really, what did you do?

EMMA: Well, I just hung out with my friends; we went to the mall and stuff.

INSTRUCTOR: What did you do at the mall?

EMMA: Can I tell you about the toothbrush now? I'm going to forget.

INSTRUCTOR: Oh, I apologize; I don't want that to happen. Sure, you can tell me in just one moment. So you went to the shopping mall, and did you buy anything?

EMMA: I bought a T-shirt.

INSTRUCTOR: Great, what color was it?

EMMA: Brown.

INSTRUCTOR: Nice. Okay, talk to me about the toothbrush.

EMMA: Well, I can't remember that much now.

INSTRUCTOR: Well, give it a shot.

EMMA: It is pink, it has lots of bristles, and that's all I can remember.

INSTRUCTOR: Good effort, but remember it also had a Mickey Mouse picture on it and the bristles were colored blue. Does anyone have any comments to add?

NIGEL: Well, I would say you were being unfair to Emma. She would have probably got more details right except that you kept on talking and putting her off.

INSTRUCTOR: Would anybody else like to add to that?

SARAH: I think Nigel is right. I don't see how she could concentrate after you started talking about all those different subjects.

INSTRUCTOR: Good observations. In fact, I did all of those things on purpose. I wanted to put Emma off to challenge her memory and her concentration. While I was trying to change the topic to something else, Emma was still trying to think about the toothbrush. So in other words, I was becoming a distraction. Can you give me an example of how you could apply this to an acting experience?

EMMA: Well, it is not exactly the same, but if you are in a play you have many things to remember and people in the audience could be talking or moving and this may affect your concentration.

INSTRUCTOR: Emma, this is an excellent example, the only difference is they are generally not trying to affect your concentration on purpose, but this can happen. Now I want to take this exercise a bit further. I would like one more volunteer. Okay, Esperanza. Now Esperanza, let me remind you of what I want you to do — I want you to tell me everything you can possibly think of about this object. Okay, your time starts now. *(The item is a matchbox.)* All right, time is up. Now, before you begin I want to help you a little and give you one thing. A matchbox is made from card, which is made from paper, which comes from trees.

ESPERANZA: Okay, you want every single thing I can think of. I would say it is a small gray box with a blue zigzag pattern on the top of the box. It has a red stripe down the side of the box, which probably has a trace of gunpowder. The texture of the box is slightly abrasive, and I would say it weighs about one ounce. So it is made from a type of card, which means it must be made from paper, paper is made from trees, and trees were cut down by people. So it was probably cut down at a sawmill, which means there was some kind of fuel-powered saw, so I suppose there was also gasoline involved. Gasoline is produced from oil, which would probably be found deep down in the earth. So it could be linked to mud, soil, and nature, which could therefore be linked to the universe, and the formation of earth.

INSTRUCTOR: I would say you just about covered everything. That was really excellent, Esperanza. Do you see how you have to think outside the box? Just remind me again, what does it mean to think outside the box?

BILL: Not to just think about the obvious, but to look at all the possibilities.

INSTRUCTOR: So what I'm hearing Bill say is that you should involve all your creative sources, and not just follow the predictable and the

125

obvious. Often in acting you are asked to do the thinking yourselves and discover the different possibilities. Okay, class, excellent job. Who wants to go next?

I will not break up the variables, discussion, and purpose; I think we covered most of it during that conversation.

63. Descriptive Story

Have your students sit in a circle on the floor. Tell them that in a moment you will choose one student to think of a noun, for instance, a cathedral. That student should have a picture in his mind and know exactly what it looks like. Now he can give the group one clue. This clue needs to be fairly general, so for instance, the student might reveal that his object is made of brick. When the other students think they have an idea what the object might be they can add to its description. If Fred thinks he is catching on he might say, "It has oval-shaped windows." Bear in mind that Fred really doesn't know for sure what the picture is and he may be envisioning a castle. And so the activity continues. Other people will add to the description based on the information they have heard.

The aim is still to try to come up with the original person's picture; however, it may not work out this way. This is not a guessing game, so do not have the students guess out loud. If students think they know the picture they can add something that describes it. As the activity continues, allow the students to get a little bolder in their choices. The end result is not necessarily going to be the original picture. It is the exploration process that is most important. Remember, this is not "Twenty Questions." The person who began the activity should not be shaking or nodding his head; rather he should just sit and observe. You may want him to add another part of the picture every so often if you choose.

Variables:

If you are using this activity with younger students you might want to narrow the field of topics; for instance, you may ask them to picture a fruit.

Discussion:

"In what ways do you have to explore in this activity?"

"Would you say this activity was simply a guessing game? Explain your answer."

"Why should the actor who started the activity not signal to the rest of the group when something is right or wrong?"

"Explain to me why an actor should have a good descriptive ability."

Purpose:

To encourage exploration

The students will go through a journey of exploration during this activity. The only person who knows the original image is the person who started. Everyone else must work from that point. As they continue on this journey the students may not be sure they are on the right track. It is great if they get the right answer; however, the journey is the most important part.

I especially like this activity because the exploration takes place as an ensemble. As the activity continues, more and more people will add to the picture. If I say, "It has a padded seat," I might be thinking of a throne. The next person might say, "The seat is fairly narrow," thinking of a motorbike.

Exploration is an important part of the acting process. Through exploration the actor can come up with an interpretation. For example, one actor might play the part of King Lear and interpret him as callous and jealous, while another actor might play the same role, but find more sympathy for the character. Both will have come to these decisions partly through exploring their characters.

To develop descriptive ability

This activity relies partly on subtlety. For instance, if the person who begins the activity is thinking of a cathedral and says, "It has large church windows," he has effectively ended the activity. There is no need for the rest of the cast to explore different possibilities because the answer has already been given. The situation may have been different if the actor had said, "It has beautiful, oval-shaped windows that sparkle and shimmer in the sunlight." Now the actor has been descriptive, and he has hinted at the correct answer without giving it away.

The use of descriptive language can often be an actor's friend. An actor may be given the line, "I ate the tomato." While this is okay, it does not give the actor too much to work with. A more descriptive version of the same line might be, "I took a bite into the red and juicy tomato, and as I bit into it I tasted its sweetness and zesty tang all at the same time. The juices dripped over the corner of my mouth as I took a deeper bite into that flavorful tomato." By using descriptive language the actors are hopefully able to create a more vivid and real image.

64. Let Me Have It

Have your students form a circle. I often start in this way because it helps to create an ensemble atmosphere. After they are in a circle, explain the game. The dialogue might go as follows:

INSTRUCTOR: Okay, ladies and gentlemen, in a moment I am going to ask two of you to come into the middle of the circle. Let me ask Jana and Porche to demonstrate. Now Jana, you want something from Porche, let us say an orange. The challenge is that Porche has no idea what you want and you are not allowed to mention the object. So Jana might want to start with something like, "I sure am hungry." Jana, what else could you say?

JANA: I might say, "That looks really tasty."

INSTRUCTOR: Good, so Porche would now know you are referring to food. Porche, how might you respond?

PORSCHE: I might say, "It's my favorite."

INSTRUCTOR: Good, this shows us that even though you do not know what the specific food is, you are moving in the right direction. Now I chose food as an example, but you can choose anything you want. Perhaps your partner is wearing your favorite hat or playing with your computer game. I would like you to lead in gently by starting off with questions that are fairly subtle. If you find that your partner has no idea what you are talking about you can start to make your questions more obvious to help him out. Also, do not feel you have to just stand facing each other. If you feel there is a moment where you need to sit, then go ahead and sit. Any quick questions? (I will literally only spend two or three minutes on questions. If you find during the activity there is need to clarify further then go ahead and do so.)

Variables:

You could choose a specific topic to work with, such as jobs or pets.

Discussion:

"Talk to me about the importance of words for this activity."

"How could miming be beneficial in this activity?"

"In what ways do the actors have to think outside the box?"

"'The actor who is asking for something must understand his objective.' What does this statement mean?"

Purpose:

To encourage actors to read

Because they cannot refer to the item specifically in this activity, the actors must use different words. These words are related indirectly to the item. The actors really have to search their vocabulary to describe what they want. This activity can often be a wake-up call for many students to let them know that their vocabulary is more limited than they thought. One way to improve this is through reading. I tell my students that I do not really care what they read so long as they are reading something.

Reading has other benefits for acting apart from just increasing vocabulary. You might live in Texas, but the book you are reading might have been written in Zambia. By reading books students learn all about different aspects of life and are able to become more aware of the world. It is important for actors to have knowledge about the world and various walks of life because many characters have totally different backgrounds than the actors playing them.

To develop creativity

One of the aspects of this activity I love is that the actors have to be creative. If the actor wants some peanut butter but cannot mention these words then he is forced to come up with an alternative method. We have mentioned the importance of vocabulary; however, there are other pieces that factor into this equation. Through his creativity the actor might choose to lick his lips to show that he is hungry or that the item seems tasty. This action could be classed as mime, or perhaps body language. Of course, depending on how it is done the receiver may interpret this action simply as flirtatious. The actors' creativity soars in this activity as they attempt to convey a message.

65. If This Person Were a Shoe

This game is a more advanced version of "Twenty Questions." It should be used as your actors become a little more experienced. To begin, have everyone sit in the middle of the room. They do not need to be in any kind of formation. Explain the game as follows:

"Today's game is called, 'If This Person Were a Shoe.' In a moment, I am going to send one of you out of the room. While the person is outside I will choose a person in the room to be the subject. Everybody needs to know who the subject is, but this must all be done without vocalization so that the person outside cannot overhear. So to choose the subject I will pat someone on the head and then that person will raise his hand so everyone knows who it is.

"At this point, we will bring the person who is outside the door back in and he has to guess who was chosen. He is able to do this by asking questions; however, he has to ask his questions in a specific way. An example of what the questions should sound like is, 'If this person were a movie, what type of movie would he be?' If the person we chose was someone I think is funny, I might answer, 'A comedy.' Or I might want to be more specific and name a particular movie. There is no right or wrong answer; however, you should aim to describe the individual as accurately as possible through you answers. What about the question, 'If this person were a car, what type of car would he be?' If I knew this person was a fast runner I might say that the subject would be a Porsche. Remember, there are no wrong answers! The only answers you need to avoid are ones that are personally attacking or of a derogatory nature." (You have to be careful here. Students may try to push the limits on what is acceptable, or just honestly not realize something is offensive, so you will need some discretion.)

"The challenge is just as great for the people asking the questions, because they have to come up with an array of topics to keep the game going. A few more examples could be, 'If this person were a food, what type of food would he be? If this person were a book, what type of book would he be?' Is everybody ready to begin?"

When asking the questions it is good if the questioner asks a number of different people. It is okay if he happens to ask the same person twice. If the subject is asked a question, he must answer like everyone else without drawing attention to the fact that he is the subject. I tend to allow the questioner three guesses and about ten to fifteen questions. One reason I do not go much higher than this is because it becomes difficult to come up with so many questions. I do not spend too long on this exercise in a session and may use it only once or twice.

Variables:

I bet there are some. Come up with your own ideas.

Discussion:

"How hard was it to guess the subject?"
"What part did body language play in this exercise?"
"Were you at a disadvantage if you did not know the person very well?"
"What did you do when you had no idea how to answer?"
"What was the most difficult aspect of this exercise?"

Purpose:

To develop specifics

We have mentioned before that generality is an enemy in acting, so this game is great for the students. Although there is no right or wrong answer, the students are guided toward specificity. The fact that they are answering the questions for one individual means they have to be as specific as possible if the answers are to give any real clues. Some scripts will say, "The character is called Jane." This is fine, except that it creates a sense that the person is not real. If my student came to me with this background information I would ask her to invent a last name for the character. This is just a tiny example of getting specific.

To broaden actors' imaginations

This is probably harder for the questioners than anyone else. They have to come up with a variety of questions, and sometimes that can be tough. I know I talk about imagination again and again, but without it an actor is lost. We have talked about how imagination is essential for plays, but it is just as important for TV or movies. If you were making a film set in the Sahara desert and you filmed it on location you might ask, "Why do I need to use my imagination?" Well, let's say you were supposed to be alone in the desert, but it just so happens there are 150 members of the technical crew on the set, including cameramen, producers, light and sound crew, not to mention the director. It takes a great imagination to pretend you are the only soul in sight.

Just like working out in the gym, all of these skills need to be exercised and developed. You don't just walk into the gym and suddenly find you have a great body. You have to work at it with dedication and commitment. This is doubly true for actors, who must constantly be developing their craft. Concentration, memorization, teamwork, imagination, attention to detail, purpose, and risk taking are just some examples of skills to hone. Students should be constantly training at their craft, whether they know it or not.

66. Ball Toss

Have your students form a circle for this activity. You will need two or three items that you can use for throwing. I would suggest a beach ball, a hacky sack, and a beanbag. Start off by throwing the ball to a student and saying his or her name. As each student catches the ball he or she will throw it to someone else and say that person's name.

Practice that for a while and then tell the class you are going to change the rules. This time as the ball is thrown they have to say a color. If Simon throws the ball to Mark, Simon might say, "Red." Once a color has been said it cannot be repeated. Choose a leader to run the activity and change the topics as often as he likes. He might start with colors and then change to movie titles, states, clothes, and so on. This game is best played at a fast pace, so the leader may want to have thought about a few topics beforehand.

If actors drop the ball (beanbag), repeat a color, or simply cannot think of anything to say they are "out" and have to sit down in their spot. Do not have those students who get "out" leave the circle, but just sit down where they are. This way they still feel they are participating to some degree. If they leave the circle they will probably start wandering around or talking, the whole dynamic of the activity will change, and the focus and concentration in the room will most likely disappear. You want to have all your activities well organized and thought through to get the most out of them. Once you have a winner, you can try this game again with a new leader.

Variables:

Although I said you might need two or three items, so far I have only used one. If you find this activity appears to be too easy for the students, add another item. While the ball is being thrown across the circle and the students are naming colors, the beanbag can be thrown to the tune of movie titles. If the students are still breezing through, add another.

Also, you could vary this so that instead of being out students simply have to go down on one knee when they miss the ball or an answer. If this happens again they must go down on both knees, next they would have to put one arm behind their back, and finally they would be out. If they are on one knee and succeed the next time the ball comes to them they can stand up again. If they have one hand behind their back and are successful they can now use both hands. Beware that this could really extend the duration of the game.

Discussion:

"How might this activity be linked to improvisation?"

"When someone is out why do I ask him or her to remain in the circle and not just go sit somewhere else?"

"Is there any way you can prepare ahead of time to be more successful in this activity? If I know the topic is colors I might think of five or six colors before the ball comes to me."

"Why is the leader's job vital in this activity? In what way does the leader drive this exercise?"

Purpose:

To increase improvisational skills

The students have very little time to think in this activity. They really have to be creative and think fast. They may have a color prepared, but if the topic changes to Olympic events just as the ball is being thrown to them, they have to react quickly. This activity is excellent at keeping the students on their toes.

We have often talked about the benefits of improvisational skills during performance, but they can also be extremely useful during the rehearsal process. The director may feel that the scene has become stagnant and wish to change things up a little. She may ask the actors to put their scripts down and run the scene using improvisation. She might say, "You know the general outline of the scene, and so work from this premise. Do not even worry about using the words from the script or the blocking. Let's run with it and see what happens." Sometimes using improvisation in a scene will help free up the actors.

To enhance multitasking

The link between the mental and the physical in this activity is apparent. The students must throw the ball while at the same time think of a response. Because this activity works at a fast pace they really do not have much time to separate the two. Therefore the mental and the physical are very much intertwined. It is important for actors to realize the importance of the connection between the two. A director may tell an actor that he needs to be angry in this scene. This is a very vague statement for the director to make. If, however, the actor is chopping wood with an axe (physical) and he cannot break through the wood this might cause him to become frustrated and angry (emotional). This connection will solidify the emotion for both the actor and the audience.

Chapter 10
Improvisation

67. Improvisation Dance Circle

To start with ask everyone to stand in a circle. (Why do we stand in a circle so much? I find it is an excellent way to demonstrate an exercise, but it also keeps the class working as a close-knit unit. I do not use this positioning on every exercise, but it is certainly very effective for many.) You will need a stereo and some upbeat music for this exercise. (It's more fun if you find music the students can relate to.) What happens is one person does some form of action and then everyone does it together. Demonstrate this before you put the music on. An example of an action could be jumping up and down or shaking your arms; these are essentially dance moves, but it is better to phrase it by saying, "Everyone will come up with his own action, which the others will then copy." Some students may not feel as comfortable if you tell them they have to come up with a dance move. Go around the circle and do this one at a time. Once you have been around one time, go around again, maybe in the other direction this time.

Variables:

Come up with your own! If we are trying to stretch the students' imaginations, shouldn't we, as leaders, follow the same process?

Discussion:

"Who felt embarrassed when it was your turn to start the next move? Why do you think you felt that way?"
"Why do you think I asked everyone to repeat the move?"
"How is this activity related to being an ensemble?"
"In what way can this activity serve as an icebreaker?"
I usually do not have a discussion with this game because I feel it is enough that the students participated.

Purpose:
To break the ice

This game is an icebreaker and it can work really well at helping the students lose their inhibitions. This is excellent preparation for a performance. If an actor becomes self-conscious onstage, the audience will see it and it will detract from his performance. This activity will help the students to lose their inhibitions so that they can concentrate on the performance.

To work as an ensemble

The students are beginning to work as an ensemble. One person makes a move or an action and everyone mimics him. Why is working as an ensemble important? There are numerous reasons, but let me give you one for starters. You are performing a play and it is going well; however, one member of the cast is not paying attention and forgets to make an entrance. When he remembers two minutes later, he stumbles onstage and trips. When he gets up, he cannot remember his lines and run offstage crying. An extreme example, to be fair, but this is what the audience would remember. Not the excellent performances, not the wonderful costumes, but the person who tripped. Your cast must work as an ensemble throughout their performance if they want to do it justice. Among the group there might be one person who takes a leadership role, but this does not negate the importance of the other members. According to Lee Strasberg, "In every collective work, the important feature is that you must have a leader, but everything must be done by the group."[1] There is no getting away from the responsibility of the group.

68. Who Am I?

Explain this game as follows:

"I need four or five volunteers. Okay, Mark, Jane, Anita, Dan, you four come up onto the stage. I need one more person ... okay, Claudia. Claudia, you have been invited to a party, but you do not know who you are. While you are at the party the other guests will drop subtle hints to help you figure out who you are. For example, if you were Santa Claus, when you come in Jane might say, 'Wow, it sure is cold outside today!' And Dan might add, 'Yes, I heard that you had to visit a lot of people.' These clues are not too big, but they will hopefully guide you in the right direction.

"Now there are two objectives here: one is for Claudia to discover her identity; the other is to keep the party going. There should be music, food and drinks, and presents to open, and all of these things should be mimed. Throughout the activity the host should constantly make sure his party is going smoothly. What you want to avoid is everyone just standing in a huddle asking questions. Claudia, when you are trying to figure out who you are, you might say something like, 'Oh yes, it was cold outside, but it was okay because I came on my sleigh.' In other

[1] Lee Strasberg, *A Dream of Passion* (New York: Plume Books, 1987), 66.

words, you are not just guessing and destroying any realism in the conversation. At all times, everyone is to keep the conversation going. "It is also important that the clues are not too obvious. For example, when Claudia walks in the door you don't want to ask, 'How is Rudolph today?' However, if you have been playing for five minutes and not made progress then you can start to drop bigger clues. If the host guesses who the person is then this should be acknowledged with an exit, such as, 'Thanks for having me to your party but I really must be leaving.' This way the illusion of the party is not broken.

"Claudia, you are going to go outside the room for a minute, while the audience decides who you are. When you come back into the room you are going to go toward the side of the stage, ring the doorbell, and wait for someone to let you in because the party is at your friend Anita's house. Okay everyone, let's begin."

Variables:

In "Who Am I?" you can change the number of people who are at the party.

You could also have more than one guest come to the party so that two people have to guess who they are.

You might limit the character possibilities, so perhaps the guest has to be a famous movie star or a singer.

Discussion:

"How did you keep the party going while dropping clues?"

"Were some of the clues too big too soon?"

"Which person was the most entertaining? Which person was the most believable? Is there a difference?"

Purpose:

To practice improvisation

There is very little time for planning here; the cast acts out their scene without having time to prepare. This can be very interesting to watch as it leads to unpredictable results. It is also a great challenge for the performers as they have very little time to think. As Carla Blank and Jody Roberts put it, "When performing an improvisation you will need to 'think on your feet.'"[2]

---

[2] Carla Blank and Jody Roberts, *Live On Stage!* (Palo Alto, Calif.: Dale Seymour Publications, 1997), 41.

Improvisation is a very useful skill for actors. If actors are in a live performance and someone forgets his line it might throw off the rest of the cast. Perhaps the other actors are unable to pick up their cues. What you may then see is a few moments of improvisation while the actors find their footing. The actors have to be able to trust that they can do this. If they don't, the outcome can be undesirable.

I once saw a college performance of *Three Sisters.* Everyone was in the dining room and someone accidentally knocked over some cutlery. Instead of just picking it up and continuing with the scene, everyone froze for a moment, looked at the knife and fork, and kept on going as if they were not there. Well, having had their attention drawn to these items, the audience became fixated on them and could not take their eyes off them, myself included! We were all wondering when someone was going to pick them up and it did not happen until the scene change. I probably missed about three or four minutes of the show because my focus had been drawn elsewhere. I probably lost another five minutes thinking about what had just happened. I wish someone had just improvised and picked the things up! These improvised moments can be the most beautiful because they are real.

To remember your objectives

We have talked before about how important it is for actors to know their objectives. This is one reason why I am particularly fond of this exercise. If you just play out the scene at the party the guest will never be able to guess who they are; on the other hand, if you just spend your time giving clues we will not believe you are having a real conversation. The actors have to remember both objectives for this activity to work.

69. Automatic Writing

To start this activity, give you students five minutes to write a story. The story can be on any topic at all; the only guidelines are that they must not think before they start writing and they must not stop writing from the moment they start. Tell them not to worry about grammar. After five minutes ask them to put their pencils down. Then go around the class and have them read their stories. You might want to start by having some students volunteer to read their stories.

Variables:

I will discuss this more in the purpose section; however, you can use this technique for different topics. The students can use automatic (free) writing for characters, objectives, and plot outlines.

Discussion:

"What was the point of that activity?"
"Talk to me about the stories we heard? Did any of them have value?"
"Who found that they could not automatically write the whole time? Why do you think that was?"

Purpose:

To improve improvisation skills

I believe that automatic writing is very closely linked to improvisation. The actors are not given time to think and have to go with whatever comes to them in the moment. It is the same in improvisation; if one actor tries to plan a scene or a moment, another actor in that same scene may have already moved on to a different idea. So because the actors cannot plan in this writing exercise it will complement their improvisation.

To develop characters

Students can use automatic writing to get them started on background for a character. Perhaps they have a clue about their character from the play, such as "John is obnoxious." They could spend the next thirty seconds free writing and see what they come up with. "Obnoxious, silly, annoying, dumb, vermin, skeptical." Those are the words I came up with in fifteen seconds. These descriptions are not fact about the character, but they might help an actor move in the right direction. Sometimes scripts are very underdeveloped or the actors might be writing a play themselves and this kind of exercise can be useful.

70. Freeze Tag

This is a well-known activity used by many acting groups. It is especially popular with improvisation troupes. I am going to show you different levels that increase in complexity and difficulty. The reason I am putting them all together is because I would usually use them in the same session, one after the other.

To start with, have half your actors move into your acting space, while the other half observes. Explain: "All right, in a moment I would like one of you to start to moving around the space. You can move in any way you like. When someone else wants to start moving he must clap his hands and at that point the previous person will stop moving; there should only be one person moving at any given time. As you move around the space, try not to imitate someone else's movement but use your imagination and be creative."

After the first group of students has completed this exercise, switch groups so that the observers are now the participants. Your aim is to try to get everyone to move at some stage, although you don't want to interfere too much. You may need to jump in if no one is taking the initiative. On these occasions you may want to call out a name of an actor who then has to start a new movement.

Now explain the next stage of the exercise: "Okay, we are going to continue with this exercise. What I would like you to do now is very similar. You are still going to move around like before, only this time you are going to add a sound to your movement. Try to keep the movement and the sound compatible. For example, if you are walking around and making a chopping motion with your hands then you would probably want a short, brisk sound to accompany the movement. Apply the same rules as before: If you are going to take over please clap your hands to signal the other person to stop. Remember that only one person should be moving at a time. Let's start with the second group this time, while the first group can observe."

Once you have finished with both groups you may want to have a short discussion before going on. Let me give you a sample of a direction that discussion might take.

INSTRUCTOR: Excellent work, everyone. So what do you think we are trying to do here?

MARK: Free us up.

INSTRUCTOR: Good, can you expand more?

MARK: Well, there really is no right or wrong so you can move in any way you want.

INSTRUCTOR: Nice, you are not restricted in your movements, as long as you use spatial awareness. What else?

JUDY: You have to put your voice and body together so that when you move you add a sound to that movement.

INSTRUCTOR: Excellent, so what I am hearing you say, Judy, is that we are connecting the movement and sound. How does that relate to acting?

CAMERON: When you say something in a play you can just be moving around the stage.

INSTRUCTOR: Great point! So in other words, my body language will give away how I feel; it is connected to the words.

Do you see how you can take what your actors have said and help them shape it? Often they have excellent comments, so you can say it back to them in a way that is clearer for others to understand. Only do this if it is necessary. Also, try to keep away from telling your actors, "No, that is wrong." Once they hear this they will stop volunteering their ideas. You probably also noticed that in different exercises we raise the same ideas time and time again. I do this on purpose; as someone once said, "Repetition is the mother of skill." If you teach something one time it will go into short-term memory. If you teach something over and over, it will go into long-term memory. Another way to ensure the material is stored in long-term memory is to have the actors participate as opposed to always giving lectures.

Once you have finished this part of the discussion, move on to the next part of the activity. Again, you will want half of the students to observe while the other half participates.

"Okay, what I want the person in the middle to do this time is move somewhere in the space and talk. You are not going to talk to anyone else; it will just be a conversation on your own. So perhaps you are going over some thoughts or ideas or maybe a shopping list, except that you will vocalize these thoughts. I am not going to ask you to match the way you move with what you are saying. I want to use a slightly different rule now: if you want to take over you have to shout 'Freeze!' Remember, only one person should be talking at a time. Let's begin!"

Do this activity with both groups, and when you are ready, proceed to the next phase, which can be explained as follows:

"Now, we are going to take this exercise one step further. This time the person in the middle will go up to someone else in the playing area and start a conversation. You can approach anyone you like. There are no ground rules for what you should discuss, just make sure that both of you are participating and the conversation is not one-way. When someone says 'Freeze,' he or she can either go to the group that has already started a conversation or approach a new person. No group can have more than three people in it at any time. We are still following the rule of the action taking place in just one area at a time. As soon as someone says freeze all other conversations must cease as a new one begins. Okay, off we go."

Repeat this exercise with both groups before proceeding. Even if you only have ten students, I would still split them into observers and participant at this stage. The actors will learn an incredible amount from watching each other.

Before I move on to the final stage, a word of warning: You may not want to add the last part of the activity on the same day. You have to consider where your actors are in their work and decide at what point the exercise will be of the most benefit to them. The fifth part to this activity is the most well known and it utilizes everything we have done so far.

"Okay class, please form a circle and remain standing. Now this activity is called 'Freeze Tag,' but it is not like the game of tag that I am sure you all know. Two of you will go into the middle of the circle and one of you will start a scene. For example, you might say, 'But Dad, that's not fair! Why can't I go and play with my friends?' In this scene, the first actor has chosen the role of a young child. He has also decided that the other actor is his dad. This means that the second actor must go along with the scenario and play the role of the dad. You are given no scripts and there is no specific movement you have to do. The only thing you have to do is keep going until someone else says 'Freeze.' There is no rehearsal time, so the scene is purely improvisational.

"Now, to end the scene, one of you from the circle must say, 'Freeze.' At the same time, you have to tag one of the actors inside the circle. At that moment, the scene ends and you, the new actor, will take the other actor's place in exactly the same position that he was in when he froze. So if the actor was sitting down with a hand over his mouth, then this is the exact position you must start from. You are also the person who has to start the new scene. Once you are in the middle you only leave once you have been tagged, so it is possible to be in for several scenes in a row.

"Now there are some restrictions on what you can do once you enter the circle. You have just taken over the other actor's positioning, and now you have to justify it. For instance, if you have your hand over your mouth, you might say something like, 'Shh, someone's coming! Let's hide!' Perhaps you are stowaways. Or maybe the hand over your mouth indicates that you are feeling sick. In other words, you have to justify the starting position, and whatever position you start from is what establishes the next scene. Alternately, you cannot continue the last scene. Once you freeze a scene you have to start a totally new scene.

"Now, with improvisation and freeze tag there are a few basics we should discuss. First, don't negate your partner. For example, if actor one says, 'Dad, can I go out?' the other actor should not say, 'I am not your dad!' This scene has nowhere to go because one of the actors refuses to cooperate. So if your fellow actor says, 'Wow! It is cool being here on the moon,' go along with it. This does not mean you have to agree with everything your partner says, but go along with the premise.

"Another important thing is to keep your scene going. In other words, do not stop your scene and say, 'The end.' You cannot stop your scene until someone else says 'Freeze.' If you have an audience watching, you cannot end the scene until you are asked to do so. The audience wants to see you squirm as you are forced to come up with ideas to keep the scene going. This leads us to another question. Can someone die in a scene? The answer is yes, if it is justified. But that person then has to somehow come back to life during the scene. So the idea is that you have to keep the scene going no matter what.

"Now let's talk for a moment about going into the middle. We already said that you have to say 'Freeze' before you take over, but you must also tag the actor simultaneously. This keeps the time between scenes to a minimum; it also means you can take over the actor's position more accurately. So please do not say 'Freeze' and then walk into the middle; be more prepared.

"When you go into the middle do not think too hard. If you are waiting for the right moment to come along, by the time it gets there you might miss it. What I mean by this is that the players might freeze a moment after they were in the position you wanted and now you have to come up with a totally new idea. The best option is to go into the middle, say 'Freeze,' and just do the first thing that comes into your head. In other words, don't think! If you over analyze, the scene will become stilted and stagnant, and it will be very boring to watch. Remember, we have talked about taking risks. This is the perfect opportunity to do just that. This is a time when your characters can be as wacky and outrageous as you like.

"I am also going to ask you to wait at least fifteen seconds before freezing a scene. It will be more interesting if we let each scene run for a short while. If every scene is stopped in the first five seconds the actors will have no time to develop it and the scenes will probably be boring to watch. I would like you to decide for yourselves when to go into the middle. However, if a scene goes on too long, I will shout 'Freeze,' and just call out one of your names. Whomever I call will then have to go into the middle. All right, let's begin."

I know this sounds like an enormous amount of information to throw at your students, but they will get it. I like to give them a really good grounding of what we are looking for in this activity, as there is so much for them to think about.

Variables:

We have played this where there is no time limit for the students to freeze a scene and where I am not allowed stop a scene until someone freezes it. This can lead to some very interesting results.

Another way to vary this exercise is to ask the students to really develop their characters. In other words, John should not go in as John, but as the character he is portraying. Ask your students to think about their vocal quality, their physicality, and their world views, to name just a few. You may think these are obvious; however, I usually do not start the activity off with these criteria. The actors will have enough to do as it is. I would save this variable for your more advanced students.

Discussion:

We have already looked at some questions you can use in your discussion stages. I say "stages" because we really looked at five separate exercises that all complement each other nicely. The discussion for this activity will run itself to a large degree. The students will want to stop during the activity to ask each other questions. You might guide their comments like this:

CLAIRE: Some people are going in the middle too soon; you need to let the scene run a bit first.

INSTRUCTOR: That's a good observation, Claire; does anybody else have a comment?

PATRICK: Well, I just think of something and go in. I don't keep track of exactly how long it has been.

INSTRUCTOR: That's a very good point, Patrick. You go in because you find a good opportunity, and you get so caught up in the activity that you forget to wait fifteen seconds. Both of you have made good observations. I am still going to ask you all to try to wait about fifteen seconds because that's an outline we are trying to stick with for the moment. Although I totally agree with Patrick that this can be difficult at times when you are all wrapped up in the activity.

Purpose:

To loosen inhibitions

In the first two parts of this activity the actors used movement and then movement plus sound. By starting with very basic instructions, the actors feel less inhibited and recognize the opportunity for succeeding in the activity. They will not want to volunteer if they think they will fail. With the first activity you are just asking them to move around the space; even though they have to do this on their own they usually feel little inhibition. Then you ask them to add sound to the movement. They already felt they succeeded in the first assignment, so adding a sound is not such a big deal. You may not be setting your actors up to pass or fail, but many of your actors will probably set themselves up mentally. Try to build their confidence by ensuring that they feel each step is an accomplishment or a learning experience.

Let me tell you a story I once heard that parallels this idea; I do not remember the story exactly so I will use my imagination to fill in the gaps. A young man who worked for a charity knocked on a door and asked the gentleman inside if he would mind wearing a badge that said "I support giving blood." The gentleman, who had no particular interest in giving blood, said that he would. After all, this young man had not asked for any money. A month or so went by, and the gentleman was still wearing the badge. Many people commented on it and what a good thing it was that he supported giving blood. At this time the young man from the charity came back and asked the gentleman for a small donation. The gentleman was only too happy to comply and said it would be a pleasure. About a month went by and the young man came back. He was happy to see that the gentleman was still wearing his badge. This time he asked the gentleman if he would consider giving blood. The gentleman was only too happy to comply. After another month or so went by, the young man knocked at the door once again. He said that they were looking for bone marrow donations and that he would like the gentleman to think about it, although he did not want him to make a decision at this stage. So the gentleman said he would think about it. After a little while, the gentleman phoned the young man to tell him he would be happy to be a bone marrow donor. This is an extremely painful process, and yet this man, who just a few months ago had never considered giving blood before, was willing to help. By taking tiny steps, one at a time, the charity worker was able to build leverage with this man. He was also able to give the gentleman a new set of references. The most powerful was probably asking him to wear the

145

badge because he automatically became an advocate for the cause. Find ways to give your actors new sets of references, to make them feel like they are always progressing. Point out something they did that you liked or that worked and allow them to build off these references. By building their confidence in this way, it will be much easier for them to accept constructive criticism when it is given. If we want to get the most out of our students we need to ensure that they have a positive self-image. As Maxwell Maltz puts it, "The self image is the key to human personality and human behavior. Change the self image and you change the personality and the behavior."[3] If students believe they can't act, then they are probably right. If you foster your students' belief in their own potential then anything is possible.

To develop improvisational skills

I really love "Freeze Tag" and have always seen it as the ultimate improvisation activity. The scenes are usually changed once or twice a minute and it moves at such a fast pace that the actors have very little time to think.

Improvisation is so complementary to the technical aspects of acting because we can add the freedom of improvisation to the structure of technicalities. Improvisation will allow the actors to make choices and follow them through. Sometimes in a play something might go wrong; even if this happens just momentarily, it is improvisation the actors will use to pull themselves through.

Improvisational skills can be of great benefit to the beginning actor. It offers students the opportunity to perform in front of others without having to have mastered some of the technical aspects of acting such as line learning and blocking. Viola Spolin says that, "Everyone can act. Everyone can improvise. Anyone who wishes to can play in the theatre and learn to become stage worthy."[4] I am not saying that improvisation is a simple skill; far from it. I am, however, observing that it can be a good building block for actors. A director should always look for a way to hook his students into acting, and I have found that improvisation is one such hook for many young actors. Having said this, do not rely on improvisation alone. It should be just one piece of the acting puzzle.

---

[3] Maxwell Maltz, *Psycho Cybernetics* (New York: Prentice-Hall, 1960), ix.
[4] Viola Spolin, *Improvisation for the Theatre* (Chicago: Northwestern University Press, 1983), 3.

71. Touch and Go

For this activity, have your actors sit so that they are facing the stage area and ask two volunteers to come up onstage. You may want to have a chair or two available. Tell them that they are going to improvise a short scene. Let us say for a moment that one person is going to play the employee and the other person is going to play the boss who needs to let the employee go. There is a slight twist to this activity in that every time one of the actors speaks he must touch the other in some way that is justified. So the boss might say, "I'm sorry, Jane, we are going to have to let you go." At this moment she might choose to pat Jane on the back. Jane might become very upset and start to cry on her boss's shoulder and say, "But why?" So every time an actor speaks he must touch the other actor in some way that is justified. The actors also have to make sure that they alternate lines so they both get equal time to speak.

This exercise will be a great challenge for your actors. You may have the topics prepared or you may accept suggestions from the audience, but try to choose topics that allow for physical contact. Some examples are a breakup, an argument, and a board meeting. Remember, if the topic is incredibly static it might be very difficult for the actors to justify touch. Of course, this might be just the challenge you are looking for.

Variables:

You could try this activity with three or more players. Of course, this will make it more complex and challenging. You might want to give the actors a prearranged order before they begin.

Discussion:

"Explain some of the challenges of this activity."
"How might the necessity of touch make the scenes more powerful?"
"What were some of the ways the actors justified touching their partners?"
"Why are the topic choices very important for this activity?"

Purpose:
To help actors become more aware of their actions
In this exercise we have said that every time an actor speaks he must touch his partner in some way. To do this in a way that is meaningful can be quite a challenge. The actors start to realize just how difficult a task it can be to justify every action they take. Even though this is done in an

exaggerated fashion in this activity, it highlights the importance of the actors' connection to their actions. If, in a movie, a general patted an enemy soldier on the back, this action could have enormous connotations. The audience could perceive this action in a number of different ways. If, when asked at a later date why he performed this action, the actor said, "Because it seemed like a good idea at the time," this does not show the involvement of any thought process. Of course, actors should have freedom and spontaneity; however, we should also be aware of the messages our actions send. Actors sometimes forget that the audience scrutinizes every move. This is even more apparent in film, where we see the actors close up and enlarged. There is a lot of truth in the saying "Actions speak louder than words."

To demonstrate the power of touch

When the actors first start this activity they sometimes perceive it as a bit lame. They do not always like the idea of having to justify each touch. What becomes interesting after a short while is not only do they strive to justify each touch, but they also find a variety of ways to do so. They start to experiment with touch in ways they had not even considered before. We see a touch given through love, hate, tenderness, hurt, pain, disgust, animosity, lust, greed, confidence, and determination, to name but a few. It is powerful to see the actors' eyes when the light comes on and they start to understand the power of touch.

Chapter 11
Action and Reaction

72. Dog, Dog, Dog

Have the students stand in a circle. Go around the circle and have everyone come up with and say the name of a different animal. The animals need to be fairly simple, so a long-haired elephant rabbit would not work. Once everyone has said an animal, go around the circle again. This time tell your students that they need to know what animal people are. Have one student go into the middle of the circle. The person in the middle must try to say any animal three times before the person who chose that animal can say it once. Let's say Mike is in the middle and he knows Fred is a cat so he says "cat." If Fred manages to say his animal once before Mike can say it three times, then Fred has won and Mike remains in the middle.

When in the middle, a student can say anyone's animal. He doesn't even have to look at the person, but he has to say the animal audibly. If it is not understood, then the student has to stay in the middle. (You are introducing them to good diction without even telling them.) Students on the outside can only answer to their own animal.

Ask your actors to come up with animals that have no more than two syllables. If a student chooses a really complex name it usually never gets called, and then he becomes frustrated that no one mentioned his animal. No two people can have the same animal, but they can have the same animal group. If one person chooses to be a pigeon, another can choose to be a dove. The students usually love this activity, so you may want to play for a good ten or fifteen minutes.

Variations:

You could try having students say the animal names in different multiples, perhaps five times instead of three, to make it harder.

Discussion:

I tend to keep the discussion light on this exercise, but you will want to address a number of areas.

"Why was concentration an issue in this exercise?"

"Some of you got caught out on different occasions even when you were concentrating; why do you think that was?"

"Why did I ask you to stand up rather than sit down?"

To help them really become alert, you can change your students' physical stance even further. Have them lean in slightly with one foot forward; now they will be really alert. It is as if they were about to start a race from a standing position.

Purpose:

I love this game and the students love this game

This is as good a reason as any to include this exercise in your repertoire. You may think I am being casual to talk about fun, but shouldn't this be part of the learning process? If the students are never able to enjoy themselves, it is very unlikely they will become enthusiastic about the subject you are teaching. If you make sure there are fun activities included in your teaching, you will find the students learn a great deal more than you ever imagined. You will find them more amiable when it comes to challenging material.

To demonstrate listening as an important factor

You always want to look at the bigger picture. How can you apply this exercise to acting in other ways? There is nothing worse that an actor onstage who is simply waiting for his line and obviously not listening to the other actors. I often talk about this concept somewhere in my discussion.

As you can see, quite a few skills, such as focus and concentration, seem to be utilized in many different activities, so you can take any of these activities and mold them according to your needs. Do not feel you have to talk about focus and concentration in every activity for which they may be relevant. One day you might play three games without any discussion. This is okay; remember, the actors will still be learning through other means. When choosing my activities I usually look for ones that complement what I am teaching that day. For instance, if we are studying mime, then I may use an activity that enhances nonverbal communication.

73. Hot Potato

Explain this game as follows:

"The game we are about to play is called 'Hot Potato' because that is what I decided to call it today. In a moment, one of you is going to stand in the center and everyone else will have to touch this person with one finger. Your fingers must be above the waist and in a non-intrusive area. Do not touch the face please. When I blow my whistle the person in the center will try to tag as many people as he can; however, he cannot move off the spot he's in. He must pivot. Participants, you can move off of your spots as soon as I blow my whistle. Please be careful not to crash into other people around you. If you are caught you will then join the person in the middle on the next round and also be a tagger. This means that those left in the game will put a finger on you or any of the other taggers.

"A few more rules before we start. If you are in the middle, you must use caution when tagging. You cannot slap someone; you must tap. Alternately, if you are trying to escape, you cannot dive into or push people out of the way. You must think of safety first. Remember there are many other people around you, so be conscious of your surrounding area and the other people in it. If you are not already touching someone when I blow the whistle to start then you are out. This game works best when played at a fast pace, so there will only be about ten seconds between rounds."

Variables:

You could start off with more than one tagger.

You could also change the rules about what part of the body the players may touch, i.e., just the arms.

Discussion:

Remember, if you have a discussion after every game the students will get frustrated. You will still have taught them something even if you do not explain it. It also means they are not able to predict the sequence of each exercise. This will keep them on their toes.

Purpose:

To act and react

This is a great exercise for developing reactions. It will help the students to stay alert and focused. The tagger tries to tag as many people as possible: action. And the participants attempt to move out of reach: reaction.

To improve spatial awareness

This game does not stress teamwork, but the players certainly must consider spatial awareness so as not to crash into each other. Of course, it is loads of fun. However, when there is a game the students absolutely love, do not play it all the time. You will find they will soon tire of their favorites if you use them too often. I am not showing an exact sequence these exercises should go in or putting them into complete lesson plan format (that would be another book); rather, I am leaving it to you to add them to your bag of tricks.

74. Simon Says

This is a game we all played when we were children; the trick is to understand how you can link familiar games to the training of actors. How can you use even childhood games to enhance actors' abilities? Let's find out! You may want to introduce this game like this:

"Okay, I'm sure you all know this game already, but let me quickly go through the rules for you. Pat, come over here and demonstrate for me. Everyone else, I need you to go to the center of the room and stay standing; you must be facing Patrick. The leader in this game is called Simon. Simon's job is to give commands and your job is to follow those commands if and only if they are preceded by 'Simon says.' For instance, if Patrick says, 'Simon says put your hands on your head,' he will put his hands on his head and everyone else should do the same. If, however, he says, 'Put your hands on your head,' and you do it, you are out. You should only copy Simon if he starts his sentence with 'Simon says.' If you start to move and then change your mind, you are still out. If you are out, take a seat where you are. Simon, you want to keep the game moving fairly quickly so that you can catch people off guard, but you must still make sure that what you say is audible. All right, let's begin." (You will be amazed that even with these well-known activities some students will know different versions, so I always recommend you go through the rules before you start no matter how redundant that may seem. You may also want to consider changing the leader during this activity; that way even when students are out they can still be utilized in another way.)

Variables:

The leader could make his actions and his commands incongruent. For instance, Simon could say, "Simon says put your hands on your head," and he could put his hands on his feet. This would confuse the players even more. Remember, they have to do what Simon says, not what Simon does.

Discussion:

"What skills were important for this game?"

"What happened when Simon did not speak clearly?"

"How easy was it to follow Simon's actions?"

"How influenced were you by other people around you?"

Purpose:

To practice action and reaction

In this game, Simon acts and the class reacts. Simon puts his hands on his head (action) and the class reciprocates (reaction). In acting, the phrase that is often used is "act and react"; the actor responds to whatever stimulus he is given. His wife enters the room (action), so he goes over and hugs her (reaction). The alarm clock rings (action) and she wakes up (reaction).

To interpret subtext

Subtext is also important in this game. The subtext is what is really being said, what is behind the sentence. "Simon says put your hands on your head." (Subtext: I really want you to put your hands on your head.) "Put your hands on your head." (Subtext: I want you to put your hands on your heads so you will be out.) When actors are interpreting a script they are constantly looking for the subtext. "I love you." (Subtext: I really care about you as a friend. / I cannot stand you! / Marry me!) I am not saying that all of this is being taught through "Simon Says"; however, it can certainly be a beginning. I am not asking you to mention all of the above in a discussion; it is enough that you are aware of the future value of what they are learning. Many of these exercises should be seen as building blocks for future exercises. This is not supposed to be a replacement for other actor training; it should be seen as complementary, but most definitely necessary.

75. One-Word Story

Introduce this activity like this:

"All right, now I need everyone to sit down in a circle. This game is called 'One-Word Story.' We are going to tell a story as a group in which each person will add one word to the story and no more. So for instance, John might say 'There,' and Monica might add, 'was,' and Simon may follow with, 'a,' and on it goes. That is all I am going to tell you about the exercise for the moment. Just remember you can only say one word until it comes back around to you again. Okay, let's begin!"

After your students have played a couple of times stop the game and start to adjust the rules: "Now I want to add a couple of adjustments to the exercise. This time I want you all to move in so that you are sitting shoulder to shoulder and there are no gaps from person to person. Also, try to speed it up this time so that there are no gaps in between when one person speaks and the next person does. In other words, it needs to flow a lot better. Okay, let's start with Brad."

Allow them to play this way for a couple of times before you change it again. Notice that I am giving them very little feedback and making only a few small observations. You do not want to give them too much information; allow them to discover for themselves.

"Good, now let's try it again and let me get a little more specific with you. Remember I said you needed to let it flow better. What I meant by this was 'Don't think.' Some of you are planning what to say way before the story gets to you. You are trying to come up with something funny and make other people laugh. The challenge is you have no idea how the story is going to develop, so even if you do plan a word it may make absolutely no sense by the time it gets to you. So what I want you to do this time is to clear your mind and not plan anything. Wait for the person who speaks before you and just react with the first word that comes to mind. This may mean that our story may not make much sense, but that is okay. It may actually lead to some very interesting results. So stop thinking. I am not saying you have done anything wrong before; I just want you to try something new.

"One more thing, during your story I want you to mention three separate things, which can be as imaginative as you want. I will give you the first one. Somewhere in your story you have to come across an elephant that can sing. Okay, now you give me a couple other suggestions."

MARIO: McDonald's.
SARAH: A giant talking carrot.

"Okay good, so remember those three topics have to come up in your story. Do not just say one after the other for no reason; we should not hear about McDonald's and the carrot in the same sentence. Allow them to come up when they do. Okay, let's start with Patty."

Allow them to experiment with this a few times before moving on. You may find that you have to stop and start them a few times. One challenge is to get them to really focus and to stop thinking. Every time a student pauses or is thinking I stop and make the group start again. So this time you will want to intervene if necessary and not just observe.

After they have completed a few rounds, introduce the final element: "Very good. We are going to do it one more time, and this time I want you to try it with your eyes closed." You will want to come up with three more suggestions of topics before you begin. Also, if you work your students hard, make sure you praise them at the end. You can use constructive criticism, but if you never praise them they will begin to tune you out.

Variables:

This game has built-in variables.

Discussion:

This is an exercise where you may find a lot of the discussion develops as you go so you may not need a discussion at the end.

"What difference did it make when I asked you to stop preparing ahead of time?"

"What happened when you had to add topics to the story?"

"Could you tell when people were planning ahead of time? How?"

"Did it make any difference when I asked you to scoot in or when you had to have your eyes closed?"

"What might you have gained from this exercise?"

Purpose:
To make discoveries

You do not want to spoon-feed your students all the time. This game allows them to learn as they go. By giving them one piece of information at a time I allowed them to experience for themselves instead of just telling them "the right way." The students will learn a lot more from making mistakes on their own rather than being given the right answers. If you are doing a play or making a short film, the students should do their own research on background and history and then report back to you on what they found out. You will see some directors who get up onto the stage and show the actors what they want them to do. I totally disagree with this approach. This will lead to imitation from the actors, but they have not had to think for themselves. The discovery process can be one of the most exciting experiences of an actor's work.

155

To create an ensemble

At first glance this activity may look like it has no relation to teamwork; however, as you can see, it very much rests on the group as a whole. If one person is not paying attention he will forget it is his turn and the exercise will come to a halt. The exercise may also founder because a student tries to be clever and come up with a funny word. The story may become totally nonsensical or there may be a long pause as the student tries to come up with something clever. As Stanislavski puts it, "There must be mutual responsibility."[1] If one person in a play does not work as part of the collaborative then the whole performance could be in jeopardy.

76. Fruitcake

Here is a fun little activity you can use. Have all of your actors sit in a circle. Introduce about four different fruits, for example, a banana, a mango, a kiwi, and a pineapple. Go around the circle having the students call out one of the four fruits in consecutive order. In the end, you should have one fourth of the actors with each fruit.

Put one of the actors in the middle of the circle. He will call out one of the fruits, let's say, "Banana." When this happens all the bananas have to get up and switch places. The actor who is calling out the fruit will also try to sit down by stealing a seat while all of the "bananas" are out of their spots. The last person standing goes into the middle of the circle and becomes the new leader.

There are only a few more little details. The actors in the center should change the fruit they call out as much as they like. So they may say "Banana" twice in a row to see if the bananas are awake. Also, if the person in the middle wants to be really sneaky, he can say, "Fruitcake." At this point, all of the actors change places at once. Remember to talk about spatial awareness so that the game is kept safe. This game is excellent for ages from about four to one hundred.

Variables:

Of course, you can use as many fruits as you want. Perhaps you want six groups.

[1] Constantin Stanislaviski, *An Actor's Handbook* (New York: Theatre Art Books, 1994), 57.

You could also switch from fruit to, say, famous people, and tell the students that they have to move to a new seat while impersonating their character. If you do this you will want to find famous people who are relevant to your actors.

Discussion:

Generate your own questions. There are certainly benefits for the actor with this exercise; I do not usually have a discussion here because I like to use this activity to springboard into something else.

Purpose:

To break down barriers and create an ensemble

I mentioned earlier that you could use this with four-year-olds. When I was living in London I used to work for a children's theatre company. We would often go to children's birthday parties as hired entertainment and work with children who were four or five. We would use this activity just to help them relax more and have some fun. Although small children have fewer inhibitions than adults, they can still be painfully shy around those they don't know. After running around as a banana or mango for a few minutes the kids would often be much more at ease. The younger kids would often laugh just when they heard the name of the fruit.

The reason I am talking about young children is to remind you that you should not feel limited on where and with whom you can use these exercises. This game would work very well with young children or with professional actors. The key for you as the instructor is to ask yourself, "What is my purpose for using this activity? What do I hope to achieve? What do I want my students to learn?" For four-year-olds, the goal may be to help them feel more comfortable and learn that if they participate they can really have a good time. If I was using this exercise with professional actors I might want my actors to develop as an ensemble, to develop spatial awareness, and to enhance their senses, such as their listening skills. So with my more advanced actors I might have many goals in mind. It does not mean that after the exercise they would have to be proficient in all areas, but hopefully we addressed them in some way.

I am looking at these activities from the standpoint of acting, but you could apply them in many different arenas. Don't restrict the benefits of these exercises to actors alone.

To develop heightened reactions

As actors, we always want to be aware of what is going on around us. In this activity, the actors are forced to pay attention. If they are not paying attention they may not hear their fruit and will then end up in the middle. You can parallel this to theatre and television in a number of ways, such as knowing when to come onstage or listening to the film director say "Action." This activity can be very interesting because it goes one step further. Not only do the actors have to be listening, but they also have to react quickly. You may have heard your fruit being called out, but if your reaction time is slow you may still be the last person. In a play an actor may hear the cue line being said and he may know it is his line next, but if he does not allow it to roll off his tongue it may sound false and stagnant. This game helps to enhance our reactions and our timing.

Chapter 12
Trust

77. Airport

You want to have this exercise all set up before the students arrive. Make two rows across the room and set up obstacles within each row, for instance, plastic cones, chairs, buckets, or whatever is available to you. You'll need two rows because two teams will play at the same time. Explain the game as follows:

"In a minute I will split you into two teams and you have to stand with your team at the start of your obstacle course. Pretend you are at an airport and two of you are the airport signalmen who have to land the planes. Each member of the team must have his or her eyes closed and be guided one at a time around every obstacle on the course (the runway). Each team member must go around every obstacle without touching it or that person will have to start again. You have two signalmen you will want to work with. The signalmen have to guide the actors (pilots) by giving them direction; they cannot touch them in any way. So they may say things like, 'Take two steps forward.' The first team to get their entire team around all the obstacles will win."

Variables:

You can have more than one student moving around the obstacles at a time.

You can make the obstacles as difficult as you wish.

Discussion:

"Is it more helpful to have two signalmen working together, or is it more of a hindrance?"

"If you were a signalman, did you find a way to make your directions more specific? Explain."

"If you were the pilot, were there any challenges in communication?"

"How did it feel moving with your eyes closed?"

Purpose:
To learn to trust others

There are elements in this activity that make trust a very important issue. The pilot has to give his trust to the signalmen. If the signalmen ask him to take a step to his left, then this is what he must do. In a play, actors have to trust the crew in terms of light, sound, scenery, and so on. The actors cannot take responsibility for all of these things, and must therefore put their trust in others.

To learn to direct others

The players who are the signalmen are getting a sense of what it is like to direct. They have to make the decisions and guide their team around the obstacles. They will start to realize that they need to be specific in their direction. Asking a player to "take a step forward" is not as specific as telling him, "Slide your foot forward about six inches." They will have to decide what is working and what is not. A film director might be going through a scene and decide it is not working. He could keep working the scene the same way, but this may just achieve the same results. He may then decide to work the scene using a different approach. This activity gives the students a taste of the role of the director.

78. Trust Exercise

Directions for this game may go as follows:

INSTRUCTOR: Okay gang, I want you to form a circle. Good. Now, this game is a trust exercise so we all have to work together if we are going to do this. Before we start, I need you to close up the circle so that we are all standing shoulder to shoulder. In a moment I am going to ask one of you to go in the middle of the circle. Now all of us on the outside of the circle are going to hold our arms out in front of us with our palms facing forward. You want to keep those positions the whole time. The person in the middle is going to close his eyes and lean backward. Sounds scary, huh? Well, it is a little at first. As he leans backward he will fall toward someone in the circle (who does not have her eyes closed) who will then gently guide him back to the middle. This is not a push or a shove, but needs to be more gentle and slow, so as to help the person in the middle gain confidence. If the person in the middle falls toward several people they all need to support him and guide him back to the center. Another key to this exercise is that, if you are the person in the middle, you need to let your body relax enough so that your teammates can guide you. If you become too rigid your body will hardly move and you will probably just open your eyes and stop.

Remember, we all have to work together; out of all the exercises we have looked at so far it is probably most imperative that we are paying attention here. If somebody falls to the floor it could cause serious injury, so you must never take your eyes off the person in the middle. Any questions before we begin? Allison?

ALLISON: What if the person is really heavy?

INSTRUCTOR: That's a good question because even when people are quite small, in a relaxed state their bodies will feel very heavy as they fall toward you. Remember that you have to work as a team. Those falling are not moving too fast for two or three people to work together to catch them and guide them back toward the center. Simon?

SIMON: What if we do not want to go in the middle?

INSTRUCTOR: Very good question. In this exercise I will not ask you to go in if you do not want to. Your comfort level is very important. However, once students have been in the middle they usually find they like it a lot. It really is quite an interesting experience.

This exercise works best in small groups of about eight to ten students. I do not often have question and answer sessions before games. However, there are some for which it really is necessary, and this is certainly one of those in my opinion. I also like to play this one along with my students because it is so important that you create safety and trust. As they gain experience, perhaps you can just become the observer. I would do the same thing with adults. Remember, although you are often trying to facilitate, you must still have ultimate control when necessary. I always feel like the more control I have, the more I can back off.

Variables:

To start, you want the students to stand very close together so that you create a safe environment. This means there is only a limited space for the student to fall back. Once the students seem more confident you can ask them to step back and spread out a little more. This requires even more concentration and trust and should only be attempted once the students have developed a higher level of confidence and understanding.

Discussion:

"Why do I limit the group sizes to about eight to ten people?"

"Why is it necessary to start so close together?"

"Why do we not force everyone to go in the middle?"

"Why is it necessary to try to let your body relax when you are in the middle?"

161

"In what way does everyone have to work together?"

"What is the purpose of this exercise?"

Remember, the students may take the discussion off in many different directions. Do not stick to a rigid script; however, you still need to guide it so it does not go too far on a tangent. Make sure that all of the important points are covered.

Purpose:

To learn to trust each other

In this exercise, the actors are putting their trust in someone else. They are allowing another person to control their outcome. This takes a lot of courage. In a play, for example, actors must trust the rest of the cast and crew on many issues. They have no control of whether the lights will come up onstage, or if the doorbell sound cue will happen; they have to trust their fellow cast and crew members for these developments. This exercise can help performers move away from the spotlight attitude toward teamwork. This mindset will help the actors to become more humble as it becomes clearer that the show does not center around them individually, but is a collaborative effort.

To sense the moment

When the student in the middle is falling back the students behind him must guide him back toward the center. They have to sense when they are needed to do this. As the person falls backwards he may start by falling in one direction, but actually end up falling in another. This also means those in the circle must be alert and focused.

79. Tour Guide

This is another trust exercise. To begin, ask the students to find a partner and sit together in the middle of the room. Ask them to designate themselves as *A* and *B*. In a moment, the *A*s will lie down on the floor with their eyes closed and, after a minute or so, the *B*s will go over and help them slowly to stand up. Tell them they have to make sure this is done with absolute care and that they must not yank their partners up. The idea is not to scare their partners, but to gain their trust. Once they have them standing, the *B*s have to take their partners by the hand and slowly guide them around the room. (Some may opt to take them by their sleeve; this is fine if they feel more comfortable this way.) It is important that they take them very slowly and are aware of any obstacles. There may be a bag, a chair, or another pair or students in the path. This is not a race and needs to be taken seriously, although it can be a great experience for the students. Often the guides have to be looking in two directions: in front of themselves and at their partners to make sure they are not going to bump into anything.

Allow this activity to continue for as long as your students are absorbed; I usually allow about three to five minutes. Be sure and switch roles, too, so that everyone gets to experience being a guide and being led around the room. While your students are participating in this exercise you should be walking around and making comments wherever it is necessary. Remember, you also want to make sure that no two groups collide. It can be interesting for the guides to solve the challenge presented when they have to negotiate their partner around another pair, but their safety is ultimately up to you. Before you actually start it is a good idea to have just one group in the center to demonstrate.

Variables:

I mentioned that you should have the As start by lying on the floor. You could start off with a relaxation exercise first and move straight into the tour guide exercise. You could lead the relaxation exercise for those on the floor, but that might leave their partners with nothing to do, so you might have their partners talk them through a short relaxation exercise first. You can give them a small handout with the relaxation exercise if needed. This seems to add to the experience. I like to give them the exercise in which they tense and relax their muscles, or you could also use the "On the Beach" exercise if you prefer.

Discussion:

"Who felt comfortable being led around the room? Why do you think you felt that way?"

"How did having partners help to ease your anxiety?"

"Who still had reservations after the exercise was complete?"

"How did it feel being the leader?"

"Leaders, do you feel you did everything possible to put your partner at ease?"

Purpose:

To build trust and cooperation

This activity requires a great deal of trust. To have your eyes closed and allow yourself to be led around the room by another individual requires an enormous amount of faith and cooperation. If one student refuses to participate, the activity cannot proceed. Actors have to rely on each other in so many different ways. An actor may have to trust the director in her decision-making, a light technician on his light plot, and a fellow actor on her memorization of her blocking. When talking about the establishment of trust, Garry Izzo explains, "Trust is given, not earned, and it always represents risk."[1] One of the risks is that an actor cannot be in full control of the situation. This activity aims to help the students release some of their need for control.

To establish physical contact

I do not want to scare you with this statement, but it is something that actors need to address fairly early on. When people communicate they often touch: sometimes they may put their arm on someone's shoulder to confirm a point, or maybe pat someone on the back to wish him congratulations. These are common experiences in everyday life, and therefore need to be addressed by the students. By asking them to lead another person around the room the students will normally hold that person by the hand or sometimes they may choose to lead him by his shoulder. The participants have now established physical contact and broken down a barrier. This may make physical contact in performance less of a challenge for them in the future. Of course, you need to make sure the contact is suitable for the class and enforce strict limitations depending on the age of the students. College-level students will have a lot more freedom than junior high students. When working on a play with some of my junior high kids, they opted to handle a kissing scene by kissing on the cheek, and we made sure to obtain clearance from their parents first. I have worked with twenty-year-olds who did not want any physical contact with their fellow actors; this can be taken as very unprofessional and can lose an actor future roles.

80. Blind Run

This is the ultimate trust game. I would not recommend you use this with anyone younger than high school age, and even then you have to use your discretion. Not all of these exercises are suitable for all age

[1] Gary Izzo, *Acting Interactive Theatre* (Portsmouth: Heinemann, 1998), 22.

groups; you should decide what you feel is suitable and what isn't. It is not just the age of the students, but their maturity and experience that should also be considered.

To conduct this exercise you need a fairly large space (about thirty feet) with no obstacles in the way. Have most of the students stand at one end of the room and ask four of your physically stronger students to position themselves at the other end of the room. One at a time, have the students run as fast as they can toward the other end of the room where the four students are waiting. The challenge is that they have to run with their eyes closed. The students at the other end of the room are there to catch them; you should have two standing and two crouching. The ones who are crouching are going to try to catch the running students around their calf and thigh area. The two who are standing are going to aim for the waist and shoulder. All four students need to be careful that they don't grab the runners by their joints as this could cause serious injury. When stopping them, those catching have to be very careful to try to absorb the runners' momentum and not stop them abruptly. This means they need to give them some cushion space so it is not a jarring motion. The catchers also need to be very careful not to put their hands anywhere near the runners' faces and necks, and try to avoid personal areas.

The people who are running need to keep their eyes closed for the ultimate experience. They may find it quite difficult to run at full speed. I know when I first participated in this exercise I was scared out of my wits and moving like a snail. Try to encourage everyone to try it, but do not complain if people choose to move fairly slowly. Again, safety is of the utmost importance. This activity can be risky, but I still think you can teach exercises such as this if you choose. Boundaries will be stretched, but in my opinion, this is one of the most powerful exercises for risk taking.

Variables:

I have not seen any.

Discussion:

The questions you use can be really general and unspecific.
"Talk to me."
"Well, what did you think?"
"Anyone want to go again?"
I would probably start the discussion in this way because the adrenalin will still be rushing through the students' bodies, releasing a

165

range of emotions. You will find that they need time to bring their bodies back into balance before you move on to more specific questions. You also might want to direct these questions right away. If you leave the discussion until ten minutes later you might get some very different responses. Ask each student as soon as he or she is finished. This is when the experience will be most vivid and the adrenalin still pumping.

Purpose:
To take risks
Often actors are told to take risks. This does not mean in terms of physical danger, but is usually in relation to character or in terms of objectives. In this exercise, I would say that it does lean more toward a physical challenge. I believe an experience such as this may free actors up to take more chances in their acting and not be so tight and constrained. Actors involved in a melodrama are often asked to caricature their characters so that they are over the top. If they do not throw themselves into this and take risks they will probably end up with a very tame character.

While interviewing John Gielgud, Hal Burton asked him, "Do you think there's anything at all in the thought that great experience, in the Theatre, can sometimes lead to an inhibiting of an actor's instinct? [Gielgud replied,] Yes I think one is inclined to turn to old clichés."[2] This activity will help the students avoid that by encouraging them to lose their inhibitions.

To create an ensemble
It is very important that the whole group focuses together on this task. Of course, the four people at the far end of the room must work as a unit, but the rest of the class needs to create the right atmosphere. If a student is getting ready to run he may need words of encouragement, or perhaps the class decides that silence is the way they will prepare. Whatever method is used it will only work if there is agreement and follow-through from the whole class.

[2] Hal Burton, *Great Acting* (New York: Hill and Wang, 1967), 143.

Chapter 13
Knowing Your Objective

81. Fistorama

Have everyone come out and sit in the middle of the room. Give them the following directions: "This game is called 'Fistorama.' I am going to choose a volunteer to come forward and sit down at the front. I will ask that person to keep one fist clenched while I ask another student to come up and try to get the fist open. Here is the challenge: You cannot unclench it by force; the only way you can get the person to open his fist is verbally. Now, this person is obviously not going to open his fist just because you ask him nicely. You must use the art of persuasion to get him to comply. If you are the person with the clenched fist you cannot keep it closed unless you can justify your reasoning. Alternately, do not open your fist unless the other person really makes you feel compelled to do so."

Variables:
Come up with your own.

Discussion:
"How hard was it to get the person to open his fist? What tactics did you have to use?"

"If you were the person with your fist clenched, why did you not open your fist? When you opened your fist, what compelled you to do so?"

"Were those doing the persuasion repetitive in their persuasion or did they use varied arguments?"

Purpose:
To raise the stakes
To get the students to open their fists will take a great imagination. Here is an example of a persuasion tactic: "Ah! I saw a scorpion go inside your hand! Quick, open it up!" This is more powerful than, "Please open your fist." If the stakes are high, the student will feel more compelled to open his fist. Raising the stakes means increasing the urgency and importance of the situation. The students might choose to go with something life threatening: "I have cancer and you have the pill in your hand that could save my life!" Actors will sometimes use this technique when working on a part by imagining a sense of urgency in order to create

more realism. The people who have the closed fists must also justify their answers. So in the example above they may respond by saying, "Yes, I have your pill, but I also have cancer and I need it as much as you." Keep reminding the students that their main objective is to get the fist open and that they need to stay on task.

To know your objective
The students must know their objective (to get the fist open) and not give up until it is achieved or the instructor stops them. This is a vital part of an actor's work. Sometimes the students will go off on tangents that are interesting but do not specifically help them to get the fist open.

A given objective can be explored at a deeper level. For a movie example, let's say Jane has just killed Claire. At first glance, we might say her objective was to kill Claire, but by delving a little further we may find that her ultimate objective was to marry Bob, who was married to Claire. Jonnie Patricia Mobley describes Iago's objective in *Othello*: "In Shakespeare's *Othello* Iago, mad with jealousy at being passed over for promotion, intends to punish Othello, no matter what harm he may cause in achieving that objective."[1] So it is important for the students to define and understand their objective(s).

82. It's My Party
This game is very similar to "Who Am I?" in that it is set at a party and the actors have more than one objective. In this game, one person is at the house and starts the party. One at a time, three different guests arrive. The guests knock on the door and it is the host's job to guess who they are. This game is more interesting when the guests have some strange quirk. for instance, a man who is afraid of heights or claustrophobic and a woman who sees dead people. The guests can be as outrageous as they like; there is no need for subtlety, as they want the host to guess who they are as soon as possible. They do not have to be famous people. The host must keep the party going while trying to figure out who the guests are. If the host works out who a guest is, that guest needs to find a way to casually be excused from the party until, eventually, all the guests have left.

[1] Jonnie Patricia Mobley, *NTC's Dictionary of Theatre and Drama Terms* (Lincolnwood, Ill: National Textbook Company, 1995), 101.

Variables:

See "Who Am I?"
You could change the number of guests who arrive at the party.

Discussion:

"How well did the scenes work?"
"Did the audience give away any clues by accident?"
"What did you do to define your character? Were you specific enough?"
"What could we do to enhance this game?"

Purpose:

To know your objective

This exercise is really good training for performers as it forces them to be really specific. If the person is supposed to be agoraphobic then there cannot be a time when it is okay for him to be standing next to someone else having a conversation; he cannot join a group of people and shake someone's hand; he cannot go dance next to the other guests. Once the actor breaks a rule, he has lost his objective and will then be sending a confusing message to the host. The actor is forced to consider how his character would act and react in a situation.

Projection

I mention this at this point because this is a performance. The actors are putting on a small play so we need to understand what they are saying. As an audience member I do not want to miss one word. I said project and not shout because there is a huge difference; actors want to protect their instruments (themselves). If an actor cannot be heard, then an audience will quickly lose interest. In connection with the voice and its qualities, Cecily Berry says, "Your voice is a very particular expression of your own personality, for it is the means by which you convey your thoughts and feelings in an immediate way to other people."[2] If actors want to convey their message, it is important that they embrace the technical aspects of acting as well as the creative.

[2] Cicely Berry, *Your Voice and How to Use It Successfully* (London: Harrap Limited, 1990), 9.

83. Strike a Pose

To start this activity, have your students spread out to different parts of the room. Ask them to move around the room in any direction they want. When you blow the whistle, they must stop in whatever position they find themselves; if they have one foot in midair, this is how they must stop. Next, select two or three students and ask them, one at a time, to justify their position by acting out a short scene. For example, if one student stopped with her hands in the air she might say something like, "No, please don't shoot; I surrender!" Or perhaps she might act as if she were picking apples from a tree. Whatever position the students finish in, they must justify it. If a student has one leg in the air he might pretend to be a martial arts instructor. Each scene should only last about five to ten seconds.

I suggest you approach two or three students each time you stop, but this is entirely up to you. Approach them one at a time so that they do not know ahead of time that they will be chosen. Be careful that they do not change their position for the scene. If an actor was standing with her hand on her hip and she suddenly decided to lie down on the floor and pretend to be sick in a hospital bed, this would be unfair. She has to justify her scene from the position she finished in. You can play this game as long as you like. Try allowing the students to move in any direction and in any fashion they like, provided they are using safety awareness. This will probably make for a more varied selection of positioning. Once you have watched two or three people justify their positions, start another round.

Variables:

You might want to use music for this activity. In this variation, when you pause the music the students would freeze.

Discussion:

"What activity would you say is similar to this exercise?"
"What are the challenges of having to justify your final position?"
"What preparation could the actor take for this activity?"
"How can you condense your scene into a few seconds and still make it clear what is happening?"

Purpose:

To encourage actors to justify their actions
If an actor freezes with his hand in the air pointing toward the ceiling

he may be called on to explain what this signifies. The actor may choose this moment to point out a star he is looking at in the sky. Whatever he decides, he must make a choice. The other important aspect of this activity is that the justification has to be valid. If the actor is pointing upwards, he could not suddenly crouch down and tie his shoelace as a justified action.

This activity teaches the actors to think on the spot, but also to be congruent with their actions and their meanings. Sometimes in rehearsal you will see an actor wander onstage from Stage Left. The director might ask him, "Where have you just come from?" The actor will sometimes reply, "Stage Left." The director may reiterate the question, "No, I asked you where you were coming from." The actor will then hopefully tell the director, "Oh, I was coming from the market and now I'm heading into town." As actors we need to be able to justify our actions to ourselves, and in this way they will be more believable to those around us.

To practice preparation
Because the students don't know if they will be called on next they all have to be prepared. They have to assume every single time that they might be next. In reality, they may never be chosen, or perhaps one time out of twenty-five possibilities, but they have to have thought of a way to justify their position every time. The one time they don't bother may be the time they are called upon.

Let us say you are watching a phenomenal fight scene between two best friends in a movie. The action is terrific, but you look at the crowd in the background and happen to notice that someone is picking his nose. It is obvious that this has nothing to do with the story line; nevertheless, it catches your attention. You stop watching the powerful scene in the foreground and get caught up in the amusement of the man picking his nose. It is possible that you have just missed the most important part of the movie.

We could say that this man was not focused or not concentrating, but we could also say he was not prepared. He could have thought about this scene before he went on. He might have asked himself a number of questions: "Where was I just before this fight took place? Am I late for a meeting? Do I care that these two strangers are fighting? Are they strangers? Perhaps one of them is a good friend of mine." By preparing ahead of time, the actor is now invested in the scene. The scene has value for the actor, which translates to the audience.

171

Chapter 14
Life Experience

84. King and Queen

This exercise is a lot of fun for the students, and I usually use it if we have been talking about persecution in a historical context. Directions and discussion can be given as follows:

INSTRUCTOR: Okay, I need everyone to go sit on the stage. Now let me choose a volunteer. Okay, Samantha, come on down. Samantha, you are queen for the day. Because you are the queen, you rule over all these subjects and you can tell them what to do. Being the queen, you really don't have to give them a good reason. If they displease you then they are out. For instance, you can say, "I don't like the way you are smiling, you're out!" Or you may say, "Eric, give me twenty pushups ... Too slow, you're out!"

Now, subjects, Samantha does not have to give you a logical reason for taking you out; remember, she is the queen and what she says goes. She does not even have to ask nicely, although she cannot say anything that is personal or attacking. Again, she can ask you to do anything she wants within reason. She might give the command, "Sing a song, jump up and down on the spot until I ask you to stop, and do an impression of a monkey!"

When you are out, come and sit in the center of the room. The object of the game is to be the last person out. I will switch the queen or king every few minutes, so be prepared because it may be you. (One reason I do this is to show different ideas and different styles of leadership; also, students tend to run out of things to say after a while.) Oh, by the way, you cannot argue with the king or queen. Why do you think this is so?

GARRET: Because they would chop your head off?

INSTRUCTOR: Good! What else, Lisa?

LISA: Because it is disrespectful.

INSTRUCTOR: Very good! Remember that you could not be disrespectful to a king or queen or it may have cost you your life or gotten you thrown into the dungeon. As we play this game, I want you to imagine that this really is the queen or king and you know what the consequences will be if you disobey.

Remember, if you have just taught a unit related to some sort of persecution, such as the Salem witch trials, it would be a good time to use this activity. You are not trying to trivialize the issue of persecution; rather, you want to give the students a small experience of how it feels to have no control and to experience a situation in which the results are not always fair. What you are doing, in effect, is creating more life experiences that your students will then be able to put into their acting. I like to discuss these issues in the game explanation. I ask questions such as, "Why are we playing this at this particular time? How might this relate to our history project? What are the serious implications of this game?" You should always be striving to get as much out of these exercises as you can. Building moral and ethical character in your students is of the utmost important to you as a facilitator. When you feel all bases have been covered, begin the activity.

Variables:
If you want, you can keep the same person as the leader the whole time. Maybe you could try having two leaders at once (a king and a queen).

Discussion:
Please see game explanation for discussion ideas. I would advise you to hit a large part of your discussion before you proceed with this activity. The key is to make the students aware of the serious implications of this activity. Sure, they can have fun with it, but you want them to have the underlying sense of the illogical nature of persecution.

Purpose:
To utilize life experiences
As actors, it is useful for us to have an array of personal experiences. Through this activity, the actors will be given a sense of how it is to be treated unfairly. This may be a resource they can tap into at a later stage. Stanislavski believed that, "Every moment onstage must be filled with belief in the truthfulness of the emotion felt and the actions carried out."[1] By utilizing their own life experiences it is possible that the students can bring more honesty and truth to their performances.

[1] David Allen, *Stanislavski for Beginners* (New York: Writers and Readers, 1999), 68.

To create conflict

I know this does not sound particularly sportsmanlike and seems to go against everything I have said an actor should be, but read on. Conflict is a key element in many plays and movies, and one of the reasons is that it holds our interest; it gives the story some backbone. Without conflict, the audience may feel there is nothing to be concerned about. In this activity, when actors are told they are out they may feel this is totally unreasonable. This may make them mad, although they cannot show their feelings. What will have been created for that moment, even without words, is tension and conflict. Joseph O'Conner and John Seymour talk about the role of conflict in our everyday lives: "Everyone lives in the same world, and because we make different models of it, we come into conflict."[2] If conflict is part of our lives, then it is something that actors must be aware of.

To have fun

Yes, believe it or not, another purpose of this exercise is to have fun. I have used this activity quite a lot and my students love it. They always ask, "When can we play 'King and Queen'?" You want to create an atmosphere that leaves your students hungry for more. They don't mind the hard work, as long as it is offset with fun. Combine the two and help them build a passion for acting.

85. Arm Levitation

This is an exercise many students have come across before and it yields interesting results. Have three students come up onto the stage and have one of them stand in the middle. Tell the middle person to let his arms drop by his sides. Have the other two players grab the player just above the wrist and just above or below the elbow, one on each side. It is important that they are not holding at the joints as this could cause injury. Now, tell the middle player to try to push his arms out sideways as much as he can. He has to commit for one minute without easing up on the pressure regardless of the results. It will be a little uncomfortable at times, but tell him he has to commit. The other two players need to hold his arms down as best they can, and make sure

[2] Joseph O'Conner and John Seymour, *Introducing Neuro-linguistic Programming* (London: HarperCollins Publishers, 1993), 141.

175

they are holding as opposed to squeezing. Tell the player that after one minute he can relax his arms and let go of all the tension. At this point the two players holding his arms should release their grip. Then simply tell the students to observe what happens.

You should find that the student's arms will start to rise on their own. They start to float outward toward the sides. The amount that this happens will vary depending on how much the student was really pushing and whether he committed himself for the entire minute. Also, it is linked to how much he relaxes at the end. The experience can be a little unnerving for some students, although many seem to get a pleasant surprise. Convincing the audience is another story. You will have some skeptics who believe the players are lifting their arms themselves. Set enough time aside so you can try this exercise a number of times.

Variables:

After you have conducted this exercise one or two times you can split the students into groups of three or four and have them continue the exercise in their groups. Make sure you reiterate that they should not put their hands over the person's wrist or elbow joints. This is likely to cause hyperextension, which can lead to serious injury. Safety, safety, safety! As well as exploring the body, we should know its limitations.

Discussion:

"Why do you think the arms were able to rise up like that?"

"Why did individuals' arms move in varying degrees? Was part of the responsibility that of the two supporters?"

"Talk to me about body awareness in relation to this activity. How did you feel when you saw your own arms move?"

Purpose:

To create new life experiences

We talk about how actors can glean resources from all of their life experiences and from the environment around them. This exercise adds another resource, a new experience to that toolbox. It is great that actors have training, but to emulate life, we have to experience it. This is one reason why actors spend so much time "doing."

To isolate body parts

When the actors push their arms out to the side they will create an enormous amount of tension in their arms. This can feel painful or at the very least uncomfortable. It would be quite easy for the actors to feel tension in their entire body, but the aim is to isolate just the arms. If an actor is in a very moving scene and puts her hand to her lover's face and strokes it, it might be totally inappropriate for her left leg to slowly start bouncing up and down. This would totally take the focus away from where it needs to be. In order to control this movement, the actor has to be aware it exists.

86. Arm Zapper

I am fairly convinced that this activity will be new to you. A famous marathon runner showed it to me in a health seminar I attended. It works in a similar way to "Arm Levitation," except you only need two people. Have one person hold an arm out straight in front of him at a ninety-degree angle from his body. Now, the other person is going to try to push his partner's arm down using only one hand. He will probably be able to do it, but it will not be easy. Now offer the first actor a segment of orange. Tell him he does not have to eat it, but can simply bite into it. Now have him raise one arm again and ask his partner to try to push it down. Try one more time, and this time give the student a salty peanut. (Make sure he is not highly allergic to peanuts first.) Tell him to just suck on the peanut and then repeat the exercise again. It is important that the actor have the peanut or fruit in his mouth the moment his partner tries to push his arm down.

What you will find is that some people's arms will automatically go down. They will not be able to hold them up no matter how hard they try. The students will look on dumbfounded, but the explanation is a fairly simple one. These people are to some degree allergic to either oranges or peanuts. They don't break out in hives, but it drains their bodies of the energy they think they are getting. The famous marathon runner told me that people eat oranges in the middle of a marathon thinking they are giving themselves an extra boost, but for some people the effect is the exact opposite.

You can start this activity off with one pair and once you have shown the activity to them you can split all your students into pairs. Remember, not everyone in the group will get the same results. You may find only 10 percent of your students react in the way we described. (Always check with your students to see if they have serious allergies. I know a number of people who have to be hospitalized if they eat almonds. I don't want to make you panic, but always err on the side of caution.)

Variables:

See "Sink to the Floor" and "Arm Levitation." These exercises are on a similar footing.

Discussion:

"Were you surprised by the results?"

"What did you learn from this activity?"

"Why is understanding our bodies important for acting?"

Notice that on this last question I am pointing the question in the direction I want it to go. I have been very specific in my line of questioning. Look at the previous question, which is asking the students what they learned. It is much more general. So although you don't want to put words in your students' mouths, you have some control over where the discussion to goes.

Let me point out that many of these activities were not designed with acting in mind. They come from all walks of life. I picked up one exercise at a business convention, another in a massage therapy course, a few games in teacher training courses, and I even picked up some of these games on the school playground when I was a kid. The point I am trying to make is that actors' resources are all around them, and so I collected these ideas from every resource I could find.

Purpose:

To increase body awareness

This activity is another example of learning how our body works. We have mentioned that actors' bodies are their instruments; the more we understand how it works the better we are able to play it.

What I like about this activity is that the results are so evident. The students see the results visually by watching or experience them kinesthetically by feeling them for themselves. The results are very abrupt: If the arm goes down, the evidence is right there. You are giving your students something tangible, something they can prove or disprove. (Of course, they could still argue that the results are not conclusive and could come from a number of variables, such as inconsistent pushing.) There are times when I will sit with a group and read from an acting book, but I also like them to experience what we are discussing. This is one of the great things about acting; we spend a lot of our time "doing," rather than just talking about what we could be doing.

87. I Like You Because/I Love You Because

I was introduced to this activity on the first day of a massage therapy course I was taking. I have given it two titles so that you can use either one depending on the maturity of your students.

Split your students in half and have them stand in two rows. Designate one row as *As* and the other as *Bs*. Have the students turn so that they are all facing someone from the other row. Now, tell them that in a moment the *As* are going to spend one minute telling the *Bs* what they like about them. However, they have to start each sentence with, "I like you because ... " and then they can add anything they like. Some examples are, " ... you have a nice smile," " ... your eyes are green," " ... you seem friendly." Tell them they have to talk for the whole minute without long pauses and that the aim is to keep the comments as sincere and honest as possible. After a minute have all the *As* move down the row one space and do exactly the same thing with the next person. When students reach the end of the line, they just go back to the beginning. I would have the *As* speak with three or four people and then switch and let the *Bs* do the talking. A lot of the students may find this activity particularly difficult depending on their age, so bear with them. The hardest thing will be for them to be sincere, so continue to stress this point.

Variables:

I also said this game was called, "I love you because ... " When I originally played it, this is what we had to say. It was on our first class of massage therapy training and the teacher used it to break down barriers. He told us that after this experience we wouldn't be embarrassed by anything else in the class. It was a real jolt to the system and it was very effective. You will want to use this phrase with your more mature students. It is not necessarily age or knowledge of acting that counts; you decide which version is best.

You can also vary when you use this activity. You might want to use it on the first day of class as an icebreaker, or you may feel it is better to use later on as a team-building activity.

You might want to change the number of students participants have to interact with. This is entirely up to you. I would have them do it at least three times each, so that they get a good sense of the activity, but you may decide it is going really well and do it six or seven times.

You can change the amount of time they talk to one another from one minute to three minutes per person. None of the rules I give you are set in stone; look at the needs of your students and see what works.

179

Discussion:

"How did it feel saying these things to another classmate for a minute?"
"Were there any surprises?"
"Did you break down any barriers?"
"Did it change the classroom environment?"
"Is it important for actors to break down physical and emotional barriers? Why?"

Purpose:

To break down barriers

If you use this the very first week of class you will find that you have changed the dynamics of the class. Some students may not like the activity, but by the time it is finished, more than likely you will have brought them closer together. One reason is because the students are saying personal things to someone they may hardly know. Another reason they will feel closer as a group is because you have only asked them to say positive things. Feeling closer and more relaxed as an ensemble may lead to students taking greater risks in activity work.

We always need to look for ways to help the students become more relaxed and more comfortable with themselves. This activity is aimed at helping students break down any barriers that are self-created. Jerzy Grotowski explains the importance of moving away from constraints in the body: "If the actor is conscious of his body, he cannot penetrate and reveal himself. The body must be freed from all resistance. It must virtually cease to exist."[3] You may choose never to use this activity, but if you do, you are guaranteed some interesting results.

Remember how we talked about a safe environment? You might feel this activity will put too much pressure on some students and cause excessive amounts of embarrassment. You can usually get around that by the fact that everyone is doing the activity at the same time and everyone participates. I have never done this with two volunteers by themselves. I prefer it when no one knows exactly what to expect.

88. Surprising Surface

In this activity the students are going to walk barefoot around the room as if they are on different surfaces. You can do this with the whole

---

[3] Jerzy Grotowski, *Towards a Poor Theatre* (London: Methuen, 1991), 36.

class at once or you may want half to participate while the other half watches. Ask the students to start off by just walking around the room. Now ask them to walk around as if they are walking on sand in the desert. Talk them through the rest of the exercise: "How does this feel to walk on? How do you have to adjust your body? Is their some give in the knee joints? Ankles? You are now walking on extremely hot sand and your feet are burning, but there is no shade. (As you change to different surfaces keep the story and the movement flowing.) You are now walking on cool grass; the grass is lush and soft, and as you walk across it, it cushions your feet. The grass blades get in between your toes and it tickles slightly. As you continue walking, you find yourself in really gooey mud up to your ankles. Your legs become slow and heavy, and as you try to keep moving forward you find the task slow and difficult. The mud has now become knee high; you keep wading through as best you can. As you carry on, you find yourself on the moon. You are now incredibly light. Each step you take seems to be pulling you upward; you are finding it difficult keeping your feet on the ground. You cannot move as fast as you would like and you feel as if you are floating in midair or flying. You feel yourself coming back down and you now find yourself back on earth, walking on egg crates. You have to walk very delicately so as not to break the eggs; you have to pull your body upward so as to make yourself as light as possible. All right, nice work, class!"

Variables:

You can use as many different surfaces as you like. Come up with some more of your own, such as snow, ice, gravel, and a shallow riverbed.

You can talk them through the activity as I just did, or you can simply tell them the surface they are walking on and change it sporadically.

Discussion:

"Who broke the eggs?"

"In your mind's eye, did you see yourself walking across the egg crates or were you just pretending?"

"How did your body feel when you were walking on the hot sand?"

"Talk to me about your imagination in relation to this exercise."

"How did you transition from one surface to the next?"

"Which was your favorite surface area?"

Purpose:

To utilize life experiences

I like this exercise because there are some parts in which the actors can really utilize their own experiences. Most of them will have played in soft grass at some stage in their lives, walked on a hot beach, or tromped through the mud. They could utilize these experiences for certain aspects of this exercise. It's unlikely that any of them have been on the moon, but most of them have probably been on a trampoline and would have some idea of the feeling of weightlessness. Sure, we want to stretch the imagination, but we don't just have to work in areas that have no relevance to our immediate life, such as, "Suddenly you come across a dinosaur." Utilizing life experiences can help the subject matter become more meaningful to the audience. Andre Van Gyseghem talks about the influence of the theatre in Russia: "Under the new system the role of the theatre was to assume tremendous importance; its influence was to spread to the darkest corners of the land."[4] By understanding our own experiences we can better influence others.

To improve spatial awareness

I have mentioned the benefits of this skill on a number of occasions. I like to do this exercise with twenty or thirty actors all at once because they really have to become aware of their environment. It is just another obstacle to overcome, another technical aspect that must be dealt with. I like to throw things at actors so that they have to deal with many different issues all at once.

---

[4] Andre Van Gyseghem, *Theatre in Soviet Russia* (London: Faber and Faber, 1943), 11.

Chapter 15
Spatial Awareness

89. Arm Link

Learning how to explain a game with clarity is just as important as playing the game. If the students cannot see you or do not clearly understand what is required, the game will not be played to its full potential and it may become disjointed as the students continue to stop you to ask questions. Have everyone sit down while you explain this game.

"In a moment, everyone will stand and link arms with a partner somewhere in this room. Please keep a space between you and other pairs. Now, there is going to be a chaser and a runner. Leah, can you help with an example? Let's say Leah is the runner and her job is to not get caught by me. I am going to try to tag Leah. In order to accomplish her objective she has to run away and link arms with someone in another pair. No pair is ever allowed to become a trio, so once she links arms with someone, that person's original partner becomes the runner. The task repeats itself, and the only way to safety for the runner is to link arms with another pair, remembering that whoever is left dangling on the end of the three must now run. If the chaser tags the runner before he or she can get to safety the roles are switched and the runner now becomes the chaser."

Sound complicated? When played at a fast pace it can become very confusing, so you have to be paying close attention to keep the exercise moving. You should do all that explaining while the students are in their seats. Before they get up, find out if there are any questions (there will be!). Do not allow too much time for questions; the students will discover a lot of the answers as they play. Once the students are in position, explain the game again briefly. Some games need more clarification than others.

Variables:

If you were really crazy you could try having two runners and two chasers (good luck!).

Discussion:

"What did you think of that game? Did you enjoy it?"
"What skills did you need to utilize to play this game?"
Possible answers here are focus, concentration, teamwork, speed, agility, and common sense. You may believe that some of the terminology applied can only be used with young adults and older. This is not the case; I have used all of these phrases and terminology on

students starting at about ten years of age. If there is something they do not understand, just rephrase it another way. You might even want to raise the issue of the complexity of playing this game. It can certainly become very confusing at times. How might that apply to a play? How about in a farce where everyone is constantly running on and off the stage? The actors will certainly need to know their blocking inside and out. You should constantly aim to not only discuss the specifics of each game, but to show its linkage to acting as a whole whenever possible.

Purpose:

To stress the importance of agility

It is not enough to just be a fast runner in this activity. If a student wants to avoid getting caught he is also going to have to be able to move quickly in different directions. Some words for this are agility, suppleness, or nimbleness. When actors are developing a character they will want to use their agility. The characterization of an eighty-year-old woman with scoliosis, for example, will take subtle yet precise movement.

To improve concentration

Concentration is certainly of the utmost importance, as is focus. It goes without saying that this game is a load of fun and can be used in between a more cerebral activity. Be clever about how you set up what you want to cover that day. Look at your material and break it up accordingly. If you have a one-and-a-half-hour voice class, be careful of spending all that time working on diction. Give your students a little fun in between to break up the hard work they are doing. If you want to keep them on task, find a game where use of voice is paramount. That way, even the workaholics among them will still feel they are on task. You must stimulate their brains in a variety of ways.

90. Arm Tangle

Talk about this activity before you ask any of the students to move:
"This activity is called 'Arm Tangle.' Let me talk about it for a few moments and then you will split into groups of about eight to ten people. For this activity you will stand with your group in a tight circle so that you are shoulder to shoulder. Next, everyone will put one hand into the center of the circle and grab someone else's hand; try not to make it the person standing next to you. Then you will put your other

hand in and grab another hand. At that point, you will be holding two hands, which will more than likely be from two different people. The idea of this game is to untangle yourselves as a group without anyone letting go of a hand. Some people will have to go under, while others may have to go through the middle. At the end, your whole team should be back to your original circle, facing either completely inward or completely outward. There are no prizes for finishing first; this is not a race. We have to put safety first, and it is the discovery that will be interesting. If Fred needs to crouch down, he has to remember he is holding Sarah and Emily's hands, and Emily is already overstretched. You have to talk to your teammates and see what will and won't work. Nobody should make any sudden movements; we don't want to have any broken arms. Is everybody ready? Okay, then let's begin!"

Variables:

You can change the number of players on each team. You may recall that I said eight to ten on each team. This size of group is large enough so that the students can get tangled, but not too large so that the activity becomes ineffective. I have tried this activity with twenty students and found that they couldn't keep hold of hands and everyone was getting overstretched. I also did not feel it was safe. When an exercise seems futile, the students will soon lose their interest. If the students become really good, you may want to go up to twelve or fourteen in a group.

Discussion:

"What did you have to do to be successful in this activity?"

"Was there any time when you felt like giving up? If you gave up, why did you do so?"

"What happened when someone made a sudden movement?"

"When you repeated the exercise, what could you apply from what you had learned the first time?"

Purpose:

To make adaptations

As the students try to solve the problem they must be ready to adapt at any given moment. If someone moves to the left, perhaps he will have to climb over someone else who is kneeling down. It is the constant willingness to adapt that will make this activity a success. Directors often ask actors to adapt their thinking. If the director has one vision and the actor has another, more than likely the actor will need to

185

bend to help create what the director is looking for. As Stanislavski puts it, "All types of communication ... require adjustments peculiar to each. If people in ordinary ... life need and make use of a large variety of adaptations, actors need a correspondingly greater number because we must be constantly in contact with one another."[1] Actors must continuously be able to adapt to any given situation.

To develop leadership

You will usually find that someone takes control and instructs the others on what they should do in this activity. This can be very successful, or sometimes it can cause conflict. I would not compare the leader with a director; he or she is more like a stage manager, who takes control of many of the decisions and gets the actors organized.

To improve spatial awareness

In this exercise, the actors become aware of the space around them. They start to sense where the other people are. If not, they will step on feet, bump into people, and sometimes fall over. Onstage, actors have to be aware of their space, because this is often what creates the illusion of the setting. They may have ten feet of stage space that is supposed to signify a three-hundred-mile-long forest. They have to understand how to utilize the space around them.

91. Sock 'Em

Have your audience sit in the center of the room facing the stage. You will need five actors to start this activity. Bring them up onto the stage and give each one a sock. The socks need to be fairly long, like the ones soccer or volleyball players wear. Now tell the actors to take the sock and tuck it into the back of their pants. If any students are wearing a T-shirt, they need to tuck it in so that the sock is clearly visible. Explain that the actors will all be given the same role to play, which they must carry out convincingly.

The actors have two objectives; one is to convince the audience in their role. For instance, if they are magicians they have to act out magic tricks convincingly. The other objective is to try to get the socks of their

---

[1] Constantin Stanislavski, *An Actor's Handbook* (New York: Theatre Art Books, 1994), 17.

opponents. They cannot just grab the socks, but must make it seem totally natural. So perhaps they bend over to tie their shoe and remove a sock on the way down. The audience will judge whether they feel the actor was grabbing or whether he was believable. Every few minutes you should stop and have the least convincing player voted off by the audience. Each time you stop, give the performers a new character: world-class chefs, zookeepers, or aerobic instructors, for example. These are just a few possibilities of what you can use.

Perhaps the most important element in this activity is that at all times the actors must be performing for the audience. They must also consistently be trying to get the sock from their opponents, but this must be done in a subtle or tactful way. The winner will be the last person in, who must also still have his sock. Try this with the first five students and then switch and try another group.

I like to use the following step in the same session as a progression. For this part, you will need two players. Have them come up onto the stage and then position their socks as before. Tell them that their aim is still to take the other person's sock, but this time they will have to do it while acting in a small scene. Perhaps they are a brother and sister who meet at the airport. They have not seen each other since they were babies, which was ten years ago. This is obviously a very emotional time for them and they will probably want to hug each other. The idea is to make it as difficult as possible for them to achieve the objective of sincerity while protecting their socks. That is why I suggested they would probably want to hug. By the way, they cannot protect their sock by holding it, but they could, for example, move or turn around, provided the action is justified. I have seen these mini scenes go on for six or seven minutes and have the whole audience in stitches. The key here is for the actors to commit 100 percent to both objectives. Come up with your own scene that leads the actors into close proximity. For this step, they do not have to be performing out to the audience as they did in the first part.

Variables:

In the first part of the activity in which the students are acting out a character of some sort, you can start with as many as ten to twelve players. The key is to make sure you have a fair-size audience at all times. So don't have one person watching with twelve onstage. In the first exercise it is the audience that forces the actors to keep them entertained.

Discussion:

"What part did the audience play in the first exercise?"

"How do you think the audience influenced the actors?"

(These two questions are fairly similar. I will sometimes ask leading questions, the second of which I will use only if the information I was looking for was not discussed in the first question. Remember, if you extract the information from the students, it is more likely to stick than if you just tell them what you want.)

"In the second part of our activity, what made the scenes believable?"

"Was there a way of taking the sock and making the action appear justified?"

"If you were onstage, tell us about some of the pressures you faced."

Purpose:

To improve spatial awareness

The actors have to carry out their objectives of defining their characters and acting out their scenes, but at the same time they do not want to lose their socks. This means they do not want to get too close to another person, or if they have to get close they want to have an idea of the boundary they need to protect their sock.

To highlight audience participation

In the first half of this exercise we give the audience the power to decide who stays and who has to leave. This means that the actors feel a lot of pressure to perform for the audience. Actors often feel this pressure in the theatre as a whole. They may notice halfway through a show that the audience isn't laughing and become distracted from their objectives. Trying to gauge the audience reaction through vocal response can be very misleading. Edwin Wilson and Alvin Goldfarb explain that the audience response is not always what it seems: "At a comedy, on some nights the audience laughs at everything. On other nights, audience members may enjoy the show just as much, but they barely chuckle and seem never to indulge in a hearty laugh."[2] We cannot help but be influenced by our audience to some degree, but I like the fact that this exercise takes it to an extreme. It allows the actors to realize just how powerful and controlling their audience can be if they let it affect them.

[2] Edwin Wilson and Alvin Goldfarb, *Theatre the Lively Art* (New York: McGraw-Hill, 1991), 44.

Chapter 16
Motor Skills

92. Mirroring

Have everyone in the class find a partner and designate one person as *A* and one person as *B*. Once all the students are paired up, tell the pairs to spread to different parts of the room so they have some space. In a moment, *A*s will start to move very slowly and *B*s will try to mirror their movements. Explain the exercise as follows:

"*A*s, you can move your body however you want; you can lift your legs and your arms, but you must stay on the same spot. It is imperative that your movements are slow and flowing so that your partner can really follow them. The idea is not to trick your partner, but to help them. There is no talking during this exercise."

Once everyone is ready, dim the lights to low if you can and turn on some music. Choose your music carefully because it will really set the tone. I like to use something with a rhythmic, trancelike quality. While the students are moving I like to walk around and observe. You will find that people often giggle when they start this exercise. Do not reprimand them but see the funny side with them and then help to get them back on track. If you see students making sudden movements, compliment them for working so well and then recommend that they try moving at a slower pace to help their partner even more. Once you feel it has been enough time (around two to five minutes), switch so that *B*s are now leading.

You could stop here, but I recommend you continue with different mirroring exercises. You can have the students do the same exercise, only this time allow them to move slowly around the room. While one person is moving slowly his partner should follow him, mirroring his every move. This will make the game more challenging, as the partners are able to move off their spots.

Once they have completed that task you can have them continue so that both partners are leaders and during the exercise they will switch back and forth. This part of the exercise can be done either in a static position or with the actors moving off the spot. If they can keep their movements close together there will be many times when they do not even know who is leading. Everything we have done so far could have been done in one continuous flow without stopping the music.

Next have one group at a time come up onstage and mirror each other for the class. We usually watch each group for about a minute. Remember to have music playing during this section. Now ask everyone to sit in the center of the room facing in different directions. Choose one person to be the leader and ask the entire class to follow. They do not all need to look at the leader. As long as a few people can see the leader, the rest of the class just has to look to those students and copy them. As long as everyone can see someone else, this activity will work. Students do not have to make any eye contact for this activity to succeed. Change the leader every twenty seconds or so. I love this activity and it is an excellent visual spectacle. If you've made it this far, you have probably just spent a good forty-five minutes on mirroring activities! Great!

Variables:
Included in the game description.

Discussion:
"How did you like the mirroring activity? Which part did you enjoy the most?"

"When did it become difficult to follow the other person?"

"Why is this activity helpful to us as actors?"

"What was interesting about everyone mirroring at the same time? Did this involve any form of teamwork?"

"What happened when you momentarily lost your concentration?"

"How did it go when you were not watching the leader?"

Purpose:
To learn to cooperate with others
What an excellent exercise for cooperation and teamwork! Students have to work with their partners for this exercise to be a success. Cooperation is of vital importance to actors. If two actors are in a scene and one believes he is the star and tries to outshine the other actor then there is nothing authentic to watch. Actors must work together, act and react; you cannot react if you are too into yourself and have no idea what the other person just said. Working together in the mirroring exercise will get your students on the right track. Focus and concentration go without saying. Also, the actors are again becoming more aware of their bodies and how they work as we strive to enhance our motor skills (hand-eye coordination).

To de-focus
Actors often spend too much time looking directly at one another. This can be due to nerves, bad acting, or any number of reasons. This

activity encourages the students to be aware of everything around them. In order to mirror their partner they need to be looking in the vicinity of the other person, but they will discover that they do not need to make that much eye contact. Michael Shurtleff says, "Don't see eyes, see images."[1] In this activity the actors are asked to gain a larger focus.

93. Ventriloquist

To start, have the class sit facing the performance area. You will need two participants and one chair onstage. It is better if it is a narrow chair or one that has an open back. For this game the students onstage will present a topic. Examples would be how to drive a car or how to bake a cake. The students are going to show and tell us how to do this activity. However, to do this they are going to act as one person.

One of the students has to sit on the chair and be the spokesperson. The other person should go behind the chair and keep his head out of sight. He needs to stretch his arms through the chair from the back to be the arms for the person sitting in the chair. The person sitting in the chair should put his arms toward the back of the chair and keep them out of sight. Try to find a plastic chair that accommodates the players as much as possible. It is important for the person at the back to keep his head down; otherwise it becomes obvious that there are two people. It is much more amusing when it looks as if there is just one person.

Remind the student who is the arms to be sure to move them for expression. People move their hands all the time for expression. It is important for the arms not to become static. Of course, people use their hands to demonstrate, i.e., baking the cake or turning the steering wheel, but they should also be used to express moments of thought or frustration. I usually have the participants demonstrate something, because this seems to make the task more complex.

This game can lead to some wonderful results. You want to make sure that the speaker does not comment on his hands and say things like, "What are my arms doing now?" Believe me, this will happen unless you make a point to bring it up. Remind the students that we want to laugh with the performers and not at them. Try to have quite a few topics prepared in advanced. You want these to be some form of

[1] Michael Shurtleff, *Audition* (New York: Bantam Books, 1978), 161.

presentation; possible examples are performing magic tricks with the help of audience members or teaching someone how to drive a car, how to put on makeup, and how to build a house out of matchsticks.

Variables:

Have two chairs on the stage with two people sitting down and two people behind the chairs. Instead of demonstrating something they should just be having a conversation. An example could be a boyfriend and girlfriend at the movies. This game can be quite complex with four people in control of two characters.

Discussion:

"How important is it for the two people to work together in this exercise?"

"Why is it important for the face not to be seen behind the chair?"

"Why should the hands sometimes be moving even when they are not demonstrating something?"

"Talk about the importance of hand-eye coordination for this activity."

Purpose:

To develop motor skills

The students are working together to coordinate motor skills with information gathered through their senses. This is really a benefit for the people sitting in the chair. They have the advantage of being able to see the hands and can coordinate their dialog accordingly. The people behind the chair are going to have to utilize their sense of hearing in this activity. If they hear their partner telling the audience to put the cake in the oven, they will have to respond accordingly.

To develop teamwork

The two players must work together in many areas. Safety is an issue because if you are the arms you must be careful not to hurt your partner. Also, you have to be able to trust the arms in their actions. So, while they will certainly have fun, the students must keep a mature attitude.

To develop discipline

Many novice acting students see acting as a fun subject where they get to just play around. As they develop their skills they realize that a tremendous amount of discipline is needed to learn lines, develop characters, and understand motivations and actions. The sooner we can get them on this track of self-discipline the better off they will be in the long run. Russell Grandstaff explains, "To be a good actor you almost must have the stamina of a mountain climber, the endurance of a marathon runner, the patience of a turtle, the strength of a weight lifter, the courage of a lion trainer, the memory of a computer, the agility of a gymnast, the imagination of a child, and the confidence of the devil."[2] To achieve these outcomes requires discipline that will come mainly from self-motivation. The following passage from *Drama on Stage* highlights the extreme level of dedication and discipline of Moliére, the famous French playwright and actor of the seventeenth century: "During the performance he suffered a hemorrhage but played the piece out to the end. That night, in his house in the Rue Richelieu, he died."[3] I am certainly not suggesting that you die for your art, but it does highlight the level of discipline one can work toward.

94. Clap Out

Have everyone stand in a circle. One reason I prefer to have everyone stand is that it keeps the energy up and it helps your students to stay alert. You can try it both ways, sitting and standing, and see what works for you. Choose a person to start; that person should say the number one and the next person, number two. The third person has to clap, but not say three. The next person will say four, the next will say five, and the following person will clap. So every time you get to a multiple of three, that person has to clap instead of saying the number. If a person says the wrong number, claps at the wrong time, or says the number and claps, he is out. If he pauses too long and then claps, he is out. You decide when a pause is too long. As participants get out, just ask them to sit down where they are.

Next, add in multiples of five so that now every time they get to a multiple of three or five they have to clap. This makes it a lot more complicated. I start this exercise off fairly slowly, and then we speed up to a faster pace. It gets really intense. To start with, do not allow anyone

[2] Russell Grandstaff, *Acting and Directing* (Lincolnwood, Ill.: National Textbook Company Publishing Group, 1975), 1.
[3] Ralph Goodman, *Drama on Stage* (New York: Holt, Rinehart and Winston, 1961), 201.

to be out. I like to build everyone's confidence. So for the first few minutes just use it as a warm-up. You should consider doing this with all exercises in which there is a process of elimination.

Variables:

I would suggest that you change the numbers and use different multiples.

Also, when I was about five or six my mother taught me a game that is very similar, except when you get to multiples of five you say "buzz" instead of clapping your hands.

Discussion:

"What was the point of that exercise?"

"Were there any tricks that made it easier to know when to clap? Was there a sequence you could use?"

"How did adding an extra multiple affect the game?"

"Could you work as a team?"

"What are motor skills? How do they play a part in this activity?"

Purpose:

To develop motor skills

This exercise is interesting because not only do the students have to be constantly thinking so they know when to say the next number, they also have to be ready physically. They have to know when to speak and when to clap. They have to allow the mind and physical body to work simultaneously. If you think about motor skills, we might train a young child to catch a ball. The child sees it and must use his hands to catch it. So what has this got to do with acting? Good question! Well, when actors are in a scene they have many things to remember, but let's just take one example. In most performances actors will have some lines to learn. They go home, learn their lines, and tell you they know them perfectly. Then, they come in for rehearsal and look as if they have not even attempted to learn them. Did they lie to you? Probably not. The problem is they may have gone home and sat in a nice comfy chair and learned their lines. There was a thought process in learning the lines, but no physical connection. So when they have to stand up and add movement and purpose and objective, everything starts to fall apart. They wonder why they cannot remember anything. I am not saying you have to learn your lines in rehearsal. There are many different approaches to this memorization. I am saying that for actors it is useful to connect the mind and the body wherever possible. They are not separate entities; rather, they complement each other. This is why I like the game "Clap Out"; you have to connect both the mental and physical. As Anthony Robbins puts it, "Everything that we feel is the result of how we use our bodies."[4] As actors, we can take advantage of this if we are able to manipulate our bodies. This activity requires the body to be alert and energized; it is up to the student to discover how to create this feeling.

95. Popcorn

Have the whole class come and form a circle. Then explain the game as follows:

"Okay people, this game we are about to play is called 'Popcorn.' As you know, when popcorn is being made the kernels pop open, which makes them fly up in the air. I want you to imagine that you are pieces of popcorn and in a moment you are going to jump up in the air. The only thing is that when you are in the air you have to clap your hands one time. Now, that sounds easy enough, except you cannot clap your hands at the same time as anyone else. So while you are up in the air you have to time when to clap your hands. You can do it on the way up or on the way down. If you clap at the same time as someone else you are out. If you jump up and don't clap, you are out. If you stand for a long time and don't jump, you are out. You do not have to jump constantly, but you cannot just stand there and watch everyone else. Also, you cannot fake jump. If you start to jump you have to go through with it. If you get out, please sit down where you are. You will then be the judges. Those of you who are left in, if someone says you are out then you are out. It is really hard for you to see everyone, so we have to trust the judges. At the end of the game there are usually two winners. Now, I cannot always tell if you are out or not so I am going to trust you to use your integrity. If you know you are out, please take a seat. Remember, there is no leader, and you do not all have to jump together. Okay, let's begin."

Variables:

When the students jump up they could snap their fingers instead of clapping.

[4] Anthony Robbins, *Awaken the Giant Within* (London: Simon & Schuster, 1992), 161.

You could vary the clapping. Perhaps participants have to clap twice instead of only once.

Discussion:

"Was there a formula to being able to last longer in this activity?"
"What difference, if any, did it make if you could jump higher?"
"Did the same people last longer on a consistent basis or was it more random?"

Purpose:

To improve timing

As each participant jumps in the air he has to time when to clap so as not to coincide with anyone else. Although this is not a precise link, it parallels the timing that actors need to develop. In a comic play, it is not just the lines that are funny. It is the way the actors deliver them and the way they lift them off the page. Actors must develop a good sense of timing.

To build character

For once I do not mean in terms of a part in a script. In this exercise, I ask the students to admit when they are out and then I ask them to judge when others are out. I could take more control than this, but this way they have to consider their own honesty and the motivation for how they respond. Some will swear that they are not out and get very frustrated when they have to sit down. Others will just accept it with good humor. It is very interesting to watch. In either case, we want to push our students toward a sense of noble behavior. We want to guide our students toward having the utmost respect for themselves and for others. Actors will find there are many situations in which being of good character will serve them well. Sarah Duncan explains some of the important steps in the audition process: "Always be polite to anyone who checks your name off the list, or hands out scripts."[5] Students will find that developing a good nature puts them in good standing on- and offstage.

[5] Sarah Duncan, *How to Become a Working Actor* (London: Cheverell Press, 1990), 54.

Chapter 17
Nonverbal Communication

96. Tell the Truth

To start this activity, you are going to send five students outside the room. While they are outside they have to come up with a true story that happened to them at some stage in their lives. It could be something similar to, "When I was seven I fell out of a tree and had to go to the hospital and get some stitches." Or, "When I was seven I met the Queen." Whatever the story is, it has to be completely true. The more interesting the content of the story the more interesting the game will be. My students always seem to like the ones that involve some sort of injury.

Although all five of the students outside will be thinking of things that have happened to them, they will only end up using the story that they, as a group, think is the best. They should be careful that the story is not one that all of their friends inside already know. When they go back into the classroom they will line up at the front of the stage and you will ask each person one by one to tell the story. They will all recite the same chosen story, but for one person it will be a true story, and all the others have to pretend it happened to them. Everyone will repeat the opening sentence, "When I was two/seven/fifteen ... " and then tell the story in his own words, as if it happened to him personally, although this is only true of one person. Each person has the responsibility to persuade the audience that he is telling the truth.

Following the stories, go around the audience and allow each person to ask one question, such as, "John, where were you when you hit your head?" "Sarah, did you have to go to the hospital?" It is important for the audience to name the person to whom they are asking questions and to try to avoid repetitive questions. You may find that even though the contestants say how old they were in the opening statements, someone will still ask this question. Do not give them another question; it was their responsibility to be focused and attentive. You will also see someone come up with the question, "Are you telling the truth?" Well, if you are telling the truth this is easy to answer, if you are not then this is still easy to answer because you are going to lie and say, "Yes, I am telling the truth."

The contestants can make their answers as long and interesting as they like. In fact, when the participants give detailed answers they are usually more convincing. Remember, the idea is to fool the audience into believing you are telling the truth. Also note that when answering the questions the contestants may come up with totally different versions of the same story. This is great and will simply make it harder for the audience to decide who is telling the truth.

After you have been around the entire class, you should give the audience about a minute to make up their minds about who they think is correct. Then take a vote and see how many in the audience vote for each contestant. The person telling the truth wants to get the least number of votes and the goal of the liars is to get the most votes, so in effect you can have two winners in one game. You may want to come up with small prizes. I will warn you that the students love this activity, and once you have played it they will ask to play it again and again.

Variables:

I usually have five people go out of the room, but you can change this number.

Another way to play this game is to give the students an unusual object. Give one of them the true definition of the object, but do not tell the others what it is. Now when they go back into the room they all have to pretend they are the only one who really knows what the object is. You can also do the same thing with words. Find a really unusual word in the dictionary and give its true meaning to only one of the students. Proceed with this activity in the same way as before. (See "Wacky Word Wizard.")

Discussion:

"What did you notice about body language in this activity? Did any of the storytellers give it away through their nonverbal communication?"

"Which type of answers did you find the most believable?"

"Were some stories more interesting than others?"

"How important is it for the students to come up with identical answers?"

Purpose:

To improve nonverbal communication

This game is excellent for studying nonverbal communication. While the students are standing onstage they are fumbling, looking at the ceiling, swaying from side to side. They are giving so much away and they do not even know it. The audience will usually pick up on what they see, but not always know why. After you have played this game a couple of times you should point out to those playing that they need to sound confident and try to stand more grounded to make it harder for the audience to read into anything. You should then tell the audience to pay close attention to the storytellers' body language. Remember, it is better to let them play it their own way first. Do not tell them all this information right at the start. Part of their learning and developing will come from making some of these discoveries on their own. If actors are fidgeting onstage because they are nervous, this is what the audience will see. Being aware of nonverbal communication is, therefore, of great importance to actors.

To know your objectives

One of the things I love about this exercise is that in order to convince others that you are telling the truth you have to know your objectives. For instance, your objectives might be "to convince classmates that I am telling the truth and to prove that I am the one who fell off the wall." Students must have their objectives clearly realized in their minds so that they are congruent. This means that if they look confident then they also have to sound confident. When preparing for a role, Sarah might say, "The character I am playing, Jane, hates Erica." As she delves further she may say, "Jane wants to be more popular than Erica; her objective is to become prom queen and Erica is her biggest rival." Now we understand why Jane dislikes Erica and what her objective, or motivation, is. So our fun game, which the students love, has also helped them think about their objectives.

97. Freeze Frame

This game can be explained as follows:

"Okay people, please get yourselves into groups of five, and then find a space and sit down with your groups. In a moment, you will choose one person in the group to be the director. The director will then direct the rest of the group in a small scene. Here is the interesting part. The scene is actually a still picture, or tableaux. It could be a poster, for example. What I would like you to do is come up with two totally different advertising ideas and present them through your still pictures. Perhaps your advertisement is for a food or drink product, or perhaps it is for a vacation to London. Remember that there should be one person in each group who is going to decide ultimately how he or she wants the pictures to look.

"I would also like you to make your pictures aesthetically pleasing. The way you arrange the shapes and angles of your picture should appear pleasant to the viewer. I might say it is not aesthetically pleasing to see everyone stand in a straight line; however, if one person were standing, one kneeling, and one crouching, that could be aesthetically pleasing. Please make your two advertisements contrasting, and remember they have to be still and without dialog. Off you go!"

Give them about seven to ten minutes for this activity and then have them come back into one big group. Give each group a number so they know when they are performing. When a group is about to perform, have the director go up onstage to make sure the actors are set exactly how he or she wants them.

Variables:

You could have two directors per group, one per picture.

Also, although I told the groups to come up with advertisements, you can change this to any theme you like. Perhaps you ask them to make their pictures related to outer space, or maybe family photographs. There is no hard and fast rule for what you can do here.

Discussion:

"Were there any challenges in trying to get your information across through a still picture?"

"Directors, tell us what the important aspects of your job were for this task?"

"Link this exercise to nonverbal communication for me."

"How important was detail for this exercise? If I was supposed to have my hand on my hip, did it matter if I then put it by my side instead?"

Purpose:

To improve nonverbal communication

This exercise is great for forcing the actors to get their information across through their body and facial expressions. I find this exercise very effective; it also goes one step further than mime in that the participants cannot move. A danger for actors can be that they rely too much on their voice and the words on the page. We want to get away from letting the words tell the complete story, because after all, nonverbal counts for about 80 percent of all communication.

To give the actors the opportunity to direct
In this activity the director makes the final decision, and the director is not you. This is a great learning experience for the students. The director may find it is not just trying to get the task done that can be the challenge, but also knowing how to work with the cast. Perhaps one person disagrees with the director's idea, or maybe someone else is not listening or doing what he is supposed to.

It is also interesting for the cast, who has to follow the ideas of one of their peers. I always stress to the actors that the final decision will lie with their director. This is important because some of the more vocal actors will find this to be an enormous challenge. They will also find it difficult to accept that their ideas are not always used. This helps the actors work more toward the ensemble, which is so important.

The role of the director has changed immensely over the last hundred years. While directors are now considered a key part of the process, they have not always been given the respect they deserve. Mary Henderson notes that "before 1900 few directors in the American theatre got program credit for what they did."[1] This activity will encourage the students to respect the director's decisions as final.

98. Commercial Capers

I like to do this activity alongside "Freeze Frame" because it connects nicely. After the students have done their advertisements in a still frame I have them do the activity again, only this time I ask them to act out the advertisements as a TV commercial. Have each group take their still pictures and turn them into moving ones. Each commercial should be between about thirty seconds and one minute in length. Now, I will usually ask the groups to change directors for this activity. The aim of each commercial should be to persuade us to invest in the group's product. Give the students about the same amount of prep time as before (seven to ten minutes), and then have them come back and perform the scenes one group at a time. It works really nicely if you can do "Freeze Frame" and "Commercial Capers" in the same lesson.

Variables:

I stuck with the topic of commercials because that was what they

[1] Mary C. Henderson, *Theatre in America* (New York: Harry N. Abrams, 1986), 100.

had done in "Freeze Frame." There are no limitations to the topic you use. In fact, there does not have to be a connection between the still pictures and the ones they do in the scene work. I just find it has more coherence that way.

Discussion:

Remember that discussions can happen before, during, and after an exercise.

"Which did you think was more effective, the still pictures or the commercial capers?"

"Directors, what challenges did you face in this activity?"

"Was the ensemble unit more important in this activity or 'Freeze Frame'? Could you expand on your answer?"

"How does movement and voice affect our nonverbal communication?"

"What did you do to make your commercials aesthetically pleasing?"

Purpose:

To compare and contrast verbal and nonverbal communication

I find this activity very effective when it immediately follows "Freeze Frame." The students take the same idea and then add movement and sound. It really highlights for the students the difference between verbal and nonverbal communication. It also seems to reinforce that they can get their message across without words or gestures. We are working to enhance the belief that the actors need to rely on more than just the written word. In "Freeze Frame," the picture must be very specific and concentrated. In "Commercial Capers," the actors have different challenges; however, there is more room for dilution as the actors can use all areas of their communication skills. It is not easy, by any means, but linking the two exercises highlights for the actors that they should not rely on one discipline over the other.

To win the audience to your side

In this activity, to sell the product the actors will have to convince the audience that they need it more than anything else. To do this, the actors have to gain the audience's trust. Actors constantly have to persuade their audiences to buy into their "product." Let us say actors walk onto a stage, which for this scene is supposed to be forest. The stage gives the impression of a forest with a few fake trees and a backdrop, but to the audience it is obviously not a real forest. Through their actions and reactions to their environment, their mastery of spatial awareness, their absolute conviction that they are in a forest, and their congruency in their body language, the actors pull the audience into their world. The audience may say: "I know that this is not a real forest, but I want to believe you are in a real forest." And this is where the magic begins. David Wood and Janet Grant talk about the involvement of children as audience members. "One minute they listened attentively, the next they participated with ear splitting excitement."[2] This does not mean your students should bend to every whim of the audience, but they should not forget they are there, either.

99. Social Status

Have two students come up to your playing area while the rest of the group sits as audience members on the floor. Choose a short scene from a play and have the actors perform the scene for the class. Perhaps they could do a short scene from *Romeo and Juliet,* or you can take a scene from a film script that you like. Limit this scene to about two to three minutes in length.

After they have performed the scene once through, have the actors do it again. This time, change their physical levels randomly throughout the scene. Let's say that at the start of the scene they are both standing up facing each other. Shortly into the scene, have one of them kneel, and then a bit later perhaps one of them could sit on the floor or stand on a chair. Keep changing the levels during the scene so that at some point they have both been standing over the other one. During these transitions ask the audience who seems to be in control of the scene.

To exaggerate these movements even further you can add another step to this exercise. When the actor is sitting on the floor, you might also tell him that he cannot look at the other actor. Tell him that whatever happens he cannot make eye contact. At the same time, you could tell the other actor to try to make eye contact and to continually stare at the other actor. Again, you can pause the scene and get some audience feedback.

These do not have to be scenes that the actors have learned; you can just hand them a script and they can take the scene out of context if you wish. I like to limit these scenes to two or three minutes because it is long enough for you to play around and get an idea of what is going on. It also enables you to work with a number of different actors.

[2] David Wood and Janet Grant, *Theatre for Children* (London: Faber and Faber, 1997), 3.

Variables:

I said you could work with fresh scenes; however, you might want to work on different scenes from a play your actors are already rehearsing. This could be effective, as it would add variety and unpredictability to your rehearsals.

Discussion:

"How does this activity relate to nonverbal communication?"

"In what way did the actors' different levels change your perception of their social status?"

"Discuss the word *control* in relation to this exercise. Was there a time when the actor who was at a lower level was more in control? Perhaps you told the actor who was standing on a chair that he could not look at the other actor, and the actor who was sitting on the floor was told to attempt to make eye contact. How would this affect the scene? Could it lead to a reversal in status?"

Do not tell your actors that they are wrong if they do not come up with results that you expect. For instance, they may tell you that the character who was sitting on the ground seemed to dominate the scene. This is great, but do not just leave it there; have them explain their reasoning.

Purpose:

To highlight nonverbal communication

I say "to highlight" because in this activity we are really exaggerating nonverbal communication. When we ask the actors to stand on a chair or to lie on the floor we are really taking the scene out of context. However, this is okay because the main aim is for the audience and the actors onstage to notice how these adjustments can totally change the meaning of the words. This can also help the students understand what it means when we say that it is the actor who brings meaning to the words. The words themselves can be portrayed in myriad ways.

To increase knowledge of movement and positioning on the stage (blocking)

You want to encourage your actors to think for themselves and to be in a position to make their own choices. That way, if you have your students do scene work and you ask them to direct themselves, they will be able to apply the knowledge they gathered from this exercise. If they had a car thief sitting in a chair being interrogated by a police officer who is standing up, they would know that the balance of power would probably be swayed toward the police officer. If they wanted to show the car thief as being in control at a certain moment, they might adjust the blocking accordingly. They could have the car thief stand and the policeman sit. Of course, I am oversimplifying and there are many other things to consider besides just blocking. However, the more tools you can make available to your students the better. The more knowledge they have the more they will be able to explore.

100. Action Charades

You will need a set of note cards for this activity. On each note card write a list of five verbs. Some examples are jumping, running, yawning, and walking. Split your students into two groups and pick someone to go first. Give this student a note card and instruct him to act out the verbs listed on it. Let's say the first person to go is from Team One. He will act out his list of verbs for his teammates, who have to guess each of the verbs. The group has to guess all five, but the actor can perform them in any order he chooses. (Do not tell the students this unless they ask.)

The goal of this exercise is to get the fastest time possible. Limit the time to one or two minutes. Be prepared with a good number of cards already made for this activity. After you have played an agreed number of rounds, let's say fifteen, add up the times to see which team has won. The verbs do not have to be too complex; this activity should be fast and furious.

Variables:

I use five verbs, but you could change this number to whatever works for you.

Discussion:

"In what way do you have to work as an ensemble for this activity?"
"At what point should a person just give up?"
"Discuss mime in relation to this activity."
"What tactics could you use to help you in this activity?"

Purpose:

To encourage the students to think for themselves

In this activity the students are given a list of verbs to mime. They are not told that they have to do them in the order that is given;

205

however, they are not told that they can change the order either. It is up to them to make this discovery on their own. This could also be described as coming up with their own tactics. The students may leave the difficult words and start with the easier ones. In a play, a director may find she is having problems blocking a scene. She might decide to spend the rest of the rehearsal working with the cast to solve the challenge. Alternately, she might leave that scene and work on a different one. She might choose to come back to the problematic scene at a later date. In this way, she is using a set of tactics to make her rehearsal time more effective.

To encourage the students to persist in their task

The students will have five verbs on their cards, but if they find their team cannot guess an answer they may want to give up. Encourage them to continue until their time is up. Even when it seems hopeless they may suddenly think of something at the last moment that helps their team discover the correct answer. If the students persist, they are showing that they are a team player. Those few seconds may be the vital difference between a win and a loss for their team. They may also be surprised at what they can come up with if they persist. They will start to realize that if something isn't working they need to try something else. If an actor starts working on a play in which he has to incorporate a dialect he might find that, at first, he sounds awful. He could become embarrassed and decide to drop the dialect; or, if he persists through hard work and dedication, he might discover that he is actually pretty good. He has now added some useful skills to his toolbox: persistence and a polished dialect. You want to encourage your actors not to be afraid of hard work. You also want to encourage them to work smart. If something is not doing the trick, try something else.

101. Return of the Pink Panther

For this exercise you will probably need four or five CD players and a good selection of CDs. Have the students split up into group of about five; each group will need its own stereo. Explain to them that each group is going to select a song and act it out in the form of a mime. They must act out a complete story from start to finish based on the song of their choice. Their performance should not be based solely on the words they hear, but should also consider the tempo and different sound qualities of the song. In fact, some groups might choose a song that has no words whatsoever. The reason I called this "The Return of the Pink Panther" is because the first time I played this activity we used the theme song from *The Pink Panther.*

You may want to tell the students to bring in their music a day in advance. This way they can use a song of their choice. This exercise might also require a little more time than some of the others. You may want to give the students one session to prepare, and watch their performances on another day. I find that about forty-five minutes preparation time is more than enough; it also creates a sense of urgency. What you don't want is for a group to spend thirty minutes choosing a song.

After you have watched the presentations you might want to ask each group, one at a time, to go sit in the stage area and allow the rest of the class to make comments about that group's performance. I like to break this down into two sections. First, I ask the class to volunteer constructive comments about what did not quite work or was not fully explained. To say, "I didn't like it," doesn't help the actors improve. So I ask the students to be both tactful and specific. For instance, they might offer a suggestion such as, "You may want to face out more because I really wanted to see the expressions on your faces."

Next, I ask the students to say what they enjoyed about the performance. For instance, "It was really exciting when the fight scene occurred." I choose to start with constructive comments and then finish with things students liked about the performance; this approach allows the actors to leave on a positive note. I find finishing with constructive comments can be contradictory; it's like saying, "Yes, it was really good, but ... " I find that sometimes ending with constructive comments nullifies all the positive comments that have just been made.

Remember, some of these activities will take longer than others, so plan accordingly. I like to take some of these activities and turn them into a unit, but that would be another book! You should start looking for ways to link these activities to other material; try not to see them as isolated resources, but as a melting pot of ideas that you can link to a bigger picture. If you use an activity that is geared toward characterization, then try to link it to a section you are teaching on building a character.

Variables:

You could ask each group to use a song from a different period and see how this changes the results. For instance, one group might choose a song from the 1960s while another group might work with a song from the 1930s.

Discussion:

"Did the tempo or rhythm of the song affect your choice of movements? Could you expand on your reasoning?"

"Did you feel that you had to interpret your song literally?"

"Did the words or the music itself have a bigger influence on the way you acted out the song?" "Talk about the benefits of mime as you see them in relation to the actor."

Purpose:

To create flexible actors

This activity forces the actors to take a slightly different approach to their break down of the material. They do not have a script to which they can look for clues on their character; they must break down the song. They are still aiming to interpret the material in a clear and honest manner. By taking on this challenge, the actors are giving themselves the opportunity to become more flexible. There is a lot of experimentation that goes on in acting, so it is useful for the students to be open to this. Students also have to be flexible in terms of their expectations. John Gielgud explains, "Don't anticipate a bed of roses, for on the stage as in every other profession there are slings and arrows to contend with."[3] Some students may believe a career in acting will be glamorous. They will need to be flexible thinkers if they really see acting as a future career.

To encourage independent thinking

I have mentioned this in other activities and I don't mind mentioning it again. The students will self-direct in this activity and create the results from their collaborative effort. You should facilitate if needed, although you should steer away from directing any group. Allow them to make their own choices. A novice actor will often ask the director, "What's my motivation?" I like to see actors who can think for themselves and create their own reasoning. We do not want to create machines, but independent thinkers who are malleable.

102. Yes, Let's

In this activity, have everyone stand in a circle. Choose one person to start off; he will mime an action, for example, digging a hole. Another

[3] John Gielgud, *An Actor and His Time* (New York: Applause Books, 1997), 25.

person who recognizes the action will then say, "Yes, let's dig holes"; then the whole class will mime digging the hole together. The person who recognized the action should then start a new mime and the game continues with the rest of the class guessing. The class can only start a new mime once they have discovered and acted out the previous mime. Whenever someone is trying to guess the mime he has to start with, "Yes, let's ... "

Variables:

A more simplified version would be to have someone start an activity and say the sentence, "Yes, let's brush our hair." Instead of the class guessing it could just go from one person to the next. The only thing the class would have to do is copy each new mime.

Discussion:

"Define the word *mime.*"

"Were some mimes easier to guess than others? Why?"

"How did it affect the group mime when we used the 'Yes, let's ... ' affirmation every time? Do you think it made any difference to the outcome?"

"When the whole class acted out a mime together, what did you notice?"

You want to check how well the students are observing each other. What are they noticing about what is going on in their environment? When I am watching a movie on television I love to look at the people in the background, the extras without speaking parts. What are they doing? Are they believable?

Purpose:

To encourage the use of mime

This exercise works primarily with mime skills. It is an excellent source of nonverbal communication. Through mime, actors can show that an expression or reaction can be worth a thousand words. This activity encourages the use of mime partly through its teamwork aspect. Although one person demonstrates the action, everyone else quickly follows suit. This can help to build the confidence of those who feel shy about performing alone.

To utilize the benefits of positive affirmations

This game uses the phrase, "Yes, let's ... " after each mime. It is a positive affirmation that seems to make the group feel more at ease when asked to repeat the mime. So the terminology seems to play a large part in students' willingness to repeat.

This activity might be an eye-opener for some directors. Shouting at your actors might get results, but at what cost? If a director says something like, "Good! Now I would like you to try something different," he might get better results than if he said, "No, no, no, that was awful!" You can scare your actors or you can encourage them to explore. Positive affirmations will encourage them to participate and voice their ideas.

103. What Are You Doing?

Have everyone stand in a circle, and choose a person to start. Explain the game in a way similar to this:

"Okay, Alyssa, I want you to mime an action, for instance, why don't you act out brushing your hair. Okay, very good. Now turn to the person to your left, Molly, and continue miming brushing your hair. Molly, you now have to ask Alyssa, 'What are you doing?' Alyssa, you have to answer with something other than what you are actually doing, so you might say, 'Jumping up and down.' Now Molly, you have to jump up and down and then turn to the person to your left. That person will then ask, 'What are you doing?' And again you will come up with something different, perhaps, 'Eating ice cream,' and so on." Allow this activity to continue until you have been around the circle once or twice.

Variables:

I have never used any for this game.

Discussion:

"What did you find most difficult about this game?"

"How confusing was it to see one thing but have to do another?"

"Can you give me an example of where an actor might say something but actually mean something else?"

Purpose:

To practice nonverbal communication

This exercise is great for teaching nonverbal communication. Actors often feel that they are only acting when they are speaking, which simply is not the case. Mime is a prime example of telling a story without the use of words. Actors might believe they have never used mime during a performance and that it is a skill they do not need to develop. However, if they are playing the jury member in a court scene they may not have lines, but they will still need to react to what is being said. This reaction, if nonverbal, can be classed as mime. As actors, we are probably using mime skills a lot more than we realize. Samuel Avital, an expert in mime, says, "The art of mime, magical in many ways, is the ultimate language of silence."[4] Through this language, the students continue to communicate with each other and with the audience.

To use imagination

Imagination is key for acting. If you are on a cold concrete floor and you have to pretend you are on a sandy beach, you better have a good imagination. When students come up with their own short mimes they have to use their imaginations. For one thing, they do not want to repeat a mime that someone has already done. As we get farther around the circle, the remainder of the students will have to stretch their imaginations even more. We should not underestimate the power of the imagination. Stella Adler, who is a renowned actress in her own right, trained with Lee Strasburg and Stanislavski. Adler comments that, "Ninety percent of what you see onstage comes from imagination."[5] The more actors can stretch their imaginations, the more versatile they can become.

[4] Samuel Avital, *Mime and Beyond* (Prescott Valley, Ariz.: Hohm Press, 1985), 3.
[5] Stella Adler, *The Technique of Acting* (New York: Bantam Books, 1988), 17.

Chapter 18
Making Choices

104. British Bulldog

This game is very simple and most of the students have played something similar since they were very young. You will need a fairly large open space. Have the students sit down while you explain the game; you may find it hard to keep them quiet if they are standing up. It is no different with adults, except that they can be worse!

In a moment, ask most of the class to go to one end of the room while one person, let us say Jill, goes to the other. Each time you blow the whistle, the students will try to run to the other end of the room and touch the wall without getting tagged by Jill. In the next round they must run back to the other side of the room. If Jill tags them they must join the tagging team, so on round two there may be three people tagging, and then eight, etc. The idea is to be the last person still running.

Make sure you set tagging ground rules. Act out an example of how they should tag; preferably it will be just a tap on the shoulder. No diving or hair pulling; be very specific so you can avoid injuries. Any time you see something that looks a little unsafe, pause the game and reiterate the rules. The misconception is that running exercises in the form of a game are easy. Guiding the students so they can grow in every conceivable manner, well, that is easier said than done.

Variables:

This is one of those games that probably has many possibilities. One that I know of is called "Chain Link." You play it exactly the same way as "Bulldog," except that when you get tagged you link arms with the other taggers. This means that the taggers form a chain until eventually they become one long line. They really have to work as a team because they can only move in one direction.

Discussion:

"Would you say the fastest runner has the best chance of winning?"
"What other skills are important in this activity?"
"How did you change your tactics when the number of taggers increased?"
"How does teamwork play into this activity?"

Purpose:

To build confidence

Try to find something that everyone is good at. Some students may shy away from the games that lean more toward performance; however, they might excel in this activity. If you build their confidence in this game then perhaps they will become more relaxed and confident in other activities. One of my goals is to bring students out of their shells. I like to do it without the students knowing so that it becomes a natural process rather than saying, "Come on, you can do it." Saying this will simply embarrass most students and make them more introverted. Sometimes you will hear actors say, "I am not very talented." They may lack confidence, and just need a push in the right direction. It is quite interesting to note that actors often talk about natural talent. This is certainly a factor, but it is not the be all and end all. It is amazing how the harder actors train the more talented they seem to get. So find activities that help boost their confidence to spark their interest. We have to study to learn a language, to dance, or to play an instrument. So it follows that actors must train to excel at their craft.

To form strategies

If some students are not fast, they will realize early on in this game that they need to form strategies in order to avoid getting caught. Perhaps they decide to run behind a fast runner, or maybe they choose to run close to the sides of the room. Whatever they do, it will need to be thought through if they are to succeed. Actors often use strategies and problem solving in relation to their craft. Perhaps an actor is going for an audition and is in the waiting room with the other actors who are going for the same part. She looks around and notices that they are all sitting around looking slightly lethargic. She decides as a strategy to stay standing, as this will help her to keep her energy levels up.

105. Board Races

I especially like this activity because it has a double purpose: In addition to its benefits for actors, I also like to use this activity to help my students prepare for a quiz. It is important for actors to understand the basic terminology that is used in their craft, such as *blocking, ensemble, cue,* and *props,* to name but a few. As acting coaches, we should always look for creative ways to pass on information.

Spend a day or two reviewing your quiz questions with your students, then split the class into about four teams and divide your blackboard into four sections. Have each team sit in a row in single file. This should be their set order and at the end of each round the front person should go to the back of the line. You should pull a review question from an envelope. The question might be, "Explain what is meant by the term *Stage Right*." Now each team must send the representative who is at the front to run to the board and write the team's answer under their section. I would give them a time limit of one minute. The representative can confer with his or her team, but the time it takes to do this is part of the minute. The players must have a preselected order so that they all have a turn. As for the scoring, I will leave this entirely up to you. I usually give half a mark if they are close to the correct answer. This activity is best used when the students have already reviewed the material to some degree.

Variables:

If you do not have a blackboard, perhaps you could have pieces of paper at the front of the room where the students have to write their answers. The most important aspect is to make sure they have to leave their seats.

To make it more difficult you may want to add other factors, such as, "Once you have written your answer on the board you have to make sure the lid of the dry erase marker is back on and that it is not on the floor. Not until this point can you run back to your seat. I will also only count you as finished once every member of your group is sitting down in order." Adding extra factors such as these will not only make the activity more challenging, it may also give you better management control.

Discussion:

"Why do we need to have a basic understanding of acting terminology?"

"Why do I ask you to run to the board to write the answers?"

"Talk to me about the importance of teamwork for this activity."

"How might this activity increase your ability to memorize the necessary information?"

"Organization and acting: explain the connection."

Purpose:

To make learning fun

This may sound like an obvious statement, but I wonder how often we really live by it. What I like about "Board Races" is they give the students many opportunities to succeed. Perhaps a student did not know the correct answer, but maybe she was the first one to reach the board. This may give the student a badly needed sense of accomplishment. Because the students have to run to the board they will be increasing the oxygen level in their brains. This will help to keep them more energized and alert. This will also probably increase their level of concentration and help them to absorb the information better. If the students just sit in their chairs and are immobile, there is an opportunity for them to switch off and literally fall asleep. This activity forces them to stay alert.

As actors, it is important to have at least a basic knowledge of acting terminology. If a director asks the actor to go upstage left a bit, the actor needs to understand what this means. I would go one step further and say that as actors we should be continuously looking for new knowledge of our craft. There is such an array of valuable information out there that if we explore from now to eternity, there would still be more to discover. Let's at least make sure we are giving our students the maximum opportunity to absorb this wealth of knowledge. John Dewey, an educational theorist, explains that, "Intelligent activity is distinguished from aimless activity by the fact that it involves selection of means."[1] I would submit that "Board Races" is an excellent means by which to teach definitions. By the end of this activity the students are usually whipped up into a wild frenzy while actively engaged in learning.

To hone in on organizational skills

For this activity each team needs to form a game plan. They might decide that after they have conferred for twenty seconds they will send their representative up to write something on the board. Or they may decide that they can afford to confer for thirty seconds. They also need to decide on an order. They may have a strategic approach for whom they want to go first and so on. The more organized a team is, the better they will do. Having clear organizational skills applies to many aspects of actors' careers. Applying for auditions, sending out headshots and resumes, arriving fifteen minutes early to every audition, having their lines learned at the necessary time, and researching their characters are just a few examples. To achieve these tasks an actor must be organized and disciplined.

---

[1] John Dewey, *Experience and Education* (New York: Simon and Schuster, 1997), 84.

106. Run Around

This is an activity that comes from a game show I used to watch as a child in London, and it works best in a large space, such as a hall. Set up four signs in different corners of the room. The signs should be numbered from one to four in large, easy-to-read numbers. You should also have four cards numbered from one to four. Place these cards face down in front of you and shuffle them so that you do not know where each number is. Have your students start off by standing in a circle in the center of the room. Tell them that in a moment you will blow a whistle and they have to run to one of the corners of the room. (Students cannot all choose the same corner.) Set a time limit so they only have five or ten seconds to get to their spot. Next, you will turn over one of the four cards and call out the number that's on it. If it is number one then everyone who was standing under the number one sign is out. They can then go sit at the sides. Repeat game play until only one person is left.

Variables:

You might want to have six or eight areas; just add more signs in different parts of the room. This would make the activity easier, and it would also extend it.

This game can also be played in a smaller space if you want to make it faster and more chaotic. If you choose this option make sure you have discussed spatial awareness with your students.

Discussion:

"Talk to me about decision making in relation to this activity. In what ways do actors constantly have to make choices and decisions?"

"When might a director decide to use this activity? Please explain your reason."

"This activity relates to listening and doing. How might this apply to acting?"

Purpose:

To encourage actors to make choices

In this activity the actors are continuously asked to make a choice. They have to decide which corner to run to. They are not only asked to do this once, but must make this decision again and again. If they cannot make a decision they will be stuck in the middle, and therefore they will be out. Actors sometimes avoid making choices for fear of being wrong. Other actors choose to make the safe choice. When performing a monolog at an audition some actors will not move off the spot. They feel that this way they are less likely to make a mistake. Of course, this can lead to a totally unrealistic and somewhat boring performance. We want to encourage our actors to make choices. They may find that the choice they made was not always the best possibility. However, getting used to making these decisions will lead the actors to a greater degree of freedom and creativity in their acting.

To prepare actors for rehearsal

One challenge I sometimes find is that my actors are tired or come into class or rehearsal with little energy. This activity is great for getting actors to be alert. Because they are running around so much, they will be oxygenating their blood, which will lead to an increase in energy. Getting your actors up and moving around before rehearsal is a great preparation technique.

Chapter 19
Performance

107. Glamour Story

Have everyone sit in a group on the floor and introduce the game as follows:

"I need a volunteer who can tell us a short story on any topic. Okay, Jenny, come out front please. Now, I also need a volunteer who feels he or she has a good imagination. All right, Eric, please come forward. In a moment, Jenny, you will start your story, but you will only tell us the first line. For example, 'When I was seven years old I had a bike.' Eric, you are going to repeat the first part of Jenny's story with a slight twist. You are going to jazz it up and make it as interesting as possible. For instance, 'It was on a morning many moons ago when I was barely knee high to a grasshopper that I had in front of me my two-wheel mode of transportation,' or something like that. Then we return to Jenny, who will give us the next sentence in the story. Every time you give us a sentence, Jenny, Eric will then put his spin on your words. Make sure you give us a whole sentence; do not just say, 'There was.' Okay, ready?" After one pair has gone you can allow another pair to have a turn.

Variables:

See "Same Time Story."

Discussion:

"How did the storytellers try to make the second version more interesting? Give me some examples."

"In what way is your imagination a key factor in this exercise?"

"How would you define the term *imagination*?"

"If you told the original story, how did it feel hearing your story told another way?"

Purpose:

To perform, perform, perform!

This game is great for having students perform in front of each other. I have a small stage in my class so I like to turn out the overhead lights and put up the stage lights, which means all the focus goes to those on the stage. The rest of us then become the audience watching those onstage, but they do not see it like that; they often feel they are just playing a game or an activity. If you can get students accustomed to that feeling, you are helping them take a giant leap. As they become familiar with performing in front of others, they can start to forget (to a large extent) that the audience is there. This can apply as much to television and film as to theatre.

Feeling comfortable before an audience will lead your actors to be freer as their performance becomes less restricted and self-conscious. You find some actors who are excellent television and film performers, and yet they have never performed on a stage. Some say it is because of the fear of forgetting their lines. With recorded media there is always that safety net of doing a retake. This activity helps the students get used to performing in front of each other without a safety net.

In reference to performance in front of others, Robert Cohen explains that, "For most actors, tension, nervousness, and stage fright threaten to cancel out the careful preparation."[1] Activities such as this can therefore be useful to actors in the preparation stage.

108. Vampire

Here is an example of how to explain this game:

"Will everyone please come and form a circle, remaining standing. This activity is called 'Vampire.' Before we start, let me quickly explain the process. Eric, Nick, Claire, and Jane, would you please move into the center of the circle for me? In a moment, I am going to have you all move around the room with your eyes closed. So Claire, Nick, and Eric, would you please move cautiously around the circle with your eyes closed? Now let us say that Jane is the vampire. Her job is to move around the room and suck the blood of as many people as she can so that they become vampires. The way she does this is by putting her hands on a person's shoulders and gently squeezing. Jane, put your hands on Claire's shoulders and give us an example. Now Claire has become a vampire as well and she will join Jane in creating more vampires.

"Once you have become a vampire you can be changed back into a human. Nick, would you go up to Claire and squeeze her on one shoulder. Now Eric, would you go up to Claire and also squeeze her on

---

[1] Robert Cohen, *Acting One* (Mountain View, Calif.: Mayfield Publishing Company, 1998), 97.

one shoulder. To become a human again you have to be squeezed on the shoulder by two separate people. The only person who will squeeze you on both shoulders at once is a vampire. In our example, Jane was the original vampire and thus is the only vampire who cannot be turned into a human.

"Let me add a couple of short notes before we begin. Remember, safety first, so move cautiously around the room. Please keep your eyes closed at all times; I know you could take a peek, but that defeats the object of the activity. Also, as a vampire attacks you, let us hear a blood-curdling scream. Can anyone give us an example? (Jennifer screams.) Thank you, Jennifer, lots of blood curdles there. Please form a circle and I will choose the vampire by patting someone on the head and then you can begin moving around the room. Ready? All right, let's begin!"

Variables:

There are different ways of conducting this activity. You can have all of your actors wear a blindfold over their eyes. Another way of conducting this activity is to play in complete darkness. You may want to wait until you feel your students work well as an ensemble before moving to this stage.

Discussion:

"Who felt uneasy moving around the room with their eyes closed? Explain."

"Which role did you prefer: the vampire or the human?"

Purpose:
To loosen inhibitions

As the actors are changed into vampires they have to let out a blood-curdling scream. This takes quite a lot of guts. If the students just let the scream go they will have no control over the exact sound that will come out of their mouths. The fact that the other students cannot see them should hopefully help loosen their inhibitions even further. You may sometimes hear an actor say, "I'm saving it for performance." There are many different factors that contribute to this, but I am pretty sure that feeling inhibited plays into this equation somewhere down the line. The more ways we can find to help our actors take risks and loosen their inhibitions the better.

To enhance movement skills
This applies in more ways than one. When the students are moving around with their eyes closed they must be agile and move in a more graceful fashion. If they run around like a bull in china shop there will be injuries. Movement is a necessary skill for all actors, not just because of spatial awareness, but because the way we move also highlights our body language. If we cannot be malleable in our movement then we may be projecting a limited playing range.

109. Clap Olympics

Here is another one of my favorite activities. I explain it as follows:
"Okay people, I would like you to get yourselves into groups of five or six. Once you have your group, please make sure that one person from each group has a piece of paper and a pencil and then sit together on the floor.

"Okay, now I am going to clap some rhythms for you. I want you to listen the first time and then join in. Each group will need to write these rhythms down. Everybody ready? Here goes."

Go through about five different sequences for the students. For each sequence, perform it once through yourself and then repeat it twice with the class. They will need to write it down. Here is an example of what a sequence might look like: One two, one, one two, one, one two three, one two three. Explain the next stage of the game:

"Each group should now have all five rhythms written down. In a moment you are going to go off with your groups and learn the clapping patterns we have just gone through so that you can all do them together. When we get back together you will all be finalists at the Clap Olympics and each group will be competing for the gold medal. I am going to be the judge, so let me tell you what you will be graded on.

"Performance, first of all. I will be looking to see how well you can perform the claps together and in sync. Also, professional attitude. This means that you keep going no matter what. If you make mistakes, such as clapping at different times, you must still keep going and the audience should not see on your face that you goofed up. It is up to you to keep the performance going. Entrances and exits will be the next criteria. I want you to be lined up with your group at the back of the room. You will come toward the stage in whatever formation you choose and I will start grading you from the moment you start to move. You must position yourselves on the stage and start when you are ready. The performance will end when you have left the stage and made it back to your original starting positions. Style will also factor into your score. This is the presentation as a whole. Do you smile? Is there flair? What does your group bring to its presentation that makes it stand out? And finally, your group name. Each group needs to come up with its own name, and the more original the better. Your name should give us some clue as to what your group is all about. You have seven minutes to get that all together. Off you go!"

I know that does not sound like much time, but that is intentional. You want to give them enough time to have a shot at knowing some of the rhythms, but not enough time to get them 100 percent polished. The reason is that it is far more interesting to watch when things go wrong. They still have to try to hold things together, which sometimes becomes impossible in terms of performance, but not in terms of professional attitude. I have seen groups who have been clapping all over the place, and yet their attitudes made it seem as if that was how it was supposed to be.

Be warned! This activity will often have you all in stitches. The students love to participate in this exercise. Only one group should be up at a time and all the rest should be sitting in the audience. After each group has finished you should write down critiques for them and a score under each criteria. You can come up with what ever criteria you like. When you judge this event you must do so with a serious attitude. If you cannot stay professional then the students certainly won't. Once you have watched each group you should call them back up one at a time and tell them their scores. Give them a critique of their performance. Talk about all the areas you graded them on. For instance, you might say, "Your style was great; you all came onto the stage with big smiles on your faces." This activity will probably take about forty-five minutes, so make sure you have enough time set aside.

Variables:

You can give the students a different number of rhythms. You can also make the rhythms longer or shorter if you choose. Be careful of making them too short because you do not want to make the activity easy.

Instead of clapping you might want to use snapping.

Discussion:

"What was the most challenging part of that activity?"

"What strategy did you use to learn the rhythms and come up with a presentation in only seven minutes?"

"How did you help members of your group who were struggling?"

"What other areas could we have graded on?"

"How important was it that you had to keep going with the presentation no matter what happened?"

"How can you relate this to acting?"

Purpose:

To keep the scene going

The show must go on! This activity is often used in comedy workshops because the results can be hysterical; however, there are some very important lessons for the actor in this exercise. The students have to keep going no matter what. This can be very tough because people will keep messing up the rhythms and the audience will be laughing, yet the actors cannot break character. Some students probably will, but their main focus is to continue as if whatever happened is exactly what is supposed to happen.

Of course, this can be related to a play in which the actors must keep going in spite of missed dialogue. However, I think you can also apply it to film and TV acting. Actors seem too eager to stop a scene because they forgot a line or something did not happen the way it was supposed to. Perhaps the thing they did instead was just as good; maybe they had a moment of inspiration. You will often hear great actors say that they did something that wasn't in the script because it felt so natural and the director kept it. I am not saying that you should go out of your way to do something different from the script. But I am saying that you should keep the scene going for as long as possible, even if it takes an unexpected turn. It is the director's job to say cut, not the actor's.

To work under pressure

The students are only given a short time to complete this task so they can feel a great deal of pressure to finish. This is a good experience because it will connect to many acting projects they will be involved in. In plays, actors often find themselves under enormous amounts of pressure as scenes are changed, costumes are added, and lights and sound come into the picture. The actor must be prepared for anything and take it all in stride. In TV, the script may be changed many times and actors may get their new lines shortly before filming a scene. Again, learning to work under pressure is a valuable skill for the actor.

110. Wacky Word Wizard

This is a game that is going to take a little preparation on your part. Look up some really complex words that you think none of your actors have heard of. A history book would be a good source because you may find a whole chapter related to one word. Another good source of information is an encyclopedia. It might give you the etymology of the word and its historical context. Once you have found a suitable word, take three note cards and on one of them write the word with the correct definition. You will also want to write the word *true* on that card. On the other two cards write different words, but this time you should also write the word *false* and don't include the definition. In fact, these two other words should be made up! It's a good idea to have enough words to play the game at least three or four times; about three or four real words should suffice, along with several made up words. The trick is to have all of this organized before your students come to class.

Once the class has arrived have them take a seat so they are facing the performance area. Have three chairs on the stage, all facing out toward the audience, and ask three actors to come up onto the stage. Give each one a note card. One card will have a word with the correct definition and the other two cards will have different words with no definitions. Now, give the actors onstage two minutes to look over their words and prepare definitions. You could have them look at their words onstage or you could allow them to go outside the room for two minutes. If they go outside the room, the three of them can get together and brainstorm ideas. Of course, because the cards are labeled "true" and "false," the actors onstage already know before they begin if their word has the correct definition, but the audience does not.

After two minutes, have the actors onstage state their words and give their definitions to the audience. Do not allow them to read the definitions; more on that in a moment. That means that two of the actors are really going to have to use their imaginations, as they don't have a definition on their cards to begin with. If I were using this activity with actors who were about six or seven I might call them each a Wacky Word Wizard.

After the actors have given their definitions to the audience, the audience should start asking questions. If you have fifteen or more students in the audience I would allow them one question each; if you have less than fifteen you may want to allow them two each. Let them direct their questions to anyone they want. Now, because people may have fairly in-depth questions, it is important that you have a fairly lengthy definition or description on the "true" card. This is so the student with that card has enough information to give a sufficiently accurate description. Again, don't allow the actors to simply read their definitions off of the cards; instead they should just start with a general description. If the person with the "true" card reads the definition, he will not have any more accurate information available for answering questions and he would have to make everything up. As a result, when asked a question he might just answer, "I don't know that information." Not allowing students to read the definitions from their cards also means that all three actors can refer to their cards later on as if they are looking for more information. Remember, one person must answer only with truth and facts, whereas the other two must rely on their imaginations.

Try to guide the students in the audience to questions that are flexible and varied. You don't just want to hear, "What does it mean?" Encourage the audience to stretch their imaginations with their line of questioning. At the end of the questioning, have the audience vote on who they think is telling the truth.

Make sure to remind your audience that during this exercise they should be studying the nonverbal communication of the actors onstage to see if they can pick up any clues as to who is telling the truth. Also, remind the actors onstage that they will want to show confidence and have an authoritative air when talking. When you are finished you may want to facilitate a discussion before playing again.

Some of these activities you can use once and your actors will be okay with that. With an activity such as this, you are probably going to find that a lot of the students would like to have a turn, so you should plan your time accordingly. Students will often feel upset or left out if you do not give them the opportunity to participate, so try to include anyone who wants to play.

Variables:

I gave each actor a different word, but you could also do this activity by giving all of the actors the same word. Of course, there would still only be one correct definition and the other two actors would have to make theirs up.

Another really interesting way to do this activity is to bring in some strange objects. They have to be objects that nobody would have a clue as to what they were, and then you could proceed in the same manner.

Discussion:

"In what way is extending the vocabulary useful to an actor?"

"In this activity, the actors onstage must appear confident in answering their questions. Why is appearing confident so necessary for the actor?"

Actors are constantly faced with words they have never heard before or do not understand. This is especially true in more classical material such as Shakespeare or the Greek tragedies. It is therefore very important for actors to actively seek to increase their vocabularies. An actor should never be caught in performance saying words he does not understand.

Purpose:

To enhance auditioning skills

Actors might feel that when they go to an audition the only thing that the interviewer is looking at is their monolog or their reading. They don't realize that their personality and demeanor are also being examined. If an actor walks in with his head bent forward, does a wonderful piece, and then runs out of the room because he felt so nervous, the director will get mixed signals. She might feel that the acting was very impressive; however, she might conclude that because the actor seemed in such a rush to leave the room, he was not really interested in the part. By appearing confident in himself, the actor is able to build a more congruent picture of himself. This should also help to put the director at ease. Now you might say, "I don't feel very confident." I accept this and say just think of the "Wacky Word Wizard" exercise and appear confident. As James Duke explains, "In the course of an actor's professional life he or she is going to have literally hundreds of auditions or interviews."[2] My advice is get used to it!

To extend the actors' vocabularies

Also see discussion notes. Tadashi Suzuki explains some of the requirements for the actor in Japanese theatre: "He may have to know

---

[2] James Duke, *How to Be a Working Actor* (London: Virgin Books, 1994), 157.

the traditional vocal techniques used in No and Kabuki, as well as those used in Western popular or operatic culture."[3] In the same way that the Japanese actor must have an understanding of a wide variety of vocal techniques, we need to have at our command an extensive vocabulary so we can undertake a large variety of roles from any time period. Also, the more vocabulary we know the better we can take advantage of the huge amounts of resources devoted to our craft.

[3] Tadashi Suzuki, *The Way of Acting*, trans. J. Thomas Rimer (New York: Theatre Communications Group, 1986), 17.

Chapter 20
Thinking Outside the Box

111. Charring Cross

To begin, have your students come sit in a large circle on the floor. Now tell them that you are not really going to explain the rules to this activity; all you will tell them is if they are right or wrong. Without further ado you can get started.

You might start by saying, "I went to Charring Cross station to catch my train," and that is correct. Now, most likely the next student, who does not really have a clue what is going on, will say the same thing as you. "I went to Charring Cross station to catch my train," and that is wrong. By this time the students will be quite confused, but that is okay; keep plodding along. So that you do not get too confused, let me explain the activity.

The right and wrong answers lie not in what the students say, but in what they do. For instance, in this round I decided that before I say my sentence I must have my legs crossed. So in order for the students to get an affirmative, they must have their legs crossed when they give their answer. So if I say, "I went to Charring Cross," and the student next to me says, "I bought a pint of milk," he is still correct as long as he has his legs crossed. If you tell a student, "That's correct," do not tell him why. He may have gotten the answer correct, but he may have no idea why. You will keep going with this until everyone has caught on.

You may find that this activity goes on for quite a long time. Students will listen and listen, but because they are not paying attention to your movement they may not notice the significance of the crossed legs. At the very start of the activity I tell my students to think outside the box, and not to always pay attention to the obvious. As you progress with the activity you may want to make the leg crossing action more exaggerated. Even though you think you are being as obvious as possible, there will be a number of students who simply will not catch on. Because they are not looking for your movement, they will not find it. This game can be very frustrating for the students, but it has loads of value.

If a student thinks he knows the answer have him whisper it to you. If he is correct, have him continue to play without telling the other students the answer.

In this game I chose crossing my legs as the action, but you can choose anything you like; it might not even be a movement. For example, you might decide that saying "umm" before each sentence

229

designates a correct answer. Whatever you decide, you must stick with it for the entire duration of the activity. So if I start with leg crossing, I cannot change it to "umm" halfway through the game.

Play for as long as you think is adequate; you may not play to completion if it starts to drag. If we do not finish the activity I do not give them the answer. I simply play the activity again on another occasion. If the students all work out the answer fairly quickly, have one of the students become the leader and play again. One more thing: You can start to drop clues to pique their interest if you feel it is necessary; even as your clues get bigger, there will still be those who are totally lost. You may see a lot of frustrated faces during this activity, but continue to follow it through. It is very interesting to observe the students' reactions.

Variables:

The leader can choose anything he wants to be the criteria for correctness. He might decide it is having his arms crossed or looking up at the ceiling before talking or whatever. It can be something visual or, if he prefers, something auditory. The only rule on this is once the leader has chosen something he has to stick with it.

Discussion:

"In this activity, how did you have to think outside the box?"

"Being correct does not always indicate understanding; explain."

"I just threw you into this activity without any real guidelines; why do you think I did that?"

In this activity the students might get the correct answer, but not know why. This activity is more powerful if the students start from a state of confusion; if you sit down and explain the concept first, you have just solved half the battle for them.

Purpose:

To encourage students to think outside the box

If the students look for the obvious in this activity they will never find the solution. They have to expand their minds and look beyond the obvious. Actors often have to work in much the same way. A character might be described as a crazed, psychotic serial killer. The actor might choose to interpret this to mean he needs to continuously show this crazed person through overt physical behavior. However, if he thinks outside the box, he might realize that many serial killers often appear totally normal to their friends and neighbors. They are quite often seen as friendly and quiet. If the actor leaves himself open to different ideas he will not feel the need to interpret everything literally.

To become more aware of body language

In this activity the actors can often get the answer not just from the person who is leading the game, but also from others in the circle. When people find they have the right answer they often signal it, even if not on purpose. By really observing the entire group actors can sometimes pick up the correct answer through the body language of others. In the moment they discover they have the correct answer the players often highlight the action or sound. This should be of great benefit to those who are really observing. As actors we need to have a thorough understanding of body language and its consequences. An actor may be in a scene with his arms crossed and think nothing of it. The audience may have already interpreted this to mean the character is angry or feels negative about the situation at hand. A great way to become more aware of body language and its influence is to observe it in others.

112. Black Magic

For this activity you are going to need to have a partner who knows the game. Pull someone aside before the class and explain to her that she is going to pretend that she can read your mind. I will explain how this works in a minute. When the class comes in, tell them that you are going to introduce them to a person who can read your mind. Tell them this is a very special and rare gift. Also, tell them that it only works with you. Introduce them to the person (an instructor, student, or whomever you chose earlier) and then send the individual out of the room.

At this stage, have the students agree on an object in the room — a bottle of water, for instance. Bring the person back in the room and ask her different questions. "Is the object I am thinking of the table? Is the object I am thinking of the trash can?" Go on like this for a while. Your individual should get the right answer every time.

No, it is not quite magic. What you need to tell your partner at the start is that you will give her a signal. The signal is that any time you mention an item with the color black in it, the next item will be the correct answer. So if I say, "Is it the garbage bag (black)? Is it the telephone?" The student automatically knows the correct answer is the telephone. I do not have to mention the word *black*, but the previous item must be black.

This may sound really obvious, but you will be surprised at how few people can work it out. Each time your accomplice gets the correct answer your students will come up with different theories as to how she is cheating. Someone might say, "You are giving her a visual signal." At this point ask your accomplice to close her eyes. This time you may need to say, "Is the object I am thinking of the black folder?" As long as you do this in a matter-of-fact fashion, your students will still be no closer to figuring out the truth.

Make sure that your accomplice is trustworthy. I have worked with the same person for over three years, and so far no students have figured out the secret. Also, make sure you get together with this person well before your students arrive. It will look really suspicious if you are whispering as they are walking into the room. Remember, you have to ask the questions. You can explain this by saying your friend has learned to read only your mind. He or she is not yet capable of communicating telepathically with anyone else.

After three or four times, allow your students to have a turn. You should ask them if any of them feel they have telepathic powers and send this person out of the room. At this point, you can switch the person who asks the questions to one of the students. The person who comes back into the room usually gets the wrong answer. If they get the correct answer, have them try a second time. This is certainly a very popular activity with the students.

Variables:

When your accomplice is naming the item, she can make this more interesting. Once she knows what the item is she can continue as if she is not sure yet. So let's say the item is a set if keys; after hearing this the accomplice can just keep listening. "Is the item I am thinking of the table? Is the item I am thinking of the phone? Is the item I am thinking of the chair?" you ask. At this point, your accomplice might jump in with something like, "Hang on a minute, I am getting a message ... the item is the keys." The students will love this, and it will make them even more confused.

Discussion:

"Explain to me why problem-solving skills are important for actors?"

"How do auditory and visual cues play into this activity?"

"Was there anything about this activity that you did not feel worked well?"

"Do you believe that my assistant has telepathic powers? Explain your answer."

Purpose:

To stretch the students' problem-solving skills

This activity can be great fun, but it also has a lot of value as a problem-solving activity. The students will spend a great deal of time trying to figure out how you and your accomplice are communicating. They will watch your every move and listen to every word you say to see if they can figure it out. This takes a tremendous amount of focus and concentration on their part. It also keeps their minds engaged, as they persevere in trying to solve the mystery. Problem solving is a constant partner to the actor. An actor may be looking to define his character and yet find little information in the script; a director may be trying to block a scene, but cannot find a way to make it work. Actors are constantly faced with problems (challenges) to solve. This activity will help the actors understand how to get prepared for solving problems. It will also help them to see their challenges as things they can overcome.

To encourage the actors to move away from limitations

When the students first see this activity they always think it's a trick, and they are right. After watching it a couple of times they start to believe it is possible. They start to say, "I could do that; maybe I have telepathic powers." Regardless of whether this is true or not, the students have now started to remove their preconceived self-limitations. As actors we are always looking to remove limitations and barriers. Although actors have to be very well-grounded, they also should be able to believe in the impossible. If they want to believe they can become a movie star then they should be able to — provided they don't mind twenty years of hard work, if that is what it takes! This activity makes the impossible seem possible; it is a good reference point for the actors. Never let anyone steal your dreams!

Resources

Adler, Stella. *The Technique of Acting.* New York: Bantam Books, 1988.

Avital, Samuel. *Mime and Beyond.* Prescott Valley, Ariz.: Hohm Press, 1985.

Benedetti, Robert. *The Actor at Work.* Englewood Cliff, N. J.: Prentice-Hall, 1981.

Berry, Cicely. *Your Voice and How to Use It Successfully.* London: Harrap Limited, 1990.

Boleslavsky, Richard. *Acting.* New York: Theatre Arts Books, 1990.

Burton, Hal. *Great Acting.* New York: Hill and Wang, 1967.

Cohen, Robert. *Acting One.* Mountain View, Calif.: Mayfield Publishing Company, 1998.

Easty, Edward Dwight. *On Method Acting.* New York: Ballantine Books, 1981.

Goodman, Ralph. *Drama on Stage.* New York: Holt, Rinehart, and Winston, 1961.

Grandstaff, Russell. *Acting and Directing.* Lincolnwood, Ill.: National Textbook Company Publishing Group, 1975.

Grotowski, Jerzy. *Towards a Poor Theatre.* London: Methuen, 1991.

Hagen, Uta. *A Challenge for the Actor.* New York: Scribner, 1991.

———. *Respect for Acting.* New York: Macmillan Publishing Company, 1973.

Hendricks, Gay. *The Art of Breathing and Centering.* New York: St. Martin's Press, 1989.

Izzo, Gary. *Acting Interactive Theatre.* Portsmouth: Heinemann, 1998.

Jones, Brie. *Improve with Improv!* Colorado Springs: Meriwether Publishing, 1993.

Maltz, Maxwell. *Psycho-Cybernetics.* New York: Pocket Books, 1969.

Manderino, Ned. *All About Method Acting.* Los Angeles: Manderino Books, 1976.

Mobley, Jonnie Patricia. *NTC's Dictionary of Theatre and Drama Terms.* Lincolnwood, Ill: National Textbook Company, 1995.

Nomura, Yoko. *Pinch and Ouch.* Tokyo: Lingual House Publishing, 1982.

O'Conner, Joseph and John Seymour. *Introducing Neuro-linguistic Programming.* London: HarperCollins Publishers, 1993.

Peeters, Joelle. *Reflexology.* New York: Barnes & Noble, 2003.

Robbins, Anthony. *Awaken the Giant Within.* London: Simon & Schuster, 1992.

_____. *Unlimited Power.* New York: Ballantine Books, 1986.

Shurtleff, Michael. *Audition.* New York: Bantam Books, 1978.

Snyder, Joan and Michael P. Drumsta. *The Dynamics of Acting.* Skokie, Ill.: National Textbook Company, 1981.

Spolin, Viola. *Improvisation for the Theatre.* Chicago: Northwestern University Press, 1983.

Stanislavski, Constantin. *An Actor's Handbook.* New York: Theatre Art Books, 1994.

Stoppelman, Gabriela. *Artaud for Beginners.* New York: Writers and Readers Publishing, 1998.

Weatherford, Russ; John R. Weatherford; and Ruth Warrick. *Confidence and Clarity.* Hollywood, Calif.: The Weatherford Group, 1992.

Wilson, Edwin and Alvin Goldfarb. *Theatre the Lively Art.* New York: McGraw-Hill, 1991.

Yakim, Moni. *Creating a Character.* New York: Watson-Guptill Publications, 1990.

About the Author

Gavin Levy is co-founder of the Hollywood Stage Company with Paul Gleason at the Paul G. Gleason Theatre on Hollywood Boulevard. Their work focuses on the technique of acting and promoting the growth of working actors. Mr. Levy also instructs acting at the American National Academy in Studio City. In 2007, Mr. Levy saw the release of his second book, *Acting Games for Individual Performers*, published by Meriwether Publishing.

Mr. Levy is a native Londoner who presently resides in Hollywood, California. He received his A.L.A.M. from the London Academy of Music and Dramatic Art, and he is a graduate of the Academy of Live and Recorded Arts, completing his training in 1995. After graduating, he continued his training through the Actors Centre in London. Mr. Levy has over seventeen years of experience in acting, instructing, directing, and writing.

While living in London, Mr. Levy became involved with the Impact Theatre Company and traveled to different parts of the country performing original works. As an active member of the Dragon Drama Theatre Company, Mr. Levy continued to work as an actor as well as coordinating and instructing acting workshops.

In 1999, Mr. Levy came to the United States to continue his acting and to further pursue his interest in the technique of acting for the professional and novice actor. Mr. Levy has written several plays including *A Day in the Life of Me and My Cup of Tea* and *Adam and Martha*. Both of these plays were produced at the Jefferson Playwriting Festival in 2000. In 2005, Mr. Levy participated in The Frontera Fest as both a playwright and a director. He is looking forward to more exciting and challenging projects in the near future.

Order Form

Meriwether Publishing Ltd.
PO Box 7710
Colorado Springs CO 80933-7710
Phone: 800-937-5297 Fax: 719-594-9916
Website: www.meriwether.com

Please send me the following books:

_____ **112 Acting Games #BK-B277**   **$17.95**
by Gavin Levy
A comprehensive workbook of theatre games

_____ **Acting Games for Individual Performers**   **$17.95**
#BK-B297
by Gavin Levy
A comprehensive workbook of 110 acting exercises

_____ **Acting Games #BK-B168**   **$17.95**
by Marsh Cassady
A textbook of theatre games and improvisations

_____ **Theatre Games for Young Performers**   **$16.95**
#BK-B188
by Maria C. Novelly
Improvisations and exercises for developing acting skills

_____ **More Theatre Games for**   **$17.95**
Young Performers #BK-B268
by Suzi Zimmerman
Improvisations and exercises for developing acting skills

_____ **Theatre Games and Beyond #BK-B217**   **$17.95**
by Amiel Schotz
A creative approach for performers

_____ **Group Improvisation #BK-B259**   **$16.95**
by Peter Gwinn with additional material by Charna Halpern
The manual of ensemble improv games

These and other fine Meriwether Publishing books are available at
your local bookstore or direct from the publisher. Prices subject to
change without notice. Check our website or call for current prices.

Name: _____ e-mail: _____

Organization name: _____

Address: _____

City: _____ State: _____

Zip: _____ Phone: _____

❑ **Check enclosed**

❑ **Visa / MasterCard / Discover #** _____

Signature: _____   *Expiration*
                                               date: _____ / _____
(required for credit card orders)

Colorado residents: Please add 3% sales tax.
Shipping: Include $3.95 for the first book and 75¢ for each additional book ordered.

❑ *Please send me a copy of your complete catalog of books and plays.*